'In these ...l times we need to hear from those sage vo...s who have the expertise and experience to explain the turbulent age we live in. Books like this one could not be more timely.'
Jonathan Freedland, *Guardian*

'The world is passing through the biggest upheaval for 200 years. Power no longer belongs exclusively to the West. If Britain is to promote its interests and retain the capacity to shape events, policy-makers must understand the complexities and power shifts of the new global landscape. This set of essays, insightful and infused with realism, is an excellent place to start.'
Philip Stephens, *Financial Times*

'The debate on British foreign policy has become far too parochial. *Influencing Tomorrow* forces us to consider the worldwide challenges that Britain faces from such problems as climate change, nuclear proliferation, the rise of the East and the ever-present threat of terrorism. The analysis by expert contributors make this book essential reading for all concerned with Britain's future.'
Professor Vernon Bogdanor, Professor of Government, King's College, London

'This is a serious, ambitious and hopeful collection of essays. It's great to see a vision for British foreign policy that is pro-European, robust in its defence of democracy and human rights, embraces the rise of Asia instead of seeing it as a threat and is anchored in progressive and generous British values at home.'
Michael Ignatieff, Harvard Kennedy School

'Foreign policy is all too often both defensive and based on narrow, static and unimaginative views of self-interest ... There is another way based on a better understanding of opportunities, of the great returns to collaboration, and of a world where innovation is at the heart of progress. That is the spirit that gave us the Bretton Woods institutions, the WTO, the declaration of human rights and the beginnings of the EU ... We now need a similar spirit in tackling the problems of climate change ... and overcoming world poverty ... The challenges, par excellence, require a strategic approach that integrates foreign and environmental issues, and the economy too. We must bind these different, but fundamentally interwoven, strands together. This analytical and practical spirit runs through the chapters and the concept of this book. It is a very thoughtful and valuable ....
Lord Nicholas ...onomics and **Gove** ...d President of the**

'We live in a complex, fast moving, increasingly interconnected and unstable world. That is why the apparent unfashionable nature of the foreign policy debate today is of such great concern. In this collection of thoughtful and occasionally provocative essays Douglas Alexander and Ian Kearns have harvested some of the key issues which will face the UK in future years. These are serious matters and the contributors bring to life the dilemmas and choices an incoming government will face. For those in charge at that time, this book will be an essential primer.'
Lord George Robertson, Former Secretary General of NATO

'*Influencing Tomorrow* is a timely examination of critical issues facing Britain as global wealth and power shifts eastward. I applaud Douglas Alexander and Ian Kearns for bringing together contributions from so many commentators and thinkers into such a smart, engaging and usable book. Political leaders, policy-makers and academics are rarely on the same page, but at least they are now in the same volume. Anyone who is interested in Britain's role in the world – and the way the world is changing – should read *Influencing Tomorrow*.'
Michael Fullilove, Executive Director of the Lowy Institute, Sydney

'This book understands that the response of Western powers – individually and collectively – to Asia's rise will be key to the shape of our world in the future. Within a few years the world's largest economy will not be either a European or North American power. That will be the first time this has happened since the time of George III. It's a big deal and this is a book that gets that it's a big deal. This book offers the reader a guide to these vital challenges in the coming decades.'
Josette Sheeran, President and CEO of Asia Society

'Eliminating extreme poverty, and tackling climate change and conflict, are the gravest and most urgent global challenges facing our generation. The insights in *Influencing Tomorrow* should be required reading for all of us.'
Justin Forsyth, Chief Executive, Save the Children UK

'This is an important volume. Douglas Alexander and Ian Kearns seek to remedy that British foreign policy is too seldom and too narrowly debated. Their volume of essays offers rich pickings for those wishing to look beyond a narrow focus on Europe, the US and whatever crisis is most in the news. Influencing tomorrow, they argue, requires a fresh focus on the rise of China and Asia, new high growth economies, climate change, and the nuclear order.'
Professor Ngaire Woods, Dean of the Blavatnik School of Government, University of Oxford

INFLUENCING TOMORROW

FUTURE CHALLENGES FOR BRITISH FOREIGN POLICY

EDITED BY
RT HON DOUGLAS ALEXANDER MP
AND **DR IAN KEARNS**

IPPR

First published in 2013 by Guardian Books
Kings Place, 90 York Way
London N1 9GU

Published by Guardian Books and supported by IPPR
Guardian Books is an imprint of Guardian Newspapers Ltd

Typeset by seagulls.net
Printed in England by CPI Group (UK) Ltd, Croydon CR0 4YY

Editorial matter, selection, introduction and conclusion copyright
© Douglas Alexander and Ian Kearns 2013

All remaining chapters copyright © respective authors 2013

Douglas Alexander, Ian Kearns and the authors of individual chapters have
asserted their right under the Copyright, Designs and Patents Act 1988,
to be identified as the editors and authors of this work.

This book is sold subject to the condition that it shall not, by way of trade
or otherwise, be lent, resold, hired out, or otherwise circulated without
the publisher's prior consent in any form of binding or cover other than
that in which it is published and without a similar condition, including this
condition, being imposed on the subsequent purchaser.

A CIP record for this book is available from the British Library

ISBN 978-1-783-56006-6

FSC
www.fsc.org
MIX
Paper from
responsible sources
FSC® C020471

10 9 8 7 6 5 4

The contents of this book do not reflect the collective views of all
individual authors, or of the editors. Each of the views expressed in this
book are those of the individual authors alone. Attribution of material
to the editors, Rt Hon Douglas Alexander MP and Dr Ian Kearns, should
be limited only

This book was published with the support of the Institute for Public Policy Research (IPPR).

IPPR is the UK's leading progressive think-tank. We are an independent charitable organisation with more than 40 staff members, paid interns and visiting fellows. Our main office is in London, with IPPR North, IPPR's dedicated think-tank for the north of England, operating out of offices in Newcastle and Manchester.

The purpose of our work is to assist all those who want to create a society where every citizen lives a decent and fulfilled life, in reciprocal relationships with the people they care about. We believe that a society of this sort cannot be legislated for or guaranteed by the state. And it certainly won't be achieved by markets alone. It requires people to act together and take responsibility for themselves and each other.

CONTENTS

SECTION 3
INSTITUTIONS

SECTION 4
GLOBAL CHALLENGES

SECTION 5
POWER AND DIPLOMACY IN THE 21ST CENTURY

INTRODUCTION

by Douglas Alexander and Ian Kearns

We have written this book because we think it is needed. A number of observable global trends are affecting the UK's interests and allies and could radically alter our place and influence in the world as a result. Yet, as a country, we are not yet examining these deeply enough, nor sufficiently debating their implications for policy.

Our task in this volume is not to set out policy prescriptions, draft manifestos or dictate a policy agenda for a political party. Instead we seek to offer a detailed exploration of the range of issues affecting our world today, in order to find ways of influencing it tomorrow.

Just consider the following: after more than a decade of war abroad and amid budget cuts and political gridlock at home, our most important ally, the United States, is stepping back from its decades' long role as the world's 'policeman'. It is also rebalancing its priorities to Asia and the Pacific while reducing its level of engagement in Europe. Europe itself is gripped by an economic and social crisis on a scale not seen since the 1930s. It is inward looking rather than readily able to fill the gap being left by the United States. The destiny of the Middle East hangs in the balance as violence and volatility, more than nascent democracy, marks the wave of change still sweeping that region. And a global shift of economic power from West to East is under way, accelerated by the severe impact of the 2008 financial crisis on the West.

This latter trend is the most profound geo-economic re-ordering that our generation is likely to see and it is already bringing geopolitical changes in its wake. The relationship between the United

States and China in the Asia-Pacific region is becoming pivotal for global politics: the two countries are striving for a relationship based on accommodation and cooperation rather than conflict but a number of sensitive issues will need to be handled with great diplomatic skill if that outcome is to be secured.

Shifts in the wider global military balance are under way. That balance still favours the US and its allies overwhelmingly, but defence spending in both the US and Europe is being cut while at the same time it is rising rapidly in China, India, Brazil and the Gulf. The West may, over the long term, lose the significant military advantage it has held for decades. As rising demand for resources triggers resource scarcity, there is also already a developing international competition for influence and natural resources in Central Asia and in Africa, with the main protagonists being Russia, China, the US, India and the EU. Such geo-political consequences of economic change are likely to continue and, if anything, to become more pronounced in the next decade.

The anxiety that the future may not belong to the West is palpable. It is rooted in demographics as much as in economics. UN projections suggest that the global population will reach 9.6 billion by 2050, an increase of almost 40 per cent in 40 years (UN, 2012). Future population growth will be concentrated heavily in less developed countries and will be particularly pronounced in India, China, Bangladesh, Pakistan, Nigeria, Indonesia and the Middle East, while the population of Africa will almost certainly double. In contrast, the population of the developed world is likely to remain constant at around 1.25 billion between now and 2050, with some regions and countries – Japan, Russia and a number of European countries in particular – experiencing declining populations.

These trends will have internal as well as external consequences. The old age dependency ratio (the number of over-65s as a proportion of the total working-age population) in the EU is set to increase from around 30 per cent now to 58 per cent by 2060, raising serious questions about the long-term prospects for the current European economic model (Leonard and Kundnani, 2013). At the same time, when combined with the visible economic trends already touched

2

upon, demographic change will further reduce the strategic centrality of Europe. By 2050, the developing world could account for around 85 per cent of the world population while the population of Europe may constitute just 7 per cent of the global total, and the population of the UK just 0.8 per cent (UN, 2012).

Looking beyond the prospects of the West, other aspects of international affairs and dominant global trends provide serious cause for concern for everyone, whether one's vantage point is a Western capital or the capital of a rising power.

One such trend is the threat of climate change and environmental degradation. Together these pose real and dangerous risks to citizens and interests of individual nation states across the world. If the impacts of the financial crash and global economic crisis are likely to define this decade, it is the global climate crisis that is most likely to define the next half century. Nicholas Stern, who published the Stern review in 2006 on the impact and consequences of climate change, has long argued that 'the economic crisis is severe, but the environmental crisis is more severe' (Rose, 2009). Yet no global deal to cut carbon emissions to limit the effects of climate change has yet been agreed.

Violent Islamist terror groups continue to pose a further serious threat. There is a real risk that these groups will again revert to acts of 'mega-terrorism' on the scale of, or even greater than, the attacks of September 11 2001. Nuclear proliferation risks are growing. And despite the recent economic gains in some developing countries, we live in a world scarred by grotesque poverty, deprivation, inequality and disease.

Increased volatility is also a feature of contemporary international affairs. Nowhere perhaps, was this more starkly illustrated than in the Middle East in September 2012, when a 14-minute video from a 55-year-old man with no connection to the US government appeared to play a pivotal role in stimulating massive protests against the US across Muslim-majority countries, ultimately contributing to the events that led to the death of the US Ambassador to Libya.

Much as we would like to believe that the world is populated with strong and stable states that can readily come together to address these and other challenges, a further uncomfortable truth is that weak and failing states outnumber strong and stable ones by more than two to one (Foreign Policy/Fund for Peace, 2013). And in this interdependent world threats emerge from weakness as well as strength: these failed and failing states represent not only human tragedy but also harbour a range of dangers, from extremism and terrorism to criminality and disease.

Against this backdrop, the public and political mood in the UK and across many other Western countries is one of unease. There is a palpable reluctance to commit, after the experiences of Iraq and Afghanistan, to the human and financial costs of further lengthy overseas interventions in conflict environments. The UK, along with many of its partners, is enduring anaemic growth and high unemployment at home. More fundamental challenges, in terms of developing a model of capitalism that generates wealth, promotes fairness and protects the environment remain un-addressed. And although, as an open country, we are acutely exposed to the downside risks as well as to the benefits of globalization, the public believes policy-makers' attention should, for now at least, be focused on matters close to home.

This presents a challenging picture and it would be easy in the circumstances to be pessimistic and to turn inward, but while the context provides powerful reasons to be concerned, there is another side to the story too. Talk of relative Western decline is all too easily overdone. As Mark Leonard and Hans Kundnani recently reminded us, the European Union may have its fundamental problems but it remains the largest single economy in the world, has the second largest defence budget after the United States and has some 57,000 diplomats compared to India's 600 (Leonard and Kundnani, 2013). Talk of its demise is understandable in the wake of the euro crisis but: 'The EU's GDP per capita in purchasing-power terms is still nearly four times that of China, three times Brazil's, and nearly nine times India's' (Leonard and Kundnani, 2013).

Nor will the rising powers rise smoothly. All of them have major security, economic, political and environmental challenges that could slow down economic growth or halt it altogether if they are not properly managed. The recent protests in Turkey and Brazil may only be the start of instability that is yet to fully reveal itself in both the BRICS and the Next Eleven.[1]

Technological innovations and their wide distribution at low cost are adding to the sense that we are on the cusp of a new and at least in some ways more hopeful era. Alec Ross, Senior Advisor for Innovation to Hillary Clinton when she was Secretary of State, is right to say that the speed of communication today risks exceeding the depth of understanding, but despite these risks, technological advances do represent opportunities for real progress.

Some leading commentators, such as Fareed Zakaria, have seized on this to warn against a prevailing but excessive pessimism in the West and to talk up the new possibilities and opportunities awaiting today's graduates in an 'age of progress' (Zakaria, 2012). Kenneth Cukier and Viktor Mayer-Schoenberger, in their recent study on *Big Data*, have talked in equally upbeat tone: 'Today', they point out, 'there is enough information in the world to give every person alive 320 times as much of it as historians think was stored in the Library of Alexandria' (2013: 28). That information does not in itself empower people, they acknowledge, but as the sheer scale of the digital information available is matched with the communications infrastructure and computing power required to analyse and network it, advances in our understanding of some of the world's most pressing problems look likely to follow. Pollution data necessary to understand climate change may soon be gathered by sensors placed in hundreds of millions of smart-phones around the world, transforming our scientific understanding of the problem and allowing better, more targeted policy interventions. Linguistic differences that have acted as barriers to international and inter-cultural understanding for centuries may soon be eradicated by automatic translation systems that are accurate enough to facili-tate much deeper engagement (Schmidt and Cohen, 2013). And

[1] The BRICS being Brazil, Russia, India, China and South Africa, and the Next Eleven, as coined by Goldman Sachs, being Bangladesh, Egypt, Indonesia, Iran, Mexico, Nigeria, Pakistan, the Philippines, South Korea, Turkey and Vietnam.

wider advances in bio-technology and nano-technology promise new avenues for growth, millions of new jobs, and smarter use of resources on a planet with a serious resource scarcity problem.

Against this entire backdrop, what is striking about much of the British debate on foreign policy is how limited it is. Domestically, our debate is often dominated by three themes: the latest crisis in the news and what the British government intends to do about it; intermittent concern for the state of our 'special relationship' with the United States; and, most persistently, our relationship with the EU. The reach of Brussels makes the headlines when the big picture is China's resurgence and the prospects for an 'Asian Century'.

The result is that a wide range of important questions are relegated to expert rather than wider political or policy-maker discussion. Among them: How do we ensure an equilibrium between our ambitions and our capability in foreign policy? How do we respond to the challenge and opportunity of the rising powers? How do we focus less on debating the 'specialness', and more on building the 'relationship' we have with the United States? And how should we orient ourselves to what looks like epoch-making change under way in Asia?

How do we deal with existential threats like climate change and the challenge of an increasingly fragile nuclear order on the one hand, and with transnational threats like violent Islamist extremism and organised crime on the other? And in a world where development is progressing and hundreds of millions are being lifted out of extreme poverty, how should we act to try to help the billions still trapped by it? In addressing these questions, can we engage in an honest conversation about what resources our country can still bring to bear, what level of international ambition is consistent with those resources and how we can get the most out of them?

The problem with the status quo is not that relations with the United States or the reach of Brussels are unimportant. They obviously are vital. The problem is that under the shadow of these issues the wider canvass is too often ignored or under-acknowledged. Our view is that the changes now under way in international affairs demand a deeper re-examination of policy, deeper perhaps than any re-examination carried out by any government of any party since the end of the cold war a quarter of a century ago. It is to that deeper re-examination that we hope this book can make a worthwhile contribution.

The Book's Rationale and Structure

Implicit in the project of the book is an assumption that we cannot simply carry on as we are and expect Britain to be successful on the international stage in future. In the face of challenge and change on the scale being witnessed, long-held assumptions will need to be questioned, bedrock institutions will need to be re-evaluated for relevance, and long-standing diplomatic practices and approaches to exercising influence in the world will need to be re-thought.

With that task in mind, we have pulled together 16 essays from some of the world's leading thinkers on international affairs in this volume. Contributors to the book come from the UK and overseas, and from those with experience of very senior levels of government, the think-tank world and academia. Each contributing author was asked to focus on a particular question, to analyse the context relevant to it, and to offer thoughts on implications for Britain and its future foreign policy choices. We have also framed the book around the challenges that are likely to face an incoming government in 2015. That government is going to have to answer the central question: what comes next?

The chapters in the book are organised into five main sections to help think through the answer. The first section examines two issues that we have identified as immediate threats, namely the fight against violent Islamist extremist groups and the threat of WMD proliferation in the Middle East. Michael Clarke examines the former, and Rolf Ekeus, former Chair of the UN Special Commission on Iraq, examines the latter. The second section of the book focuses on geo-politics. Here, Mark Leonard addresses the rise of China and its implications while Xenia Dormandy explores shifting US foreign policy priorities in the wake of China's rise. Bob Legvold takes the geo-political story on and provides a view on the question that vexes many, namely: is Russia a partner or a threat? And Shahshank Joshi rounds out the section by examining change in the Arab world and its long-term implications.

In section three, we turn to institutions and examine the prospects and continued relevance of three institutions that have been central to British foreign policy for decades, namely the European Union, NATO and the United Nations. Charles Grant, Kori Schake and Michael Williams respectively bring their deep expertise and experience to bear in chapters on each.

Section four of the book puts the spotlight on a series of pressing global challenges. The former Assistant US Secretary of Defense, Graham Allison, opens the section with a chapter on the increasingly fragile global nuclear order. Jeff Mazo follows that with an examination of the other existential threat to humanity, namely climate change, and its potential human and international security consequences. Paul Collier then re-visits the theme of his best-selling book, *The Bottom Billion*, to address what steps can be taken to help the world's poorest, and the section is concluded by Simon Adams, Executive Director of the Global Centre for the Responsibility to Protect (R2P) in New York, with a chapter on how the R2P can more effectively be implemented in the years ahead.

The fifth and final section of the book is more conceptual. Larry Korb and Max Hoffman ask what power is in 21st century international politics and consider how it can be effectively exercised in current and likely future conditions. Alec Ross and Ben Scott address the implications of technology, in particular the internet and social network technologies, for the practice of diplomacy. And Robin Niblett brings the section to a close with an examination of what the UK can still bring to the table as it seeks to influence the course of international events.

We use a concluding chapter to pull together the overall themes of the book and to explore a progressive approach to foreign policy that would involve an 'Asian Step Change' that we believe can better place the UK to effectively respond to the global trends that are defining the age in which we live.

Despite the fact that the book contains 16 discrete contributions from leading thinkers in the field, we acknowledge at the outset that we do not cover the full waterfront of issues and challenges likely to face an incoming government, whatever its political persuasion, in 2015. No single volume could do that and gaps are therefore inevitable. There is no dedicated chapter, for example, on resource scarcity, though a good case could certainly be made for including one and the theme is central to Jeff Mazo's discussion of the implications of climate change. Similarly there is no dedicated chapter on the rise of unconventional energy, which offers the prospect of US energy self-sufficiency, although the potential implications for the United States' engagement with the Middle East is addressed by Shashank Joshi's discussion of the region. Notwithstanding the continuing risks to the global economy, there is no dedicated chapter on the future governance of the world economy, which could easily merit its own volume of essays.

Despite these gaps, we have tried, as we hope is evident from the structure of the book, to achieve a balance between description and analysis of immediate challenges and long-term trends on the one hand and chapters on substantive issues with reflections on underlying conceptual debates and prescriptions for the future on the other. We take licence in our conclusion to develop some specific themes and to perhaps go further in some of our policy judgments than other individual contributors to the book might prefer. Where we do so, this is either on the basis of our own research and experience or as a result of insights generated through consideration of the contributions to the book as a whole. We hope readers will find the book enlightening and challenging in equal measure, and that its contents provoke wide debate on how best the UK can most effectively influence tomorrow.

IMMEDIATE PRIORITIES

CHAPTER 1

The fight against terrorism in the UK: Are we winning?

by Michael Clarke

The degree of threat that Islamist terror – jihadism in the current political context – has posed to the UK has been a hotly debated subject since the 1990s. Some, like Simon Jenkins, have maintained that the threat has been massively overblown by the security industry and used to embellish policing and security powers that have diminished us all. 'Counter-terrorism', he has said, 'has inflated its enemies and thereby itself into an industry of cold war proportions.'[1] Others, like the former Home Secretary, John Reid, or indeed Tony Blair, have argued that the jihadist threat is real, substantial and only avoids creating great harm to our way of life because it has been handled so well to date.[2] Since the prevention of crime is impossible to measure empirically, there is no definitive answer in this dispute. But at least there are some clear foundations to make the political judgment that all counter-terrorism policies must ultimately rest upon.

---

[1] Simon Jenkins, 'Edward Snowden and his like are vital antidotes to the surveillance state', *Guardian*, 10 June 2013.
[2] John Reid, 'We must be more alert than ever: the terror threat is constantly evolving', *Independent*, 9 September 2009.

Foundations of the Argument

One foundation is that there can be no doubt that al-Qaida united a series of disparate Islamic groups and causes in the late 1990s and created some consensus about the notion of a global caliphate. Osama bin Laden was clear that this aspiration must be re-adopted (after its formal abolition in 1924 and its realistic lapse at least a century before that). On that basis he and Ayman Al-Zawahiri drew up the famous 1998 fatwa declaring war on the apostate governments in the Islamic world and on the Western powers that supported them. Long before Western powers involved themselves in Afghanistan or Iraq – in fact while they were working hard to protect Muslims in Bosnia – al-Qaida unilaterally declared war on the West. This, in any case, followed the first attack on the World Trade Center in 1993 and then two devastating attacks on US embassies in Kenya and Tanzania in 1998. While many across the world wondered for some time after the September 11 attacks of 2001 who was responsible for the atrocity, it was immediately clear in Downing Street, no less than in the White House, that it was the al-Qaida organisation that had followed up a decade of sporadic attacks with this spectacular act of terrorism.[3]

A second foundation to the argument is that while the US responded to this act of war by declaring unambiguously that it would henceforth pursue a 'war on terror', the UK did not. The UK's approach from the very beginning of what many have referred to as the era of 'super-terrorism', has been to regard it as a series of extreme criminal acts, not as a coherent act of war against the UK. This has had important consequences for the way terrorism has been tackled in this country. While the US increased defence expenditure by some 30 per cent in real terms, the UK primarily beefed-up its security services. While the US fell into the Guantanamo Bay trap of detaining almost 800 individuals without trial, but also not under the terms of the Geneva Conventions, the UK has struggled with

---

[3] See Alastair Campbell, *The Alastair Campbell Diaries: Power and Responsibility 1999–2001*, London, Hutchinson, 2011, p. 694; Tony Blair, *A Journey*, London, Arrow Books, 2011, p. 351.

Control Orders for fewer than 25 people, but has generally pursued evidence to bring individuals to trial. While the US federal authorities have pursued suspected terrorists in targeted assassinations via drone strikes and covert operations, the UK – almost certainly complicit in providing information on these targets – has studiously avoided extra-judicial killing and sought to maintain a criminal justice approach that should not be regarded as 'abnormal' in the sense that any war is, by definition, abnormal.

Of course, the UK's approach and that of most of its European partners has not been entirely consistent, nor wholly successful. The security services have had to answer many accusations about their conduct, particularly in the years immediately after 2001. The police have made some egregious errors under the harsh gaze of 24-hour news coverage; and running big military operations in Iraq and Afghanistan has drawn the UK into many of the controversies created by the US 'war on terror' approach. Nevertheless, the UK's stance has generally been vindicated by events. The US terminology surrounding the 'war on terror' was quietly dropped before the end of the Bush administration and President Obama has emphasised that he presides over an end to 'the decade of wars'. This is not to say that the US has now adopted wholesale the criminal justice approach and all it entails. Guantánamo Bay still operates and drone strikes have, if anything, increased. But the US is now closer to the European and UK outlook than at any time in the last decade.

A third foundation for the argument is the record of terrorism and counter-terrorism, as best we know it, in the UK since the late 1990s.[4] It is true that when French commentators referred at the time to 'Londonistan' they were drawing attention to the degree of toleration that UK authorities allowed for radical preaching and organisation that incited terrorism. At that time, UK security and police forces took the view that they knew about the activities of most of the suspect groups operating within the country and they tacitly acknowledge the informal existence of a 'compact' whereby some groups classed as illegal in other states were tolerated in the UK

---

[4] The following details are derived from the RUSI terrorism database.

as long as they did not attack this country. It was a shaky proposition, more believed by radical leaders than the UK authorities themselves, but the relatively relaxed attitude to their activities also facilitated the gathering of useful intelligence on many strands of international terrorism. Nevertheless, the Operation CREVICE investigation of 2003 was the first to undermine any idea of a compact since the plotters were clearly targeting the UK itself, with plans to plant massive bombs in the Ministry of Sound nightclub and at the Bluewater Shopping Centre. That investigation was overshadowed by the tube and bus bombings on 7 July 2005, which then brought home to the UK public as a whole that there was a new dimension altogether to the jihadist threat to the UK.

The London '7/7 attack' was disturbing in several new ways. It was the first example of suicide bombings in Europe, let alone in the UK; it arose predominantly from the Pakistani community in the UK, about whom the security services had less intelligence, given that they had been concentrating on North African sources of jihadism. And it was home-grown terrorism, connected to, though not closely controlled from Pakistan. It forced the UK to face up to some unpleasant truths about some sections of its ethnic minority communities – truths which the Pakistani community in the UK was slow to accept for at least two years afterwards.

The record of counter-terrorism in the UK has to be set around this particular incident. It represented a classic case of the jihadist threat to the UK as it existed in the first decade of this century. Four explosions took place, 52 people were killed, over 700 people were injured, and exactly two weeks later an attempt to replicate the atrocity only failed because the would-be bombers were less skilful than the four perpetrators of the '7/7 attack'. Until the murder of Private Lee Rigby in Woolwich in May 2013, that was the last and only successful terrorist attack in the United Kingdom.

Since 2001 there have been around 50 significant terrorist incidents targeting the UK. Richard Reid, the 'shoe bomber' tried to bring down a transatlantic flight in December 2001. In 2002, a group of would-be terrorists under the direction of an Algerian, Kamel Bourgass, tried to produce the deadly poison ricin to target connections on the Heathrow rail link and throughout Jewish neigh-bourhoods in north London. In early 2003 the British Consulate and the HSBC building in Istanbul were extensively bombed, causing 57 deaths and over 700 injuries. Then, later in 2003, two big plots, the Operation CREVICE conspiracy and the Operation RHYME inves-tigation, revealed that in addition to planned bomb attacks on public targets the intention on the part of Dhiren Barot in the RHYME case was to create the 'gas limo bomb' and a dirty radiological bomb to be used in vehicle devices against public soft targets. In fact Barot's design for a gas limo bomb seemed to have found adherents in the attempt to bomb the Tiger Tiger Nightclub in London in June 2007 and in another plot against the Bluewater Shopping Centre in 2008.

By the time of the London bombings and attempted imitation of them in July 2005 the security services knew, even if the public did not, that some very dangerous plots had been in train for some time. The trend continued. In August 2006, the Bojinka II plot was revealed that would have had a comparable impact to September 11 itself – bringing down seven aircraft simultaneously en route from the UK to the US. Despite some public scepticism about the viability of this plot the security services insist that it was entirely practicable and that it was blown (albeit unintentionally on the US side) only about three weeks ahead of its activation.[5] The Pakistan link in both this and the 7/7 plots ran through Rashid Rauf, a British national who had fled to Pakistan in 2002 following a murder in Birmingham in which he was wanted for questioning. He was believed to have provided some operational direction to both terrorist groups. In June 2007 the Tiger Tiger Nightclub attempt and the related attack on Glasgow airport occurred. In May 2008, Nicky Reilly attempted to bomb the Giraffe children's restaurant in Exeter. In April 2009 12 men, all Pakistani nationals travelling on student visas, were arrested in the north-west on suspicion of planning a series of devastating suicide attacks across the region. Again, despite some public scepticism, the security services are adamant that this was centrally directed by the al-Qaida core organ-isation and represented a genuine attempt to get a significant suicide

---

[5] Private discussions.

squad into the UK to create an impact not dissimilar to the Mumbai terror attacks. In December 2010, 12 men were arrested in Cardiff, London and Stoke-on-Trent accused of planning another series of major explosions on high-profile targets in London.

In between these various well-known incidents, the arrests and trials that were all part of the UK's criminal justice approach revealed eight significant attempts at recruitment and training for terrorism, often involving pipelines for recruits to go to Pakistan, Afghanistan or Iraq. There were convictions for creating web propaganda and attempting to procure weapons. There were nine high-profile cases of possessing and distributing terrorist material and seven cases of active planning or early action for terrorist acts in the UK, including the murder of an MP and of soldiers returning from Iraq or Afghanistan.

Dramatic as these examples were, however, it was also clear by 2010 that the pattern was changing yet again. The al-Qaida core organisation in South Asia was being severely disrupted and reduced. The locus of jihadist activity against the UK and other Western countries was shifting to routes operating from the Yemen and from Somalia. The style of attack was changing too. The relatively large – and often connected – cells of terror groups, usually very amateur but always with at least one member who had been trained and had some terrorist tradecraft, were being replaced by the 'lone wolf' terrorists. These were radicalised individuals who had very little training but high motivation and were simply encouraged by radicals in Yemen or Somalia to try their luck with whatever plans and devices they could invent. There were attempts to put small bombs on freight aircraft, moves to infiltrate 'sleepers' into airport jobs in the UK, and constant encouragement to assassinate leaders or symbolic individuals such as members of the armed forces. The murder of Private Rigby in Woolwich in 2013 represented the realisation of many such calls. The attack was not carefully planned and seemed to be relatively spontaneous when a suitable victim appeared; it was carried out with crude weapons and the suspected killers waited for the inevitable showdown with armed police. Like the Boston bombers of April 2013, they behaved as homicidal exhibitionists, who, like the Mumbai bombers of 2011, intended to go down in a public shootout. During 2012, according to the government's annual report, 45 individuals were charged with terrorism offences, 23 of them were convicted and 25 awaited trial at the beginning of 2013. More to the point, since 2008 over 150 foreign nationals have been kidnapped by Islamist terrorist groups (13 of whom were British nationals). There has also been an increase in the targeting of foreigners for kidnap in northern Nigeria, with most ascribing blame to Boko Haram's splinter group Ansaru, which has been identified as having a more international agenda.

In the face of this catalogue of terror directed at the UK, the police and security services can regard their efforts as successful certainly within the UK, if not entirely outside the country. Only the 7/7 attacks – four bombs – and the Woolwich attack – one murder – can be regarded as jihadist victories over a 12-year period. Nevertheless, it is also apparent that five other plots, involving at least nine more bombs, would have worked if the terrorists had made their devices correctly. The Richard Reid incident, the Tiger Tiger Nightclub, the Glasgow airport attack, the 21/7 imitation attacks and the Giraffe restaurant attack all evaded security and would have worked if the perpetrators had been less amateur. So the police and security services have been both effective over the last 12 years but also lucky; and they will have to go on being both effective and lucky as long as jihadism regards the UK as a key target and continues to look for novel ways to perpetrate terrorist acts.

The fourth foundation of assessment is the knowledge that the UK is regarded as a prominent target for terrorism by jihadist leaders the world over. Violent radicals in South Asia, the Arabian peninsula, east and west Africa, even on occasion in Indonesia, have repeatedly singled out the UK as one of their designated targets. The reasons are fairly clear. While the 'apostate' governments of the Muslim world are the ultimate targets of jihadism, those governments are regarded as viable only because they have been supported by the US in partic-ular, and by the corrupting forces of the Western powers in general. The US, however, is a tough target to hit, though not impossible, and does not have a social demographic dynamic that easily helps create the conditions for successful terrorist planning and recruitment.

But the UK evidently does, as witnessed by the consistency with which around 10 per cent to 15 per cent of the Muslim population in the UK express clear or very strong support for the activities of jihadists around the world.[6] More than in most Western countries, with its diverse multiculturalism and strong ethnic identities, even a marginalised sympathy for jihadist terror provides many opportunities to generate home-grown terrorism in the UK. Then too, hitting the UK is symbolically the next best thing to hitting the US itself. As the most consistent military ally of the US, the UK shares in much of the alienation within Muslim communities that has been provoked by the interventions in Afghanistan and Iraq.

In the case of the UK, Baroness Eliza Manningham-Buller, a former head of MI5, acknowledged that these interventions certainly focused and channelled tendencies towards home-grown terrorism during the decade after 2001 and in many cases increased recruitment.[7] Repeated government denials at the time that Afghanistan and Iraq were irrelevant to the terror threat in the UK were never convincing and are no longer made. On the other hand, the historical record emphasises that the jihadist threat to the UK was certainly not created by these operations. Planning for big terror attacks and some of the attacks and incidents themselves pre-dated even the September 11 atrocity, let alone the contentious invasion of Iraq in 2003.[8] The jihadist rhetoric that home-grown terror is no more than a defence against UK 'crusaders' in Muslim lands is absurd on many grounds, but certainly not supported by even a cursory examination of the historical record.

The final foundation of any judgment about the UK success in countering terrorism is the role played by the government's CONTEST strategy.[9] This strategy has four elements, known as the Pursue, Protect, Prepare and Prevent work streams. The Protect

---

[6] See ICM Poll for BBC, *Daily Telegraph*, 19 February 2006: BBC News, British Muslims Poll: key points (for Policy Exchange), 29 January 2007.
[7] *The Iraq Enquiry* (Chilcott Report), Oral Evidence, 20 July 2010, p. 19.
[8] *Ibid.*, pp. 15–16.
[9] HM Government, *CONTEST: The UK Strategy for Countering Terrorism, Annual Report*, Cm 8583, March 2013.

work stream, which seeks to create greater technical resilience in the UK to terrorist activities, has made good progress in the last eight years since the CONTEST strategy began. New buildings have counter-terrorist features designed into them and progress is being made in creating international standards for better access to technical and travel data on people moving around the world. By contrast, work under the Prepare rubric has been generally patchy. Emergency services are much better equipped to deal with terrorist events than they were before 2005, but there can be little doubt that inter-oper-ability between the joint emergency services is still relatively low and is a constant source of potential vulnerability if it were ever severely tested in the future. The Prevent side of the strategy has seen a number of initiatives to try to counter radicalisation within the UK, dealing at community level to help facilitate local communities to police themselves and to find ways of channelling political alienation into democratic and non-violent avenues. The success of the Prevent programme has been a matter of political controversy between the Labour government that introduced it and the Coalition govern-ment that has thoroughly reviewed it since 2010. Nevertheless, Prevent initiatives continue and are evolving as local communities take increased responsibility for the implementation of locally based initiatives which, in reality, are closely related to crime prevention measures in general. They vary greatly from one region to another and provide a patchy record of success across the country.

The most controversial element of the CONTEST strategy however has been the Pursue work stream, which seeks to intro-duce measures to monitor, disrupt and arrest potential terrorists before they can commit any specific acts. This strand of government policy has raised increasingly serious questions regarding civil liber-ties and rights to privacy in the UK. Criticism of the government's policy has been increasingly vocal since the Terrorism Act of 2006. A Communications Data Bill was introduced in 2012 but severely revised and then dropped in the face of intense criticism both inside and outside parliament. Similarly, civil liberties groups and parliamen-tarians attacked a new justice and security bill on the grounds that it was disproportionate to the nature of the threat. In particular, the notion that 'Closed Material Proceedings' could be initiated to allow the intelligence agencies to give secret evidence in court was regarded as a fundamental challenge to the individual rights of UK citizens to a free and public trial. Though the security services are keen to demonstrate that they can fight controversial cases by going to court to give evidence which they previously would have had to withhold for national security reasons, the greater threat to civil liberties of the notion of 'secret courts' has taken precedence in the public debate.

The CONTEST strategy is, by definition, controversial since it is an attempt to enhance the legal process to deal with the new aspects of jihadist terrorism in the UK. Nevertheless, CONTEST has also created a coherent set of measures which offer a strategic approach to counter-terrorism and provide a framework that goes beyond a merely reactive and ad hoc response. It is much admired, and imitated, by other governments around the world who also feel threatened by terrorism. CONTEST can also claim some success. Elite opinion worries more about civil liberties than does wider public opinion. This, in itself, does not make CONTEST automatically right or constitutionally justifiable, but it indicates that, as controversial as it is, the CONTEST strategy can claim some broad sense of popular legitimacy.

The Assessment of Costs

All the evidence indicates that successive Prime Ministers from the Blair era onwards have been correct in their assessments that the jihadist threat to the UK is 'generational'. The threat is generational in the sense that it is promulgated largely by an alienated younger generation of Muslims and Muslim converts, albeit directed and inspired by some older generation radicals. And it is generational in the sense that the threat seems likely to last for a generation or more. Jihadists, unlike Irish Republicans, Basque nationalists, the Palestine Liberation Organisation or Hamas cannot be accommodated with anything that the political mainstream can offer. Nothing less than a global revolution would satisfy the jihadist aspiration for a genuine global caliphate so no form of grand political settlement will ever be possible with jihadism. Yet it mobilises an anti-Western, anti-modernist alienation that is also unlikely to diminish in the foreseeable future. So a jihadist threat to Western society will be a fact of life for as long as we can imagine, though it is reasonable to expect that it will wax and wane over the coming years even as it changes its shape, and its mid-term objectives.

Judgments about UK counter-terrorism in this context are therefore not a question of defining victory or defeat in this contest but rather of balancing the relatively high success indicated by the operational record against the material and political costs of the counter-terrorism strategy and the level of vulnerability to future attacks which may now be anticipated.

If the government was right to class international terrorism as one of the Tier 1 risks in its Strategic Defence and Security Review and its National Security Strategy in 2010, then it is comparable with cyber-attacks, inter-state military crises and major natural hazards in the priority it should be given.[10] Some would dispute that international terrorism is really such a threat. The amount of damage and disruption that IRA and Loyalist terrorism occasioned in Northern Ireland and in mainland UK from 1969 to 1995 was very considerable. Jihadist terror has not come anywhere near that level so far. On the other hand, jihadists are deliberately indiscriminate in their targeting; though they often aim for symbolic targets, there is every intention to kill and maim as many innocent people as possible. And though the material costs of these attacks may be low, the political cost – and the potential political costs of a real spectacular – are very high indeed. Security chiefs worry about two particular terrorist thresholds that would have major political consequences. One is the possibility of terrorists using chemical, biological, radiological or nuclear elements (CBRN) in a successful attack. There are great technical problems for a terrorist associated with any CBRN-based device and the actual death and destruction such elements of weapons of

---

[10] HM Government, *A Strong Britain in an Age of Uncertainty, the National Security Strategy*, Cm 7953, London, 2010, p. 27; HM Government, *Securing Britain in an Age of Uncertainty, the Strategic Defence and Security Review*, Cm 7948, London, 2010.

mass destruction might cause is not likely to be so great. But the public psychology of having been subjected to a CBRN attack, the fear and uncertainty it would probably engender, would take governments into new territory in their attempts to convince the public that they were safeguarding them properly.

The second threshold is the possibility of indiscriminate 'series' attacks; a campaign such as the 21/7 bombers tried to create, that would launch attacks at regular intervals in different places to create widespread anxiety and indicate that the government was evidently unable to prevent the terrorists from attacking wherever, and whenever, they chose. Again, much as terrorist groups might like to create this situation, it is far harder to realise in operational terms than it sounds. But the political fall-out from any public perception that the government was losing control in this way – whether real or not – would be very considerable. It is the potential of jihadists to cross such thresholds and their declared intention to do so that leads the government to regard international terrorism as a Tier 1 threat.

On this reasoning, the material cost of meeting this challenge has been relatively low in terms of the threat itself. Spending on the security services (primarily MI5, MI6 and GCHQ) was increased by around 30 per cent between 2007 and 2010 and in 2008 the government introduced a 'Single Security Budget' of around £3.5 billion, covering the intelligence services, the police, Home Office and the relevant parts of other government departments. This had risen from something over £2 billion in real terms before 2001. The Single Security Budget included amounts such as £100 million on 'Prevent' activities within the CONTEST strategy and £38 million in the Foreign Office budget to promote better relations inside foreign societies that can become recruiting grounds for terrorists. Not all the Single Security Budget is allocated to countering terrorism. There are many other calls on this budget, such as non-terrorist threats to security, serious and organised crime, foreign espionage activities and so on. Around 40 per cent of the full budget is believed to be devoted, under normal circumstances, to countering terrorism from all sources, and jihadist terror makes up the greatest proportion of that.

What might be defined as the political costs, however, are a matter of perception. Civil liberties campaigners argue that the price has been far too high in terms of extra surveillance throughout society and the intrusion of the state through international intelligence cooperation, particularly with the US, into personal telephone records, emails and all forms of electronic communication. Most of all, they claim that counter-terrorism has had a corrupting influence on the principle of the rule of law in draconian new legislation – particularly the 2000 Regulation of Investigative Powers Act which covered surveillance; the 2000 Terrorism Act which broadened police powers of stop and search; the 2005 Prevention of Terrorism Act which created 'Control Orders'; and the 2006 Terrorism Act which created a broad range of offences connected with showing interest in terrorist organisations.[11] In addition is the guilt by association of the British government in US extraordinary rendition of terrorist suspects, torture and prolonged imprisonment without trial. Successive British governments have maintained that they have no truck with torture or with any unlawful behaviour on the international scene. But their necessary cooperation with foreign intelligence services, not only those of the United States, has raised a series of cases which suggest at least some real inconsistencies in this stance over the last 12 years.

If civil libertarians and parliamentarians have made a strong case that the costs of counter-terrorism are disproportionate to the manifestation of terrorism to date (if not to its potential in the future), their reservations seem not to be shared by the general public. While British public opinion is generally very sensitive to civil liberties issues on other grounds, it seems to be relatively unimpressed by these arguments in the case of terrorism and prepared to tolerate extraordinary measures on this issue that it would not on others.

Nor, it must be said, has the political fall-out from terrorism and counter-terrorism had the effect, so far, of creating a crisis in inter-ethnic relations across the UK. Despite some anxieties and a spike in relatively

---

[11] See Liberty, *From 'War' to Law: Liberty's Response to the Coalition Government's Review of Counter-terrorism and Security Powers 2010*. Policy paper, 2010.

minor incidents following the Rigby murder of 2013, the attempts of jihadists to polarise UK society by their acts has not succeeded.[12]

The final element in the equation is the level of vulnerability the UK must now accept as a result of its present counter-terrorism preparedness. No society can ever be completely safe from terrorist acts and an open, liberal society that remains near the top of the jihadists' target list must accept a certain level of vulnerability. The security services and the government's National Security Council have their own understanding of acceptable and unacceptable levels of vulnerability and these are implied in a general form in the annual National Risk Register. In general, it is fair to say that the government has put a good deal of covert effort into making the CBRN threshold as difficult as possible to cross within the UK, though it cannot do as much for British interests abroad. And there is high confidence that the police and security services have good chances of foiling the extended organisation and planning that would be necessary to set up indiscriminate series attacks. There can be no guarantees that there are similarly high thresholds against low-tech, lone wolf and lucky amateur attacks, however. And there is an expectation that these will continue to happen from time to time. Nevertheless, it is calculated that even events at the level of the London attacks of 2005 would not disrupt society to a significant extent, have a strategic impact on UK policy in the world or force a change in counter-terrorist strategy.

The answer to the essential question of this chapter must always be a political judgment. The fight against jihadism will not quickly be won in any meaningful sense. But the jihadists have so far not succeeded in any of their essential aims in targeting the UK and whether or not the country over-reacts to the threat is a matter that remains in its own hands. Jihadism is a perverted and vicious force that promotes extreme and indiscriminate violence. But for all its pervasiveness across some parts of the world, it is not, in itself, a strong force. It will only win a strategic victory over the UK if the country allows it do so.

---

[12] YouGov, What The World Thinks, 'public calm in the face of terror,' 26 May 2013.

CHAPTER 2

Iran and beyond: How do we pursue a WMD-free zone in the Middle East?

by Rolf Ekéus

The strategic environment in the Middle East has over decades been characterised by the constant tension between the major political actors in the region. If the situation on the European continent during the cold war had a distinct dual character of two secular ideological systems – democracy and communism – facing each other, both sides armed with destructive capabilities without any precedent in human history, the Middle Eastern political-strategic scenario is complex and multifaceted, both in a religious and ethnic sense and in military and strategic terms.

The centuries-old rivalry and power game between Arabs and Persians – the Ottoman and Persian Empires – or in religious terms, between Sunni and Shia Muslims, is now reflected in the tensions between Iran and several of its Arab neighbours like Saudi Arabia, the majority of the Arab Gulf states, and Egypt. The war from 1980 to 1988 between the Arab state Iraq, then under the secular Saddam Hussein, and Iran, restructured through the 1979 Islamic (Shia) revolution, had much of the character of an Arab/Persian ethnic conflict, in which Iraq's religious Shia Muslim majority clearly had chosen its secular Arab identity above its religious affinity.

In that conflict most Arab states sided with Iraq, by providing financial and material support. The USA provided military material and intelligence data to Iraq, and its European allies, as well as the Soviet Union and its partners in the Warsaw Pact, delivered large-scale material support. Notably, only one state was backing Iran in that conflict with military equipment and technology, namely Israel (if we don't count US President Reagan's personal 'Iran-Contra' initiative).

Today, after the US intervention and occupation in 2003, Iraq is subject to bitter internal and sectarian tensions and rivalry, with a negative impact on its national military capability. The country is no longer the influential strategic regional actor it once was.

Egypt, the most populous Arab state, still searching a new identity after the impact of the Arab spring events, has taken a cautious and low-key position on the ongoing conflicts. In Syria, the leadership under the al-Assad regime, father and son, has tried to maintain a secular identity to protect its minorities, but now the regime is seriously challenged by the country's revolting Sunni Muslim majority. This means that Iran, having gained influence in Iraq as a consequence of the US-led invasion having demolished Iraq's secular military and administrative structures, is now running the risk of losing its most important Arab partner, Syria.

This has tempted Iran to intervene indirectly, by supporting and encouraging Hezbollah engagement in Syria on the side of the regime. At the same time, Saudi Arabia and some of the Gulf states, especially Qatar, are providing the Syrian opposition with large quantities of military equipment. This, and the deepening engagement by extreme Muslims like the Salafists, tends to further increase Iran–Arab tensions.

The Israeli Dimension

With the establishment of the State of Israel in 1948 a new dimension of great strategic significance was added to the region. Israel, a newcomer in the contemporary Middle East, became a challenger to the political order shaped by the French and British colonial rulers, who left the region after the end of the second world war. The occupation by Israel of the Palestinian West Bank in 1967 led to increased tensions in the region. Thus to the Arab–Persian and the Sunni–Shia centuries old rivalry was added the Arab–Israeli confrontations.

A strategic Israeli/Iranian partnership followed, as reflected in Israel's material support to Iran during the Iran–Iraq war of 1980–88. This was only ended with Iran's later aggressive and threatening language against Israel as regards the Palestinian question, which was aimed at the tactical consideration of gaining sympathy among the general Arab population ('the Arab street') and thus possibly weakening the Arab leaders who were hostile to Iran and who had concluded unpopular formal peace treaties with Israel (Egypt and Jordan), or developed the Arab Peace Initiative 2002 (masterminded by Saudi Arabia).

WMD in the Middle East

Into this mix, the acquisition by Israel of a nuclear weapons capability in the late 1960s radically impacted upon Iranian and Arab security calculations.

Considerable technical and economic difficulties made the nuclear weapons option not very attractive to the Arab states but political considerations also spoke against the acquisition of these weapons. Most important of these considerations was the creation and entry into force in 1970 of the multilateral nuclear non-proliferation treaty (NPT), through which the depository states, the United States, the United Kingdom and the Soviet Union, exercised powerful pressure on non-nuclear weapons states to forego the acquisition of such weapons. Israel's Arab neighbours joined the treaty, thus forsaking the option to acquire a bomb of their own and leaving Israel as the only state in the region not to join the NPT.

Instead both Egypt and Syria followed Iraq's example and obtained a chemical weapons capability designed to serve as something of a deterrent, 'the poor man's nuclear weapon', against Israel. Thus these two states refrained from joining the Chemical Weapons Convention when it entered into force in 1996. As a consequence few specifics are known about the size and content of their chemical weapons capacity as they, in contrast to all parties to the Chemical Weapons Convention, have no reporting obligation to the Organisation for the Prohibition of Chemical Weapons (OPCW). Neither Egypt nor Syria has ratified the Biological Weapons Treaty. Iran, as we now know, has been pursuing its own discrete nuclear programme for many years.

Steps Towards the WMD-Free Zone in the Middle East

As far back as 1964 Egypt introduced the idea of a denuclearisation of the Middle East, but it was in 1974 that the Shah of Iran, supported by Egypt, launched a formal proposal in the United Nations (UN) General Assembly of a nuclear-weapons-free zone in the Middle East. Since then the proposal has stayed on the agenda of the General Assembly with the support of all states in the region.

In 1990 President Mubarak of Egypt introduced in the UN the idea of a zone in the Middle East free of not only nuclear weapons, but also of biological and chemical weapons and of all missiles for their delivery. This initiative also received a blessing from the Security Council in its chapter VII ceasefire resolution 687, which ended the Kuwait war in 1991. The inclusion of chemical weapons in the zone initiative was a reflection of the atrocities in Saddam Hussein's war against Iran and the opposing Kurds in northern Iraq, when chemical weapons had been used on a large scale.

At the same time, a prohibition of chemical weapons was being pursued in the negotiations in the Conference on Disarmament (CD) in Geneva leading to the international Convention on Chemical Weapons (CWC) in 1996.

The so-called Mubarak Plan was clearly an effort to make the idea of a zone more attractive to Israel, the only nuclear-weapons-armed state in the region, by signaling that the Arab states, Egypt and Syria, known like Iraq to have chemical weapons in their arsenals, would be ready to sacrifice their chemical weapons with the establishment of a zone in the Middle East free of weapons of mass destruction.

In 1995, when the NPT was due to expire after 25 years in force, the parties agreed on the indefinite extension of the treaty. Clearly a condition for the Arabs to accept the extension was the adoption by the NPT parties of a resolution on the Middle East calling upon all states in the region to take practical steps towards the establishment of an effectively verifiable Middle East zone free of weapons of mass destruction, nuclear, chemical and biological, and of their delivery systems. The co-sponsors of the resolution were the three NPT depository states, the United States, the United Kingdom and the Russian Federation.

After 1995, when the indefinite extension thus had been landed, it appeared that many NPT states had lost interest in the zone project, even if it was reaffirmed at the NPT Review Conference in 2000 and discussed at the subsequent NPT Review Conference in 2005.

However, even as the Israeli nuclear weapons capability remained subject to perennial attention internationally and, indeed, regionally, concerns have been growing about the intentions behind Iran's quickly expanding nuclear enrichment programme. These concerns re-energised the politics of the WMD-free zone when the 2010 NPT Review Conference assembled.

The conference, after having expressed its dismay with the absence of implementation of the 1995 resolution on the Middle East, endorsed unanimously, thus including Iran, a programme of practical steps for the implementation of the resolution. These steps included the UN Secretary-General and the co-sponsors of the 1995 resolution (Russia, the US and the UK, as depository governments of the NPT), in consultation with the states of the region, convening a conference in 2012 on the establishment of a Middle East zone free of nuclear weapons and all other weapons of mass destruction, to be attended by all states in the Middle East. This would be on the basis of arrangements freely arrived at by the states of the region, and with full support and engagement of the nuclear-weapon states. An understanding was that the participating states should be the members of the League of Arab Nations, Iran and Israel as well as the three convener states, the US, the UK and Russia.

The terms of reference of the conference would be the 1995 resolution. In October 2011 it was decided that the conference would take place in Finland in the winter of 2012. A senior Finnish diplomat was appointed as a facilitator of the conference.

The facilitator, the Head of the Department of Political Affairs of the Ministry of Foreign Affairs, Jaakko Laajava, initiated an intensive process of consultations with the states in the region on substantive and organisational aspects of the conference, modalities and rules of procedure, trying to accommodate different points of departure. On invitation, the International Atomic Energy Agency (IAEA), the OPCW, the Biological Weapons Convention Implementation Support Unit and the Preparatory Commission for the Comprehensive Test Ban Treaty Organization (CTBTO) have provided supporting documents for the conference regarding modalities for the zone.

The conference, planned for December 2012, could not take place however, as not all relevant states were ready to participate.

At the NPT Preparatory Committee (Prepcom) meeting in April 2013, the Arab states expressed their deep disappointment at the postponement, criticised the convener states and demanded that the conference be held not later than 2013. The Egyptian delegation, in a protest against the lack of agreement of a set of date for the conference, staged a walk-out of the Prepcom meeting.

In spite of this setback, the facilitator and the convener states continue, at the time of writing, to consult with states of the region and seek to hold further preparatory consultations on the conference's arrangements and the timing of the conference, still with the ambition to hold it in Finland.

The Political Dimension
and the Diplomatic Process

The eternal dilemma facing everyone who deals with disarmament affairs is whether security and stability should come first as a condition for disarmament, or whether disarmament must come first as a condition for security and stability. The same could be said to be applicable for military confidence-building measures (CBMs) – should such CBMs lay the groundwork for negotiating security structures or should established security structures be strengthened and supported by CBMs as a form of verification and compliance arrangements.

The European experience is relevant here from 1973 to 1975 and 1984 to 1990, which demonstrated that systematic efforts to build confidence between negotiating parties could make substantive and formal agreements possible, even in the context of strategic-level tensions between the major opponents in the cold war. The success of the European approaches at that time was based upon a combination of military confidence-building with political undertakings. The system of information-sharing and verifiable openness as regards troop dispositions, military training and equipment provided the confidence necessary to make political compromises and commitments possible.

An effort to transfer these European experiences to the Middle East region was made in 1990 with the Arms Control and Regional Security Working Group (ACRS) initiative as a part of the Madrid Conference on the Middle East. What prevented the ACRS from finally succeeding was the traditional dilemma facing arms control and disarmament negotiations: namely, that such agreements are difficult or even impossible to reach before security is assured, and security will only be assured when agreements on arms control are reached.

It was this fundamental tension which the negotiating parties to the European Security Conference managed to master. Participating states succeeded in combining coordinated agreements encompassing recognition of frontiers, established during the second world war, with military CBMs and substantive reductions of conventional forces.

However, one significant difference between the European security contexts during the 1970s and 1980s and the present security situation in the Middle East is that nuclear weapons in Europe were essentially a matter of superpower relations, with a specific strategic and bilateral dimension and a separate negotiating context, while the Middle East nuclear issue (as well as chemical and biological weapons) is linked to a multilateral and multifaceted security situation, with elements of legal instruments in the fields of arms control, non-proliferation and disarmament as part of regional political considerations. Obviously, conventional forces are essential for security relations in the Middle East, but nuclear weapons, whether really existing, as in Israel, or potential among other states in the region, are first and foremost instruments in a specific political setting.

Clearly, relations between Israel and its Arab neighbours is the political factor that has dominated public considerations of the question of a nuclear-weapons-free zone. It is worth noting in this regard that, in spite of the harsh rhetoric and critique of Israel, the Arabs, as regards nuclear weapons, have appeared for much of the time resigned to tolerating the status quo – a de facto but non-declared Israeli nuclear weapons status. However, considerable changes in the relative strengths of the conventional forces in the region in the last decade may have had an impact, as have, of course, the changing political circumstances in several Arab states.

While the Israeli armed forces have become generally stronger and more technically advanced, the military quality and capacity of Arab states like Iraq, Egypt and Syria have been compromised by the political events and developments during the last 10 years. It appears that only Jordan has managed to maintain the quality and operational capability of its army. Thus, even a non-nuclear Israel would be strong enough to deter its neighbours from entering into an armed conflict with it. This does not, of course, exclude the fact that the Israeli nuclear weapons capability will remain a matter of great political and psychological complication in the region, but it does mean that the context in which that capability sits has changed.

The other story, of course, though not so much in evidence in the public domain in the Arab countries, is the prospect of Iran obtaining nuclear weapons. Leading Arab states like Egypt and, even more, Saudi Arabia, warn that the realisation of an Iranian atom bomb would see, as a response, an Arab bomb, indigenously produced or acquired from abroad. Considering the growing international tensions around the Iranian nuclear programme and the potential of the outbreak of military conflict, the pursuit of a WMD-free zone in the region must now grow in significance.

When negotiators explore the best approach on how to make use of and integrate confidence and security building measures

(CSBMs) into a framework to create the zone, it will be essential to start by establishing a common base of the desirability (without binding commitment) of such a zone, and a mutual undertaking by the parties to work towards that end, by agreeing on the geographical extent of the zone and its scope.

With such fundamental understandings in place, talks on voluntary CSBMs could start with the aim of reducing tensions and suspicion, and building trust. Such steps could in the beginning be unilateral and declaratory in nature, with expectations of reciprocity. If these steps were to have an impact, talks on possible CSBMs could lead to the start of a process which should follow a step-by-step pattern, aiming at politically binding agreements, thus not necessarily legally binding in the beginning. Military CSBMs could be designed after the Conference on Security and Cooperation in Europe/Organization for Security and Co-operation in Europe (CSCE/OSCE) methods of exchanging data about military organisation, manpower and major weapons and equipment systems in Europe, as well as about military movements and exercises to be subject to transnational inspections and observation missions.

Obviously CSBMs concerning WMD-related items cannot be designed on the basis of the European experience as the nuclear dimension was not part of the CSCE work. These capabilities were dealt with mainly in a bilateral great power context. But that does not exclude the possibility that agreements and deals of a CSBM character relative to nuclear and other WMDs can contribute effectively and constructively by creating the necessary political framework of trust in the Middle East region.

Clearly verification procedures as regards the nuclear weapons issues must be much more stringent than those prescribed under the NPT. The Additional Protocol of the NPT could be a good start, but much could be learned from the successful disarmament work in Iraq by the UN Special Commission (UNSCOM) /IAEA inspection and monitoring activities between 1991 and 1998, which turned out to have a 100 per cent success rate, including with regard to Iraq's chemical and biological weapons capabilities and the missiles for their delivery.

The international institutions that have a statutory role of monitoring existing conventions, such as the IAEA and the OPCW, should be given more power to monitor and extend their activities to the maximum possible extent. Israel has in addition indicated that a verification system for a zone could also include bilateral rights similar to those prescribed in arms control agreements adopted in the context of the CSCE/OSCE, the Treaty on Conventional Forces in Europe (CFE) and the Vienna Document on CSBMs, which prevent it being outvoted by the majority in an eventual international committee tasked to monitor progress in the creation of the WMD-free zone in the region.

As a concluding remark, it is worth recalling that in the mid 1980s, when disarmament in Europe was beginning to be realised, there was no lack of suspicion and mistrust between the parties. But if the governments of the states in the Middle East could follow that pattern and openly engage in dialogue, first about modalities for talks, consultations and negotiations, and then be ready to meet, an inner dynamic may yet be realised. The nations and their governments in the Middle East need creativity and political courage to overcome all the obstacles they are facing and make use of the momentum which was created by the decision at the NPT Review Conference in 2010.

GEOPOLITICS

CHAPTER 3

Making Britain China-proof

by Mark Leonard

A Martian landing in Westminster would be forgiven for thinking that the biggest challenge to the British way of life and influence emanates from Brussels. But the truth is that Beijing raises questions of a more fundamental and existential nature.

China is already the second biggest economy in the world, the number one trading partner for 128 countries, the biggest holder of foreign reserves, the world's biggest polluter, the biggest consumer of Middle Eastern oil and gas, the country with the fastest growing defence budget and the biggest contributor to United Nations (UN) peace-keeping missions among the veto-wielding members of the Security Council. And over the next decade and a half, it is likely to be transformed not just in its relative power to the West but in the structure of its economy, politics and foreign policy. Its economy could grow to twice the size of America's. Rather than being an exporter of cheap products, it could have the world's biggest consumer market and the largest spending on R&D. Rather than being a traditional authoritarian state, its politics is likely to be transformed by the internet. And rather than having the passive foreign policy of recent years, it will become active in defence of its global interests.

British policy-makers hoped that as China became richer and more developed, it would gradually come to share our values and define its interests in a similar way. But instead, as China develops, it poses an ever greater challenge to Western ideas. Its model of state capitalism – with a key role for state-owned enterprises and closed domestic markets – is a challenge to liberal capitalism. The rise of the Chinese internet and a more pluralised civil society have fanned nationalism and belligerence rather than liberal values. And China's participation in global institutions has hollowed out many of the progressive norms rather than 'socialising' China. With a larger loan portfolio, China's development bank is now a serious alternative to the World Bank.

China does not pose an ideological challenge to the West in the same way that the Soviet Union did; it does not offer a radically different model of governance, or threaten to invade other countries or upend the international system. However, the new China will change the terms of trade on the global stage and threaten to make many of the traditional approaches of British foreign policy counter-productive. British Atlanticism risks dragging our security apparatus into a regional power struggle that we don't understand. Our commitment to multilateralism risks being turned into a recipe for global gridlock. Our commitment to free trade could see British workers trying to compete on the wrong side of an uneven playing field.

The biggest challenge for progressives is to reconcile their ideas for how the world should be with what it is possible to achieve. Nothing will expose the gulf between the two as much as China in future years. This chapter tries to explain how Chinese thinkers and officials are thinking about the next phase of their country's development before mapping out some of the fundamental dilemmas faced by British progressives in rising to the challenge of a global China.

The Challenge of China 3.0

The Chinese like to think of history progressing in 30-year cycles, and have even taken to using the jargon of the internet to describe it. China 1.0 was the three decades of Mao Zedong, the heady cocktail of a planned economy, a Leninist political system, and a foreign policy of spreading global revolution. China 2.0 was Deng Xiaoping's market revolution, which brought export-led growth, political repression and economic diplomacy. But with the 18th Party Congress in 2012, many Chinese predicted that the country not only said goodbye to some of the leading players of the last decade – it also inaugurated the beginning of a new era: China 3.0.

The real turning point was the global financial crisis in 2008, which catapulted China into the global spotlight, but also exposed many of the shortcomings of the Deng Xiaoping consensus. In 2011 and 2012 China had an extraordinary explosion of debate and discussion about its future. The Hu Jintao/Wen Jiabao duo were becoming lame ducks and the new leadership had yet to impose its authority. Many of the ideas which have worried the elite internally suddenly erupted into a public debate. Although Xi Jinping has been quick to establish his authority and to re-establish party discipline, the issues that preoccupied the country during the Beijing spring are likely to be the defining dilemmas of his decade in office. China has been facing a triple crisis of success. By 2008 China had managed to achieve each of the three goals of Deng's era – affluence, stability and power – but the policies that allowed China to reach them are now in danger of becoming self-defeating.

China 3.0 will be defined by the quest to escape each of these three traps – and the policies that are adopted will also transform China.

China's Affluence Crisis

For most of the last 30 years, China's leaders have been kept awake at night worrying about their country's poverty and the problems of a socialist economy. But today it is China's affluence and the problems of the market that are causing sleepless nights. China's leadership has spent a generation obsessively focusing on economic growth at the expense of all else, and the new vested interests that have been created are resisting the economic rebalancing required for long-term development. A surge of conspicuous private consumption and vanity projects has come at the expense of investment in public goods, such as pensions or affordable health care or public education.

On one side of the debate about how to escape from the affluence trap are economists such as Zhang Weiying, who form the core of the pro-market New Right. They pioneered the gradualist economic reforms of the 1980s and 1990s and now want the state to finish the job and privatise the rest of the economy: restart the interrupted privatisation of the state sector; give the private sector equal rights to finance; and end collective ownership of land. On the other side of the debate are New Left thinkers who favour boosting wages; ending the artificial subsidies for exports; providing access to social services; reforming the *hukou* system that ties each Chinese citizen's social rights to their birthplace, leaving millions of migrant workers without any rights and ending the 'financial repression' of artificially low interest rates. The problem for the approaches of both the left and the right is that they run into the vested interests that have grown during the dizzying two decades in which crony capitalism has taken off.

But China's senior leadership is seized of the importance of rebalancing the economy – not least because Xi Jinping and Li Keqiang will be in power for the next 10 years. China's exports to the developing world are already no longer simply cheap goods. The next phase of China's 'going out' is targeting developed markets such as Europe, which is important to China as a way of moving up the value chain, investing in high and green technology, and buying established brand names and business know-how and supply chains. One report predicts that Chinese outbound investment is likely to rise to $1 trillion by 2020, with the greater part directed towards the European Union (EU) and the US.[1] That would mean at least $250 bn in investment in the EU in the coming decade.

But more important than that are the changes to the nature of the Chinese economy if Beijing manages to rebalance. Last year saw a slew of studies and best-selling books looking at China's prospects for 2030. Hu Angang, an influential economist in Beijing who is rumoured to be one of the pens behind the working report for the 18th Party Congress that inaugurated Xi Jinping, wrote a best-selling book on *China 2030* arguing that by then China will have an

---

[1] Daniel H. Rosen and Thilo Hanemann, 'An American Open Door?', *Asia Society*, May 2011, available at: http://asiasociety.org/policy/center-us-china-relations/american-open-door.

economy over twice the size of America's. But more importantly, he says, it will be a different kind of economy from that which we have today – powered by domestic consumption rather than exports and investment. He predicts that China will be the number one import market for the world, the biggest global source of foreign investment (buying up Western companies, brands and assets with its savings); a new science and technology superpower (registering more patents and investing more money in research – both natural sciences and social sciences – than anyone else). This will make China the number one hi-tech export country – including the export of green technologies.

Fulfilling these grandiose predictions will depend on China being able to navigate some enormous challenges that it faces today: a debt crisis caused by off-balance sheet borrowing by local government with many of the characteristics of the US sub-prime crisis; the resistance of powerful vested interests particularly in the state-owned enterprises to economic rebalancing; the political challenge of managing a restive middle class that is online 24/7 through social media. However, it is clear from all this that if Hu Angang's predictions are even vaguely correct, Britain will need to rethink its policies to cope with a different China. The key questions include the asymmetry of market access – China has access to many sectors in European markets that are closed to European firms in China. Second, there are questions about how to compete with subsidised Chinese companies. Third, there is the matter of how to attract inward investment.

China's Stability Crisis

After the Tiananmen Square massacre and the collapse of the Soviet Union, China eschewed Western-style political reforms for fear that they could lead to the dissolution of the country. But during the opening of 2011/2012 the sociologist Sun Liping – who incidentally supervised the PhD of Xi Jinping – argued that the country's obsession with stability is becoming self-defeating: 'The ultimate outcome of the massive stability preservation project is in fact the intensification of social tensions.' It is true that social unrest has grown even faster than China's market – from 9,000 riots a year in the mid 1990s to 180,000 last year. That is one riot every two minutes. Privately, some scholars go even further, warning of another Tiananmen, although it is more likely to erupt on the Chinese Weibo than on the streets.

But though many thinkers privately embrace wide-ranging political reform, an equally large number have been influenced by the collapse of faith in elections in developed democracies that are beset by falling turn-outs, the rise of populism and a crisis in the very idea of representation. Thus, although they want a more institutionalised Chinese system – with term limits, public consultation and the rule of law – they do not see elections as a catch-all solution. They argue that although the West still has multi-party elections as a central part of the political process, it has supplemented them with new types of deliberation, such as referendums, public hearings, opinion surveys or 'citizens' juries'. China, according to these new political thinkers, will do things the other way around: using elections in the margins (maybe up to township level) but making public consultations, expert meetings and surveys a central part of decision-making. For example, Guangdong-based academic Ma Jun has developed the concept of 'accountability without elections'.

This move towards a more plural political system has come at the same time as the internet has transformed Chinese politics. There are now over 500 million netizens and social media sites such as Sina Weibo (sometimes compared to Twitter) have emerged as a genuine public sphere, although a stunted version that is policed by censors. What is striking about the rise of Chinese public opinion is how it has become a conveyor belt for extreme and nationalistic views – particularly on foreign policy issues. The pressure on the Chinese government to take a tough stance in maritime disputes against Japan and the Philippines seems to confirm the work of political scientists such as Jack Snyder that, although settled democracies tend to be more peaceful than autocracies, countries in transition are prone to belligerence. A populist China in quick political transition could turn out much more of a Western nightmare than the reactionary Communist leaders.

Political change in China also confounds another Western assumption. It has been an article of faith among many Western observers that the internet will eventually open up Chinese society, bringing liberal democracy in its wake. However, although there is now a lively public sphere among China's 500 million netizens, the Chinese blogger Michael Anti argues that the Chinese state has changed the internet as much it has been changed by the internet. He claims that the government's strategy of 'blocking and cloning' social media sites could actually reinforce the one-party state rather than weaken it. He argues that the selective opening and blocking of information has actually become an integral part of the party's governing strategy in a malign form similar to Western spin. In particular, central government uses the absence of censorship as a political tool to rein in local government officials. Anti's most dramatic claim is that the electronic crowds being mobilised are playing the same role as the Red Guards in China's Cultural Revolution. This arresting image shows how China 3.0 could still be defined by the political tactics of China 1.0. In that sense, social media could actually lengthen the life of the one-party state by giving citizens an outlet for discontent, while allowing the leadership to understand public opinion (and when necessary prevent political dissent and mobilisation).

China's Power Crisis
China's third big challenge is how to deal with a surge in its global power on the back of its breakneck economic growth. For a generation Beijing's foreign policy was guided by Deng Xiaoping's injunction to '*tao guang yang hui*', which literally means 'hide its brightness and nourish obscurity'. This led to a defensive foreign policy that took little initiative but reacted to Western pressure and subordinated other objectives to the imperative of creating a stable environment for China's economic development. However, since the global financial crisis, the Deng approach has been under increasing attack. China's foreign policy community knows that it is harder to sustain a low profile when your country has the second biggest economy in the world, your military spending is growing in double-digits and you have a physical presence in every continent.

One of the most dramatic changes to Chinese foreign policy is that China now has to protect the interests and safety of its citizens around the world. China has a special cabinet level position to look after the 50 million overseas Chinese (Chinese citizens living abroad and people of Chinese origin). If they were a single country they would be in the G20. Moreover, China's state-owned companies and its cohort of Chinese workers tend to be based in some of the world's most febrile trouble spots. The world sat up and took notice when China airlifted 38,000 citizens out of Libya, but millions more Chinese are working in places as unstable as Sudan, Afghanistan, Iran and Angola. Where military planners used to talk about Taiwan to make the case for extra resources, they now talk about the need to acquire a blue-water navy to protect Chinese workers and investments.

It is as a result of these factors that internationalist analysts like Wang Yizhou now call on the government to replace the low profile with a doctrine of 'creative involvement' – finding tactical ways of cooperating with international institutions in order to minimise criticism of China. Although China's foreign policy community remains cautious about getting entangled in these sorts of global commitments, the popular mood seems to be shifting towards assertive nationalists like Yan Xuetong, who argues that China needs a comprehensive rethinking of its approach to foreign policy. Instead of talking about creating a multipolar world, as Chinese officials have done in recent years, he proclaims an era of 'bipolarity', with China rising in the next 10 years to become the only counterpart to the US. Yan challenges some of the most fundamental doctrines of the Deng era: the primacy of economics (he thinks that the economy should be put at the service of Beijing's political goals), the quest for a multipolar world (he embraces an era of bipolar competition), the principle of non-alignment (he hints that Beijing should develop an alliance with Russia) and the norm of non-intervention (he has argued elsewhere that China will have the same approach to intervention as the United States when it is as strong as the United States). Yan's version of 'responsibility' is that China should provide its allies not just with economic aid and investment but also with security guarantees. If China 3.0 embarks on a series of interventions to protect Chinese interests as Yan proposes, the West may come to rue the day when they criticised the passivity of Chinese foreign policy.

Until recently, Western capitals hoped that integrating rising powers such as China into global institutions would encourage capitals like Beijing to identify their interests with the preservation of the international system. If we do not open the existing order to Chinese participation, they said, China will try to overthrow it and develop an alternative order of its own.

But seen from Beijing, there has never been a binary choice. China has always sought to take advantage of economic opportunities of the existing order while protecting its own room for manoeuvre. Rather than being transformed by global institutions, China's sophisticated multilateral diplomacy is changing the global order itself.

First, it has played a more active role in multilateral institutions such as the World Trade Organization (WTO) and the UN – and used this to minimise the constraints on Chinese sovereignty. Central to this have been Chinese attempts to build political coalitions within the order – taking part in blocking coalitions on trade in the Doha round, on climate change at Copenhagen, and at the UN Security Council on votes from Sudan to Syria. Since China's rise, the balance of power has shifted dramatically in an illiberal direction. In 1999, China won 43 per cent of the votes on human rights in the UN compared to Europe's 78 per cent. But in 2009, the EU won only 52 per cent to China's 82 per cent.

In parallel, China has long been developing what some scholars called a 'world without the West' – the Shanghai Cooperation Organisation, the BRICS, and the regional institutions it has set up to link it with countries in Asia, Central Asia, Africa, Latin America and Europe. Many of the regional groupings – like the East Asian Summit – were designed to take advantage of the US aversion to multilateralism, which led to a self-exclusion from Asian regionalism. Apart from a string of bilateral and 'minilateral' trading arrangements, the most prominent project is the BRICS Development Bank. Mark Malloch Brown claims that it could be a game-changer because – unlike the World Bank – 'it is based on a co-op structure where states pool credit and resources rather than being seen as a vehicle for one group of member states to subjugate another'.

Finally, China has tried to lessen international pressure on its client states (such as North Korea and Burma) by creating Chinese-led multilateral forums such as the six-party talks which give it control of the policy process.

Since the 1990s, China has followed a pragmatic strategy of trying in equal measure to avoid confrontation, and taking on additional international burdens. It has adopted an approach of defensive multilateralism – joining global institutions in order to protect China's interests but not to support the broader goals of the institutions themselves. Until recently this was not seen as a disruptive force because China exercised its power cautiously – for example on the UN Security Council it would often complain but abstain rather than voting against Western resolutions unless they touched on Taiwan. But in the last couple of years – as Copenhagen showed – its approach has changed.

This shows how a more powerful and active China will be more of a challenge to the West – not because they are trying to overthrow the existing order but because they will increasingly hollow it out.

Making Britain China-proof

China's scale poses a real dilemma for a middle-sized country like Britain. And if you take the trends of China 3.0 together, it is clear that we will not simply be dealing with a much bigger and more powerful China – but also one whose core characteristics will be different. In the economic sphere, China will not simply be an exporter of cheap goods but a huge source of global capital, an enormous market and a competitor at the top of the value chain. In the political sphere, China will not just be a unitary autocracy with central control of its affairs – but rather a more plural oligarchy that is swayed by waves of public opinion. And in the foreign policy sphere, China will no longer be a passive and defensive nation with a narrow definition of its interests. Rather it will be a power with interests in every corner of the world and an increasingly active foreign policy – backed by greater economic, military and diplomatic resources – to defend those interests.

It is hubristic to expect a country of 60 million citizens to be in a position to transform a country with one in five of the world's population. And yet, if you study the official statements of British policy, they claim that as our goal. I think that our policy-makers should instead have a more modest goal – of doing all we can to make Britain, and the multilateral order on which we depend – more resistant to Chinese pressure. The goal should not be to make China more liberal but to make the liberal order China-proof.

Unfortunately, British foreign policy is singularly ill-equipped to deal with this challenge.

First, for the obvious reason that, for the last 50 years, it has been a two-legged – explicitly Western – affair, balancing the 'special relationship' with the United States with membership in the EU. Today, it will need to rethink its traditional relationships for a century where both growth and insecurity are increasingly centred around the Pacific rather than the Atlantic. The truth is that both of the traditional pillars are in danger of collapsing if they are not re-oriented. President Barack Obama gives flesh to many European fantasies about American leadership, but he leads a country that is fast pivoting its energy and attention from Europe to Asia. At the same time, the EU is recasting its institutions and projects and Britain's 'half in-half out' approach is losing it influence. As one very senior official said to me: 'For the last few centuries, Britain has been in the cockpit of global affairs. For the next few we will need to get used to life on the margins.'

Germany provides a clue as to how we can avoid this fate. More than any other European country, Germany has turned around its economy, politics and foreign policy to face the new China. Although Germany's economy was well placed to take advantage of what China wanted to buy, the success has been the result of a concerted strategy by the government and German companies over decades. Moreover, Germans understand that there is no contradiction between being at the heart of Europe, being Atlanticist and engaging China – in fact Berlin sees the EU and transatlantic relationships as a uniquely valuable platform for taking advantage of China's economic opportunities.

Given the decline in US resources, the end of the cold war and the major economic opportunities and security threats in the Pacific it makes no sense to cling to nostalgia about the old West. And while we share many values and have many common goals with the United States, our interests in Asia are not identical to theirs (our ultimate goal is stability and a rule-based international order which is not identical to perpetual American military primacy).

The twin dangers of the transatlantic relationship are that the UK could become irrelevant or be dragged into the role of playing a bit part in the battle for Pacific primacy. So far, in spite of Hillary Clinton's rhetoric about 'not pivoting from Europe to Asia, but rather pivoting with Europe to Asia' there have been, at best, discussions about tactics. Former assistant secretary of state Kurt Campbell envisaged Europeans essentially acting as a Greek chorus for American policy, including by playing a more active role in multilateral forums such as the ASEAN Regional Forum (ARF), issuing statements on disputes like that over the South China Sea, speaking out on values questions, as well as comparing notes on Burma and North Korea. But that is thin gruel considering that Europeans are already more of an economic presence in Asia than the USA. Should we not be taking positions on these things, and framing them in a global, rules-based context rather than just a power-battle in Asia?

However, in order to prevent the structure of the global economy shifting so dramatically that China's huge domestic markets set all global standards, it is important for Europe and the United States to strengthen their economic base. That is what led Angela Merkel to pick up the old idea of a Transatlantic Free Trade Area in 2007. This was initially rejected but has now been expanded in the idea of a Transatlantic Trade and Investment Partnership (TTIP), which would create a vast domestic market that is currently almost half of the global GDP. David Cameron has been an enthusiastic supporter of TTIP, which the European Commission argues could bring about GDP gains of 2 per cent or more than €250 bn across the

EU (proportionately some of the largest gains being for the UK). The goal in all this is not to push China out of the international division of labour, but rather to use the deals to set the rules of the road without China and then make the market too attractive for Beijing not to accept them. In fact, some of the more far-sighted reformers in the Chinese economy, are talking of TPP (Trans-Pacific Partnership) and TTIP providing an anchor for Chinese reforms in the way WTO membership was before. As Karel De Gucht, the EU's Trade Commissioner has argued: 'This is about the weight of the Western, free world in world economic and political affairs.'

As power shifts in the world, the only way for Britain to take part in this scheme and to avoid strategic irrelevance is to combine with other Europeans – uniting the world's biggest market and the considerable political, diplomatic and military resources of Europe's nations behind a common voice.

Collectively, Europeans could be real players in Asia. The EU is China's biggest trade partner, India's second biggest (after the United Arab Emirates), ASEAN's second biggest (after China but ahead of Japan). The EU is the largest provider of development aid to Asia and the EU is responsible for 20 per cent of arms exports to Asia (compared to 29 per cent from the US).

This is in fact the best way – maybe the only way – to gain access to new markets and to have a voice in shaping the rules of engagement in the multipolar world of the 21st century. Britain will only be able to benefit from this deal and to get a handle on a country the size of China through its membership of the EU. As Tony Blair has said: 'Sixty-six years ago when the [European] project began, the rationale was peace. Today it is power.' Rather than contracting out the big decisions to Washington and Beijing, Europeans should unite in an attempt to build a G3 world where they can work with others (including Japan) to set the rules. It is worth noting that the driving force behind rules on issues from climate change to global trade and financial regulation over the last two decades has been neither America nor China, but Europe. The prize of a 'G3' world would combine US military power and consumption, Chinese capital and labour, and European rules and technology.

The idea of a G3 world seems utopian at a time when Europe is struggling economically and facing political disintegration. But equipping our economies, reinventing our social policies and boosting our foreign policies to deal with the rise of China could provide a compelling project for European action in the medium term. And, in the meantime, it will be vital for Britain to compare notes and try to develop common strategies towards China with Germany and France – as a stepping stone to eventual European action. As well as working together to advance common objectives, the three countries should agree to stand together when China targets individual countries, be it on Dalai Lama visits where the UK is currently suffering, or on trade issues such as the Chinese threats to French wine and German luxury cars in the solar panels case.

Second, British foreign policy-makers have clung to some heroic assumptions about the power of multilateral institutions to socialise emerging powers. It is vital to hang on to the values and strategy of promoting a world bound by law rather than power, but the tactics will need to be revised.

When President Obama came into power in 2009, he too hoped to integrate China into global institutions and encourage Beijing to identify its interests with the preservation of the post-war international system. But five years on, according to a senior official who talks regularly with the president, his attitude is best defined by one word: 'disappointment'. From the UN to the G20, a pattern seems to be emerging: China's multilateral diplomacy is making the institutions of the global order less effective at regulating the behaviour of their member states.

Chinese scholars such as the influential academic Shi Yinhong argue that the West should think not so much about 'integrating China into the Western liberal order' as 'adapting the Western liberal order to accommodate China'. This adaptation would involve a major redistribution of formal influence in the global financial and security institutions to correspond to the 'factual strength they respectively have and the contribution they have made'. China's rise creates a conundrum for the United States, or rather the whole West. The West is not yet ready to adapt the existing world order to meet China's aspirations to be left alone on human rights, climate change or the role of state subsidies, but nor do Western powers have enough control of universal institutions to re-shape them to their own ends. So rather than accepting the compromises required by Beijing or the gridlock of the status quo, it is increasingly developing a third strategy: the idea of routing round China – in order to change it from the outside.

In the economic realm, TTIP provides the model. But there have been parallel developments in the security realm. For example, when it comes to international interventions, the West has increasingly relied on regional organisations such as the Arab League to get things done without hitting Chinese vetoes. Even when there is a UN mandate, such as on Libya, the key decisions are taken inside a 'Group of Friends' while NATO was in charge of the military command.

In order to prevent the dystopia of a 'G Zero', where multilateral institutions are so gridlocked that rule-based international action is impossible, the West has been developing a sort of 'world without China' that mirrors China's 'world without the West'. Of course, the ultimate goal should be to deepen and unblock the universal institutions such as the UN Security Council, the G20, IMF, World Bank and other institutions. But rather than viewing these as a 'kindergarten for responsible stakeholders' that will socialise China, these should be seen as forums to manage differences or deal with crises – like North Korea – where there are common interests. The West should focus on making progress in a transactional way in these forums.

Third, the British political elite's strong belief in free trade and loosely regulated markets has prevented it from using its leverage to prise open markets in other countries, or developing an industrial policy that will allow the UK to compete with emerging economies. As Peter Mandelson has said: 'They are a state capitalist economy with subsidies operating, more or less openly, on a huge scale. Production is still governed by commercial decisions.'[2]

---

[2] Liam Byrne, *Turning to Face the East*, London, Guardian Books, 2013.

As the Chinese market grows in size, Britain should push for the European Commission to use all of its leverage to encourage a 'second opening' of the Chinese economy.[3] In theory, this should coincide with China's own objective of rebalancing its economy but there are big asymmetries between the openness of the European market to China and China's barriers to trade and investment coming from Europe. Some of the most urgent issues include restrictions on company ownership in the financial and service sectors, measures to encourage 'indigenous innovation', failure to enforce intellectual property rights, and shutting foreign companies out of public procurement. One of the reasons that the EU has been hampered in working for better market access for European companies in China is that Britain has opposed any attempt to call for reciprocal engagement. While it would be counter-productive to call for strict reciprocity – with Europeans shutting sectors to Chinese companies – it would make sense to ask for a market opening as a quid pro quo for better protection of Chinese investments in Europe, both of which could be enshrined in an investment treaty. As Mandelson argues 'Trade is all about reciprocal concessions.'[4]

At the moment, Britain exports only £50–60 bn to China – just 3 per cent of the UK total and a quarter of the exports to Ireland.[5] This is less than a seventh of Germany's total.

Britain should also develop a comprehensive strategy for attracting inward investment (yet another reason why membership of the European single market is so important). In 2010 only 0.5 per cent of Britain's inward investment came from China (less than a quarter of the German figure, and 60 per cent less than France).[6] In order to leverage Chinese investment, Europeans should collectively set some rules for transparency by state-owned enterprises. One option would be to establish a European agency that can play a

---

[3] See the chapter by Francois Godement and Jonas Parello-Plesner in *China 3.0*, edited by Mark Leonard (London, ECFR, 2012).

[4] Liam Byrne, *Turning to Face the East*, London, Guardian Books, 2013.

[5] Ibid.

[6] Ibid.

similar role to that of the Committee on Foreign Investment in the United States (CFIUS) in the United States.

Underlying all of this should be a more serious industrial policy to create jobs for the UK in a global marketplace where China is competing at the top as well as the bottom of the value chain. This means investing in sectors like health care, life sciences, civil engineering, the automotive sector, aerospace, financial services, creative industries, education, energy, financial services. As David Sainsbury has argued:

> It's about education, infrastructure, investment, knowledge transfer, and the quality of universities and science ... In every industry we should focus our innovation policies, our inward investment policies and our export promotion policies on those parts of the manufacturing chain where as a country we are most likely to be successful.[7]

As he argues, there is also an opportunity to use the £150 bn of the British government's public procurement budgets to promote innovation at a local level. Liam Byrne goes even further and suggests that the government develop a regional strategy centred around building links between the big cities – London, Manchester, Leeds, Liverpool and Birmingham – and their Chinese equivalents.

Fourth, Britain needs to overhaul its political and diplomatic links to reflect China's importance to the world. China has become part of the furniture of global politics – affecting our interests on most issues of domestic and foreign policy, from inflation and interest rates to energy prices and emissions to Iran and Syria – but we still know much less about how its politics work or how to influence it internationally than we need. If China is becoming a global challenge, it can best be dealt with through an equally global response. Rather than simply dealing with China bilaterally, Britain needs to find partners with which it can make common cause on every issue.

---

[7] Liam Byrne, *Turning to Face the East*, London, Guardian Books, 2013.

Some of the most effective attempts to influence China have come from the outside rather than the inside. For example, China was persuaded not to ship arms to Zimbabwe when European governments worked with non-governmental organisations in South Africa to put pressure on China. On Iran, Saudi Arabia's offers to cover shortfalls in Chinese oil and gas imports strengthened the impact of Western exhortations. On Libya, it was the support from the Arab League for Gaddafi's departure that persuaded the Chinese not to veto resolution 1973. And on monetary issues, Brazil's complaints about currency wars carried a lot of weight in the G20. And the modest shift in China's position on climate change in Cancun came through the EU Commissioner's courting of other G77 countries that gradually chipped away at China's silent majority. Chinese diplomats do not like to be isolated, so the most effective way of shifting Chinese policy is often by working to create wedges between Beijing and its Asian neighbours, with other BRICS or with the developing world. On many foreign policy issues the key players are Chinese state-owned enterprises – which have a presence round the world from Afghanistan to Zimbabwe – so it will often be useful to have China experts on the ground in those sorts of countries as well as on the mainland itself.

The fact that there are so many Chinese citizens at risk in global hot spots could also provide some leverage over Chinese behaviour. It is utopian to expect China to take part in multilateral interventions to support the 'Responsibility to Protect', but China is increasingly having to think about risks to its assets and citizens so there may be opportunities where Chinese and British interests are aligned to get China to put pressure on repressive regimes in order to avoid Western intervention.

Although China will never be an ally like the United States, we should try to learn some lessons from how we manage our relationship with that other superpower. Britain's links with Washington are not seen as a classical foreign policy relationship. The British embassy in Washington is like a mini-Whitehall, buzzing with officials from every part of the UK government who are working on building links with their counterparts. And the embassy is just the head of a network of posts which reach into many of the key states – building political, economic and other relationships with governors, legislatures, businesses and universities on the ground. The government also realises that, in a complex political system, government-to-government diplomacy is not enough and therefore invests in public diplomacy.

In that regard, the current government deserves praise for increasing its front-line staff in China by 50 officials and for stepping up its presence in the provinces. But the goal, over the course of a parliament, should be to have an across-Whitehall presence of trained Mandarin speakers that is as sophisticated and varied as the British government's presence in Washington. On top of that, it would make sense to establish major funds to pay for party-to-party links between each of the main parties and the Chinese Communist Party, as well as twinning exercises between British and Chinese cities. What is more, the social networking site Weibo has created a new space for foreigners to interact more directly with Chinese and is thus a new tool of diplomacy as well. The government should develop digital strategies to go beyond the stale state-driven dialogues such as the human rights dialogue and the strategic dialogue.[8]

Conclusion

Geopolitical strategists such as Edward Luttwak have convincingly argued that China's return to global pre-eminence is likely to be self-limiting. He argues that China's rise will be a lonely one if it continues to expand its military footprint and political assertiveness in line with its growing economy. Although Beijing's economy promises to overtake America's over the next decade, its economic and military power will be dwarfed by that of America and its Asian allies such as Japan, Korea, Australia, the Philippines, and friendly powers such as India and Indonesia.

---

[8] Jonas Parello-Plesner (2012) 'Weibo Spawns Wei-Diplomacy', *The Diplomat*, 13 September 2012, accessible at http://thediplomat.com/china-power/weibo-spawns-wei-diplomacy/

But for those who would like to promote a world ordered by law rather than power, China's rise poses a more fundamental challenge that cannot be countered with some soft-balancing or 'hedging'. The problem, as we have seen, is that many of the policies that were used to promote freedom and order after the cold war – such as a belief in the power of free trade, the internet and multilateralism to socialise rising powers through unconditional engagement – may end up having precisely the opposite effect in the post-financial crisis world.

The hard truth is that Western countries have relied on an overly optimistic view that engaging China and supporting its development would inevitably end up transforming its political system, economy and foreign policy. The experience of the last five years has revealed this as a faith-based approach, with nothing to show for it.

Unless British policy-makers are willing to revisit some of their core assumptions, and to group together with allies to strengthen the existing order, they could find that China has hollowed out long before any of the liberal norms rub off on it.

CHAPTER 4

How is US foreign policy changing and why should it matter to the UK?

by Xenia Dormandy

When President Obama took office in January 2009, support for him within the US and internationally, particularly in Europe, was very high. Pew Research polling showed that 74 per cent of Americans thought that Obama would 'do the right thing in world affairs', as against 37 per cent who thought this of President Bush (Pew Global Attitudes Project 2009). The divide was even greater in Europe (the UK was 86 per cent to 16 per cent, France 91 per cent to 13 per cent, and Germany 91 per cent to 14 per cent). The hopes for President Obama were great and the expectations far higher than he would ever be able to realise.

Four years later, as he was re-elected into his second term, the international public's expectations for President Obama were much more realistic. No one expects him to transform the US or the world. The past four years have seen major developments both in the international environment and the country itself that change the way the US sees its role, the way the outside world sees it, and the bounds of what is possible and what is needed globally. All these factors affect the objectives and style of US foreign policy.

America's foreign policy must be explored in this broader context. It is only with this perspective that it can be properly understood, along with its implications for the nation, its allies, and the world.

The Changing Domestic and Global Scene

Four Domestic Trends

The most significant recent development in the US, and more broadly the West, has been the 2008 'Great Recession' that started in America and spread to Europe and beyond. President Bush's last months in office were focused on responding to this downturn. President Obama's first big initiatives related to the same, and centred on a stimulus package of $787 billion (which passed in a strictly partisan vote)[1] directed at reversing America's negative GDP growth and rising unemployment.[2] Banks were bailed out and, in early 2009, so too was the auto industry.

Four years on and after a series of three 'quantitative easing' stimuli by the Federal Reserve, the US economy has returned to positive, albeit slow, growth. However, unemployment numbers, while down from their peak of 10 per cent in October 2009, are still at an unacceptably high 7.4 per cent. America's structural economic problems are as yet unresolved (as they are in many other Western countries), with the challenge of finding a sustainable balance between spending and taxation continuing to stymie politicians in Washington.

At the same time that the economic downturn hit the United States, inequality was rising. In 2011, America's Gini coefficient (a measure of inequality in which 0 signifies complete equality and 1 maximal inequality) was 0.477; in 2000, it was 0.401 (Deininger and Squire 1996, Mather, 2012). This inequality was reflected in late 2011 in the Occupy Wall Street movement that gained significant support in the months before the US elections. As a number of prominent economists have suggested, it might also have

---

[1] All Republicans voted against the bill (except one who abstained) along with 11 Democrats. It was carried by Democratic votes alone. See Office of the Clerk (2009).

[2] US GDP growth in 2008 was -0.4 per cent, followed by -3.5 per cent in 2009 and only returned to positive growth in 2010. World Bank (2013) unemployment numbers started to steadily rise from early 2007 to late 2009 before returning to a slow decline (see Bureau of Labor Statistics 2013).

implications for how quickly America recovers from the recession (Lowrey, 2012).

Two other trends became more apparent around the 2012 elections. The first relates to changing American demographics. The Latino population has become a significant minority, enough to influence the two presidential candidates' policies. In early 2013, the changing immigration positions espoused by a number of likely Republican candidates for President in 2016 are indicative of this new domestic reality. At the same time, another trend brings the US closer to the European position: recent Pew polling has also shown that the US is becoming less religious (Pew Research Center, 2012). The impact of this on policy is still to be seen.

The final major domestic trend is the rise of partisanship in Washington (Carroll et al., 2008). The 113th Congress is the most partisan ever; for the first time since records were kept the most liberal Republican is to the right of the most conservative Democrat, ensuring no overlap between the two parties. The three mainstream US foreign policy approaches today – moderate centrists, neocons and isolationists – are split between the two parties (typically, but not always, the first category are Democrats, while the last two groups subsist within the Republican Party). The divide in Republican views makes it harder for them to find a single position from which to negotiate with Democrats, so making compromise and potentially coherence, harder than ever. While partisanship is less ever-present in foreign policy than domestic policy, it can still play a decisive role such as with regards to ambassadorial appointments or, as we are seeing today, discussions on action in Syria.

A Changing International Environment

America's domestic challenges have heightened perceptions of the changing balance of (principally economic) power between the US, China, and other emerging nations. For the first time, in August 2012, the Pew Global Attitudes Survey found that less than 50 per cent of American middle class adults (43 per cent) thought that their children would have a better standard of living than they did (Pew Social and Demographic Trends, 2012). They also found that more

Americans believed that China was the world's leading economic power than was the United States (41 to 40 per cent) (Pew Research Global Attitudes Project, 2012). In fact, according to the International Monetary Fund (IMF), in 2011 China's GDP was only 48 per cent of America's and is not predicted to surpass the US in purchasing power parity until the second half of the 2010s (IMF, 2012, *The Economist*, 2011). In 2011, the United States' GDP per capita stood at $48,811, to China's $5,416.67 (IMF, 2012). While the US remains the greatest power on almost any measure – economy, military, diplomacy, media reach, academic excellence and IT saturation, to name but a few – the perception that the rest of the world is catching up remains. While the collapse of the Soviet Union led many to describe the world as unipolar, today multipolarity is more apt (some suggest the world has even moved beyond polarity).

A large element behind this change in perceptions reflects the weakening global and particularly Western economy, in part resulting from America's slowdown but also due to the eurocrisis. These have resulted in the economic balance of power moving eastward, towards Asia and a questioning of the 'Washington Consensus'. In recent years China, and to a lesser extent India, have been the key drivers of global economic growth, making a slowdown here, as has recently been the case, a real threat to the global economy and to the US and European recoveries.

At the same time as the economic balance of power is transitioning, technological developments are also having an impact on who holds power and how influence is being manifested.[3] How much a country is networked has been proposed, by Anne-Marie Slaughter (2009), as a new measure of power. Such advances are having an impact in hard security areas, where progress in drones and cyberspace are resulting in new offensive technologies that will require new responses. It is also apparent in the communications arena where Twitter, Facebook and Google are empowering the

---

[3] This trend has recently been noted both in the National Intelligence Council (NIC) *Global Trends 2030*, released in 2012, and the EU Institute for Security Studies (EUISS, 2012) European Strategy and Policy Analysis System (ESPAS) report, *Global Trends 2030 – Citizens in an Interconnected and Polycentric World*.

individual in new ways and enhancing transparency and openness in a manner to which authoritarian regimes, in particular, find it hard to respond. These trends are, if anything, speeding up and will require the development of new norms.

These changes in communications technology in particular are themselves producing another significant trend – the empowerment of non-state actors in all areas, including international affairs. More businesses are expanding multinationally, realising ever more of their sales and profits overseas. Non-governmental organisations and foundations are engaging with foreign governments and local populations to change the situation on the ground and broaden national policies. Malignant non-state actors are also having a greater impact, as terrorist groups take advantage of ungoverned territories and new inexpensive technologies that can be easily accessed and can level the playing field. More actors are finding ways to have influence and so will have to be taken into consideration in policy-making. And the US is at the leading edge of these developments.

At the same time as the actors and diplomatic tools are expanding, so too are our challenges becoming more complex. They are rarely susceptible to unilateral or even bilateral solutions. The hardest of these – from pandemics, to food and water security, climate change, energy, cyber and space security or terrorism – require regional or global responses.

While the trends listed above have transformed the context in which foreign policy is conducted, there have also been a number of significant events that have changed the situation on the ground in various regions. The most notable of these were the Arab revolutions, which started in Tunisia and moved to Egypt, Libya and Syria (as well as Bahrain and others), and led to leadership turn-overs in many of these countries. This development is not yet at an end. A civil war rages in Syria with the international community still debating what action they can take to return stability to the country. The implications of these revolutions are profound, not just for these nations and their citizens but for the broader world community.

Meanwhile, America's military footprint is shrinking fast. Where four years ago the US was involved in two wars, after 2014 it will be involved in no major overseas operations, having finally exited Afghanistan. The implications of this withdrawal are broader than just the US. Along with America's exit, so too goes ISAF (International Security Assistance Force). This will be the first time since 1949 that NATO has not been planning or fighting an operation and, as is already being seen, this is resulting in an existential debate within the alliance over its future role and responsibilities.

While this is not a comprehensive list, these trends and events provide the lens through which changes in US foreign policy must be understood. In this context, there are two questions to address: what is America trying to achieve and how is it going about doing this?

American Foreign Policy

What are America's Broad Interests?

In the words of Lord Palmerston, 'Nations have no permanent friends or allies, they only have permanent interests.' Despite the transition from Democratic to Republican administrations and back, America's broad interests remain largely unchanged. It is only in cases where the environment shifts significantly that this premise is broken (the Arab revolution is one such example). When these shifts occur, previous policy interests become untenable or irrelevant and a fundamental rethink is required from America's (and other) policy-makers.

While American interests remain largely static over time, how the US engages with and works to achieve those interests can change notably between administrations. One of the most profound transitions over the past four years, in part driven by austerity but also by President Obama's vision of America and its role in the world, is a move from an engaged neocon-led America, to one that is more wary of international action. While American leaders have for decades rhetorically rejected the role as the 'world's policeman', their actions have belied this. Obama, however, is following through on this sentiment and choosing to engage only where America's vital national interests are concerned. This comes across in multiple arenas. Where

President Bush 'promoted' democracy, President Obama 'supports' it. Even more tangibly in Libya, the United States supported France and the UK in the NATO operation to remove Muammar Gaddafi, but was not willing to invest significant US resources to lead that process. This is now playing out in Syria too.

In July 2000, a group of senior US foreign policy officials from both parties came together to create a list of America's national interests (this was an update of their 1996 publication).[4] At that time, they characterised five 'vital national interests' for the United States:

1. prevent, deter, and reduce the threat of nuclear, biological, and chemical weapons attacks on the United States or its military forces abroad;
2. ensure US allies' survival and their active cooperation with the US in shaping an international system in which we can thrive;
3. prevent the emergence of hostile major powers or failed states on US borders;
4. ensure the viability and stability of major global systems (trade, financial markets, supplies of energy and the environment); and
5. establish productive relations, consistent with American national interests, with nations that could become strategic adversaries, China and Russia.

Ten years on and, as Lord Palmerston suggested, while the details have changed, the basic tenets remain the same. As the 2010 National Security Strategy indicates, America's top national security priorities are (The White House, 2010):

1. reverse the spread of nuclear and biological weapons, secure nuclear materials and secure cyberspace;
2. disrupt, dismantle, and defeat al-Qaida and its violent extremist affiliates in Afghanistan, Pakistan, and around the world;

---

[4] The Commission on America's National Interests, 'America's National Interests', July 2000. Members included Graham Allison, Robert Blackwill, Arnold Kanter, Paul Krugman, Sam Nunn, Richard Armitage, Bob Graham, John McCain, Condoleezza Rice and Brent Scowcroft.

3. advance peace, security, and opportunity in the greater Middle East: transitioning to full Iraqi sovereignty and stability – and the pursuit of a comprehensive peace between Israel and its neighbours;
4. advance balanced and sustainable growth by focusing on the G20 as the premier forum for international economic co-operation, and pursuing bilateral and multilateral trade agreements;
5. shape an international order that promotes a just peace and facilitates cooperation capable of addressing the problems of our time (prosperity, climate change, conflict prevention, public health);
6. strengthen international norms on behalf of human rights.

America's Specific Priorities

While America's national interests have not changed, its strategic priorities develop in conjunction with circumstances and the environment. President Obama's second term objectives are becoming clearer. As he announced on his November 2011 trip to the region, the US is 'pivoting' to Asia. This is often perceived as a new initiative. However, as the National Security Strategies in the early 1990s under President George H.W. Bush make clear, the focus on Asia has been present for some decades, and America has been an Asian power for far longer.

The 'rebalancing' to Asia is also indicative, as will be elaborated upon later, of a change in how foreign policy is being implemented. When first announced, it was illustrated principally by military force projection changes, such as rotating 2,500 marines into Australia, providing Singapore with two additional littoral ships and changing the ratio of US naval capabilities from 50:50 in the Atlantic and Pacific, to 40:60 respectively. However, more recent emphasis has been on heightened economic and diplomatic engagement, as best characterised by the Trans-Pacific Partnership (TPP), a predominantly Asian-centric trade agreement.

President Obama has also moved away from a Middle East focus. While he put some effort into the Israel–Palestine peace process in the beginning of his first term, there was a clear step back subsequently as the situation deteriorated. While Secretary of State John Kerry has much experience in this conflict and has re-engaged actively (including three trips to the Middle East in his first 10 weeks on the job), it is not clear that President Obama is going to invest him with the weight and authority that would be needed to bring the two sides to the table for serious negotiations.

At the same time as the Middle East peace process has been moved to the backburner, so too have other issues of concern in the region, such as the revolutions in Libya and Syria; despite the terrible toll on the locals, Obama has not been ready to devote significant resources to helping bring resolution to the latter conflict (without first the region and the domestic opposition showing leadership, two conditions seen in Libya). The US military withdrawal from Iraq in 2011 has also freed America to pull back from the region. Egypt, on the other hand, along with Turkey, continue to attract significant US attention and resources due in large part to the important role they play in the region and their longer-term histories with the US. However, it is likely that despite US government intentions to resist being drawn in, events in this region will demand otherwise.

The other notable change in the past few years, often seen to have implications for America's Middle East policy, is the domestic energy revolution resulting from new fracking technologies. This will make the US largely energy self-sufficient in the coming decade (Hormats, 2013). However, while America's dependency on foreign oil and gas will decrease, it will continue to be part of the global energy market, ensuring that changes in pricing and access will have implications for the US along with its allies and others.

Finally, a note about US policy towards Europe. Many in Europe (and in the Republican Party) have been concerned about Obama's perceived withdrawal from their region. This belief stems in part from the Asia rebalancing policy as well as Obama's Asian background and his less regular first term visits to Europe. However, in fact America's attitude is driven by the reality that Europe is not seen as a problem area, but instead as a region of valuable resources. Europe, and the UK in particular, are partners, not challenges.[5]

This analysis is important for Europeans to understand as it, in part, explains America's strong desire to sustain NATO military capabilities. As then-Secretaries of Defence Gates and Panetta both emphasised, it is vital that NATO members retain their ability to respond to security threats and challenges. As Panetta so starkly said in Brussels in October 2011: 'budget challenges … cannot be an excuse for walking away from our national security responsibilities' (Panetta, 2011).

Meanwhile, America's emphasis with Europe in the coming years is likely to be in the economic arena, through the Transatlantic Trade and Investment Partnership (TTIP, also known as TAFTA). The strong drive to advance this initiative stems not just from the benefit to US–European trade and thus economic growth, but also the desire to set new norms and standards that it is hoped will, in time, become globally accepted.

How US Policy is Implemented

While US interests are relatively unchanging, the mechanisms through which US objectives are achieved are not, particularly as new administrations take over and events demand (or as policies are perceived to fail). In a number of areas, President Obama is trying a different approach from his predecessor.

Multilateralism: President Obama has implemented a more multilateral approach to foreign policy than did George W. Bush (something that reflects the tradition of the Democratic Party). Where Bush appointed a strong critic, John Bolton, to lead the US delegation to the UN, Obama nominated one of his closest advisors and a supporter of the institution, Susan Rice.[6] President Obama has continued to

---

[5] This is reflected in the lack of reference to Europe during the 2012 Presidential debates. This should be seen in Europe as a positive: only problems or challenges are likely to be raised in such politically fractious circumstances.

[6] Susan Rice is now Obama's National Security Advisor having missed out on becoming Secretary of State when it became apparent that the Senate confirmation battle would be tough. (The NSA position does not require confirmation.)

work closely with allies in a variety of venues, joining new established groups (such as the East Asia Summit [EAS]) and trying to develop new initiatives (such as in non-proliferation).

New Alliances and Partnerships: President Obama has expanded his alliances, formal and otherwise, and deepened those already existing. As mentioned earlier, this is particularly true in Asia, where the US has focused attention on its relationships in recent years with Vietnam and the Philippines along with Australia, Japan, South Korea and Singapore. These new links are not limited to the military arena, but also reflect interest in economic and diplomatic initiatives, from the TPP, a priority of Obama's second term, to the TTIP with Europe.

This collaborative approach even goes so far as to engage with historical antagonists. In his 2009 inaugural address, President Obama made it clear that he was willing to work with all, including Iran, 'we will extend a hand if you are willing to unclench your fist' (Obama, 2009). While this initiative has yet to be successful in this case, it could be argued that the approach played a significant role in the opening up of Burma in 2011.

The Military: The current administration has a different perspective on military engagement than did the preceding one; it is one in which the US stays out of major military operations in lieu of targeted action. This is likely to be emphasised further in the second term as the US exits its last significant operation (US–Afghan negotiations on post-2014 troop numbers, likely to be only around 10,000, are ongoing). With troops already out of Iraq, the US will have cut all large expeditionary activities. Even in Afghanistan, the role will be restricted to training and counterterrorism (i.e. no major offensive operations). As noted earlier, this new approach was evident in the style of US involvement in Libya in 2011, and more recently in Obama's visible reticence to act militarily in Syria.

With the appointment of former Senator Chuck Hagel as Secretary of Defense and Ashton Carter's continued presence as Deputy Secretary, Obama has made it clear that the priority for the Defense Department in his second term is cutting costs. Hagel is a decorated war veteran who has made clear his beliefs that the military should be used in a limited and circumscribed fashion. And Carter has been focused on budgetary issues for his past four years at Defense and prior to that in academia. With this as the priority, it is extremely unlikely that there will be any large-scale military action in the coming years. This reticence is most likely to be tested in Iran, but even here Obama is likely to try alternative tactics (e.g. drones and cyber-attacks) rather than a substantial kinetic force.

However, the military will continue to play a central role in US foreign policy through targeted action. While drones were first engaged by President Bush, their use has increased significantly under President Obama. Drone attacks in Pakistan in 2008, Bush's last year as President, were 35; in 2010 the number was 117 (although it fell back down in 2012 to 46) (Roggio and Mayer, 2013). President Obama has also approved the use of drones in Yemen and Somalia, making them a common tool of projecting force.

President Obama has also emphasised other more precise instruments. He has engaged Special Forces more overtly (such as in the operation to kill Osama bin Laden in May 2011) and, while it has not been formally acknowledged by the US government, most likely the US played a role in the Stuxnet virus in 2009, and possibly Flash in 2012, that were aimed at Iran's nuclear programme. In all these cases, President Obama shows his preference for the directed use of military resources. Given austerity and defence cuts of between $500 billion and $1.1 trillion in the coming 10 years, this trend towards the more circumscribed use of the military is likely to continue.[7]

New Non-Military Focus: President Obama and his team have also emphasised the rest of the foreign policy toolbox. While President Bush led some significant innovations in development assistance (such as the creation of the US President's Emergency Plan for AIDS Relief [PEPFAR] and the Millennium Challenge Corporation [MCC]),

---

[7] In January 2012, the US Defence Department announced cuts of $487 billion over 10 years, starting in their 2013 budget. With sequestration going through in early 2013, there are possible additional cuts of approximately $600 billion.

development and diplomacy were never a central instrument of his foreign policy (USAID was subsumed into State during his tenure). In 2009, when Hillary Clinton became Secretary of State, she launched the Quadrennial Diplomacy and Development Review (QDDR) to mirror the military's Quadrennial Defence Review (QDR), to bring a 'whole of government' approach that emphasised diplomacy and development in foreign policy. At the same time she also prioritised a civilian surge to beef up the role of diplomacy.

In support of this strategic approach, these softer tools of foreign policy have been heavily used by the current administration. America's principal response to the unrest in Egypt was economic assistance and diplomatic pressure to support civil society and political groups. America's Syria policy focused on an effort to help build a coherent opposition to Assad rather than providing it with any substantial military assistance.

There has been some confusion in the messaging, however; for example, as mentioned, the early focus of the Asian rebalancing appeared to be on enhancing military links. This is being corrected in the second term as the government turns to economic initiatives such as the TPP and the TTIP, and diplomatic efforts with allies regarding Iranian and North Korean nuclear programmes. Obama's focus on these alternate foreign policy tools is likely to be sustained or even expanded in the coming years.

Declining Perceptions Lead to Declining Influence

While the US remains *primus inter pares*, this is not always the perception. The US is seen by many to be declining as a global power, in relative if not absolute terms. Meanwhile, China's role, economically and more broadly, is perceived to be rising, raising in the minds of many the prospect of a return to bipolarity and a fear of getting caught in between these two powers. Such perceptions, even if not founded in reality, and even if limited to the economic sphere, have profound effects on America's influence and on its allies and antagonists' actions.

While the US has long been given some leeway, in the belief that when the US does the wrong thing it is often for the right reasons, this sentiment is beginning to fade. America's soft power, while still influential, appears to be diminishing, a phenomenon likely caused both by the perception of dysfunction in Washington DC (brought about by partisanship), as well as the greater reliance on hard power of the Bush administration. While support for the US rose with Obama's election, it has again declined as the international community has realised that a transformation of the US is not going to take place. To take just one example, in the UK 'favourable views' towards the United States jumped from 53 per cent in 2008 to 69 per cent in 2009, but fell back to 60 per cent in 2012 (Pew Global Attitudes Project, 2012).

Positive perceptions of the US in the Middle East and in Muslim-majority countries in particular are extremely low, with only 15 per cent of the population having a favourable opinion of the United States in Pew's average of opinions across Egypt, Jordan, Lebanon, Pakistan and Turkey (Pew Global Attitudes Project, 2012). While here too there was an upturn on Obama's election, and expectations were raised following his 2009 Cairo speech, there is a strong sense from this group that the President's actions do not match his rhetoric. For instance, in 2009, 46 per cent believed that Obama 'would be fair with Israelis and Palestinians'; in 2012, only 18 per cent believe that he has been (Pew Global Attitudes Project, 2012). This gap is damaging America's reputation and thus influence.

The perception of American decline limits its impact. Allies are less willing to stand beside the US, and some actors believe they can garner support by being seen as anti-US (as is clearly playing out in Afghanistan now). As American soft power diminishes, its values become less accepted, and the norms that it (along with Europe and others) have made global are weakened.

America's perceived weakness is also causing some countries to test the boundaries more than previously. China and Russia have taken more assertive stances in recent years, pushing back on US and Western objectives, whether with regard to Iran, Syria or territorial disputes. North Korea appears more aggressive than it has been in decades (although its relatively new leadership could be the cause of this) and Iran continues to defy the international community.

America's interests, its priorities and how it implements them come together to define America's policy on the global stage. The complex and dynamic environment, in combination with an increasing tendency to, in the words of Obama, 'nation build at home', makes a proactive policy harder still. And perceptions of diminishing power can limit the impact of American action and influence. It is in this context that the UK must consider its relationship with the United States and the implications for its own power.

Why Should America's Foreign Policy Matter to the UK?

Implications for the UK

America is Britain's strongest ally. As so many before him, President Obama, while visiting London in 2011, emphasised all that the two countries have in common:

> The reason for this close friendship doesn't just have to do with our shared history, our shared heritage; our ties of language and culture; or even the strong partnership between our governments. Our relationship is special because of the values and beliefs that have united our people through the ages. (Obama, 2011)

These connections are an enormous benefit to both countries, but they can also tie them together both in action and in the perceptions of the wider community.

America's strength can be Britain's also (and vice versa). From the US perspective, the principal benefits of the relationship are three-fold:

a. the United Kingdom as both an entrée into Europe and as a close ally whose interests align with America's and who will therefore act, in Europe, in ways that are mutually beneficial;

b.   the assets that the UK brings to the table, from defence to intelligence, economic, soft power and diplomatic capabilities;
c.   the advice and different perspective on challenges that the UK provides to the US.

At the same time, the UK also gains from the close relationship. Generally, Britain has more influence on US policy and actions than any other nation. This perception that the UK can draw upon US resources when needed allows it to broaden its reach and gives it a stronger negotiating position internationally.

There are however, some negative implications also. As America's influence and power is perceived to wane, so too does British power, leaving it more vulnerable. Similarly, if America's reputation is damaged, this will colour perceptions of the UK. As in the case of the war in Iraq, the close US–UK alliance resulted in not just the US, but also the UK, being tarred with the same brush.

There are also concrete implications for the UK. If the US gets drawn in to a conflict, the UK could get pulled in also. While other NATO members would probably engage only if Article 5 were invoked, the US would likely expect the UK to be more forward leaning. And, as the terrorist attack in London on 7 July 2005 showed, the UK can be implicated regardless of its actions.

More broadly, the UK is also affected indirectly by America's more inward vision and less assertive international presence. An America that is no longer the world's policeman providing global public goods will result in a world that is less secure. Unless Europe fills that vacuum it is likely to be filled by others who might be less supportive of the common values that the US and UK hold.

Specific Policy Changes

While America's broad strategic choices and changes in its international reputation will have implications for the UK, there are also specific policy areas in which American foreign policy impacts the UK. This is particularly the case on issues where there appears to be an increasing divide between the two nations.

China: China is of major strategic interest to the US, both as a potential partner but also a threat (economically and militarily). China's economic growth provides huge potential for access to new markets and trade. At the same time, its recent assertive and nation-alistic behaviour in its region has led many to fear that America's Asian alliances might draw the US into conflict (whether with regard to Taiwan, Japan or otherwise). This dichotomy has led to America's 'engage and hedge' policy, with emphasis often on the latter.

The British however, like much of Europe, emphasises engage-ment, seeing China principally as a commercial opportunity. The UK promotes Chinese inward investment and would like to become the principal trading venue for the *renminbi* (when it opens). While there are some signs that the UK is increasingly seeing China from a more strategic angle, the commercial incentive still predominates.

This divergence could create problems, as it did in 2004 when, led by the French, a number of European nations (including the UK) tried to get the arms embargo lifted. (Congressional Research Service, 2005) The gap in perceptions thus needs to be carefully managed.

Economics: Given the economic challenges that Europe and the US have faced in recent years, both the UK and US prioritise economic growth; to this end both are focusing on the emerging markets and, in particular, Asia. While attention will be paid to moving forward the TTIP, the US is likely to prioritise the TPP and Europe will continue to try to make progress with its bilateral trade negotiations with Japan and India.[8] Given limited resources on both sides, some of these discussions will have to take a backseat; it is possible that the TTIP, given the tough barriers that will need to be overcome, will be de-prioritised.

---

[8] The EU and Japan announced in March 2013 the launch of talks on Free Trade Agreements. It was reported earlier the same year that India and the EU were close to finalising an agreement over their own trade deal.

Defence: As stated earlier, a major implication of the current austerity is a significant decrease in defence spending on both sides of the
Atlantic. The US is going to cut between $500 billion and $1.1
trillion over the coming 10 years, and the UK up to 7.5 per cent
in real terms to the 2014/15 budget year (given the continued
lack of growth in the British economy it is unlikely to end there)
(Perlo-Freeman et al., 2012). While the UK remains one of only
two European NATO members that still spends over 2 per cent of
their GDP on defence, the loss of capabilities from these cuts will
make it even more important for the two nations to work together
militarily; but it will also make cooperation tougher as flexibility
diminishes. Defence could provide great opportunities to enhance
relations but also great challenges. At the same time, the cuts will
have significant impacts on global security.

Middle East Peace Process: There is a divergence between the US
and UK on priorities and policy on this topic. As mentioned earlier,
despite Obama's focus on the peace process early in his first term, it
is unlikely to be prioritised in the second (despite strong efforts by
Secretary Kerry). Meanwhile, however, this remains a priority for the
UK and Europe more broadly, not least given their close proximity
to the region. Thus the UK is likely to be disappointed by Obama's
lack of attention in the near term.

The balance of policies towards the Israelis and Palestinians also
provide a possible area of concern. The US is perceived by many to be
too pro-Israel, unwilling to push back on their settlement expansion.
It is possible that in his second term Obama could take a tougher
stance, however. With no election ahead of him, he might revert to
his strong early position against such construction, resulting in the
US and European positions converging.

Environmental Policy: Given Republican control of the House,
it is extremely unlikely that President Obama will be able to push
through any environmental legislation in the coming four years. Any
progress made in this area will thus be through small steps by Executive Order. Meanwhile, given the absence of federal progress, the

states might take action. While some decrease in CO_2 emissions is likely to occur due to changes in energy sources (towards shale oil), a strong environmental policy agenda is unlikely.

The UK in Europe: One final area of divergence in the coming years concerns Britain's role in the EU. With a probable referendum in the UK on EU membership in 2017, attention to this issue is only going to increase.[9] While most current polling in the UK suggests that a plurality support withdrawal (although the numbers are decreasing), American policy-makers following this issue find this of great concern (as then-Assistant Secretary of State for Europe, Phil Gordon, made clear in his 9 January 2013 intervention) (BBC News, 2013). The UK being in Europe has a number of advantages for the US: it ensures that US interests are supported in the EU; an EU with the UK as a member is stronger than one without, which makes it a more effective and powerful partner to the US; and, finally, the UK is a reforming influence in the EU. From the US perspective, Britain itself is also stronger and more influential if it stays in. Thus, if the UK continues to move in the direction of exiting the EU, while the US will continue to support it, it will prove a disappointment to many Americans and will likely, in time, lead to a more complex and weaker triangular relationship between the US, Europe and the UK.

Conclusion

America's role in the world has a fundamental effect on the UK, both directly and indirectly. One cannot just consider the specific policies the US pursues but a broader analysis is necessary, including the US's perception of itself and the role it wants to play, and others' perceptions of it – its rise or decline. These issues all have repercussions for the UK.

---

[9] While only the Conservative Party has promised a referendum, many suggest that it would be extremely hard for the other parties not to hold one if they were in power in 2017.

As the US takes a less active international role in the coming years, this could leave the UK without its traditional partner and could potentially result in a vacuum in the absence of the 'world's policeman'. At the same time, as both countries look inward, the influence of their norms on the international stage, no longer defended so actively, could weaken. However, Obama's changing emphasis on smart power has the potential to mitigate or reverse this.

The US and the UK have a 'special' and 'essential' relationship. However, they are increasingly lacking a 'strategic' one. This is not for lack of common strategic interests, but, instead, because they have for some time taken one another for granted without investing the time and resources to ensure mutual understanding and common capabilities. The lack of strategic attention paid to one another is taking its toll. Issues such as differing visions for China have the potential to divide as do varying priorities for the Middle East.

America's future is stronger with the UK alongside, and vice versa. But they are both weaker if the other is diminished. As their histories have been so close, so their futures are tied together.

There is every reason to believe that the US and UK will continue to remain the closest of allies. The US has shown its ability to regenerate, to innovate and to be entrepreneurial in its responses to the challenges it faces; there is no reason to believe that these characteristics have been lost. It is likely to remain a necessary actor – first among equals – in responding to the major global challenges that arise for some time to come; however it is not sufficient alone. It is vital that the US and UK work together, with other allies, to ensure their security and the security of the global system in all its varying aspects.

CHAPTER 5

Is Russia a partner or a threat?

by Robert Legvold

Much like a nested Russian doll, the Russian challenge for the United Kingdom comes one dimension tucked within another: the inner, small solid doll is the bilateral UK–Russia relationship. It sits inside the next doll – the interaction between Russia and the European Union (EU). The dynamic between NATO and Russia, driven by the complex US–Russia relationship, forms the outer doll.

The missing doll is the Euro-Atlantic security community that US, European and Russian leaders have regularly promised to create from the 1990 Charter of Paris for a New Europe to the Commemorative Declaration of the 2010 Organization for Security and Co-operation in Europe (OSCE) summit. Were this doll in place, were Russia, Europe, and North America working together regularly and effectively to meet the real security threats that they all face and had they made their military efforts the basis for cooperation rather than tension, much of what mars the other three dolls would disappear. That is this chapter's ultimate argument. First, however, what stands in the way needs to be explored.

Examining the *Matryoshka*

With a real *matryoshka* doll one gets to the last small doll by first opening the large outer doll, then the next inside it, and then the next. I start in reverse order, however, because the small doll – the UK–Russia relationship – well illustrates both the shortcomings of treating the challenge in bits and pieces and the consequences of skipping past the harder, deeper issues that frame the relationship's possibilities.

Of all the relationships between a major West European country and Russia, the one between the UK and Russia has been, for most of the last decade, the sourest. From the British decision to align with the US rush to war in Iraq in 2003 through the assassination of Alexander Litvinenko in 2006 to the shuttering of the British Council's operations in St Petersburg in 2008 and then soon after the Russian–Georgian war, the descent was steady and harsh. Even when the two sides gingerly set about restoring some level of comity, beginning with David Miliband's November 2009 visit to Moscow ('I'm here to talk, not growl' [Kendall, 2009]), the underlying sources of tension remained. Throughout what Paul de Quincey (2013), the director of the British Council Russia, calls years of 'a long and cold "winter of discontent"', a web of irritants, only loosely related to vital national interests, has ensnared ties between the two countries.

Friction over British insistence that Moscow cooperate in getting to the bottom of Litvinenko's murder and Russia's equally illusory demand for the extradition of Boris Berezovksy and Akhmed Zakayev may seem peripheral to the core interests of the two countries, but it has dominated an agenda largely made up of similarly grating yet secondary issues, from the harassment of the British Council to the Sergei Magnitsky case, to recurring annoyance over each side's ongoing espionage activity, British criticism of Russian human rights abuses, and even the British government's refusal to allow surviving veterans who manned the Arctic route during the second world war to accept Russia's Medal of Ushakov. At each high-level encounter, including David Cameron's visit to Moscow in September 2011, Vladimir Putin's attendance at the 2012 Olympics, and the 2 + 2 'strategic dialogue' in March 2103, the two sides' attempt to balance the sullen immobility of this conversation with upbeat talk of increased trade and investment comes up short.

While trade has increased by impressive per centages over the last several years, the fact that in 2011 Russia accounted for roughly

1 per cent more of UK trade than in 2001, and that over this period the UK slid out of the top 10 of Russia's trading partners and now represents less than 3 per cent of Russian trade, scarcely makes up for the relatively shelf-bare character of the relationship (Allen, 2012: 3, 5). Organising the recent 2 + 2 strategic dialogue between foreign and defence ministers is a sensible and potentially crucial step, but the initial session in March 2013 failed to push much beyond the rutted past, and, when attention turned to more strategic matters such as the Syria war and Iran's nuclear programme, the exchange served to underscore the new ways in which the EU context for the UK's relations with Russia adds further clutter (Golovanova, 2013, Shestakov, 2013).

In the EU's elaborate but vexed relationship with Russia, the UK's role is distinctly secondary to that of Germany and Brussels itself, and its role shrinks as the drama surrounding the eurozone 17 increasingly monopolises Russian concerns. Energy, of course, constitutes the heart of the EU–Russia relationship, an area where the UK matters to Moscow. BP's mega-deal with Rosneft in spring 2013 and Gazprom's interest in drawing Britain into the Nord Stream network represent important pieces in Russia's oil and gas strategy. Still, when it comes to centrepieces, such as the EU's third energy package and the politics of pipelines, Germany, alongside the EU Commission, controls the action.

Similarly, when the subject shifts to Syria and Iran, Britain, in the Putin regime's eyes, joins the EU troublemakers. Whether, with France, as the leader of intervention in Libya, or, again with France, as readiest to arm the Syrian opposition, or, with the United States, pressing for the stiffest sanctions against Iran, it gets placed on the negative side of Moscow's EU ledger (Harding, 2013). Russia's unwillingness to move against the Assad regime, in turn, makes Syria one more source of British frustration with Russian foreign policy.

Ultimately, however, and however close to the surface and suppurating the frictions in bilateral relations may be, the outer doll – the NATO–US dimension of the UK–Russia relationship – creates its deep underpinning. From the British perspective, Russia's alienation from a NATO-dominated Europe security system, often ham-handed treatment of neighbours, and ambiguous reliability as a critical source of European energy automatically darkens the attitude that British policy-makers bring to the table. Russia, in turn, retains the suspicion that Britain's long-standing 'special relationship' with the United States makes the country an unhappy outlier among European states. Little difference has it made that both the Cameron government and the current Labour opposition openly reject the wisdom of a partnership with the United States based on 'blind loyalty' (Ralph and Clark, 2013: 4). The most contemporary incarnation of the bias is inspired by the Blair government's co-organisation of the Iraq war, seen as but the most conspicuous of the many instances when London has fronted for Washington. But its more venerable form traces back to the cold war partnership, including the close nuclear cooperation between the two countries (Feneko, 2010).[1]

Neither Fish nor Fowl

Framing the Russian challenge in this admittedly shallow and half-sketched fashion short-changes reality, but, to the extent that it fairly captures the reality embraced by the two countries, it creates a benchmark against which to measure a more probing analysis that would better serve the foreign policy of both countries. In Britain's case, it would help to work inward by first sorting out alternative assessments of the fundamental impulses shaping Russian behavior rather than outward by stressing the immediate sources of friction in the bilateral relationship. This, of course, is easier said than done, particularly, when Putin's Russia is unhelpfully neither an ally nor an adversary – and particularly when people disagree violently over which direction the balance tilts (e.g. Lucas, 2008 versus Lieven, 2005). Underlying this ambiguous but contested spectrum are

---

[1] Feneko implies that that British nuclear forces were integrated into US operational plans. That is incorrect, and would be an important misunderstanding, if shared by senior Soviet and later Russian national security officials.

three interlinked ways of arguing about the critical characteristics of Russian foreign policy.

The first and most conventional dispute focuses on what contemporary Russia is up to. Is it bent on doing as much damage as it can to NATO, dividing Western allies, and sabotaging the foreign policy initiatives of key Western governments, including the UK, or is it more intent on counter-acting specific foreign policy initiatives to which it objects? Does it seek to maximise its power by attacking the power of these governments, or is it more concerned with influencing their use of their power? Is Russian foreign policy designed to create a 'sphere of influence' in the post-Soviet space from which major competitors are excluded or, alternatively, to enhance Russia's competitive position in what it knows will be a competitive arena? When the Russians exploit the security concerns of their neighbours are they doing so primarily to enlarge the shadow they cast, or, alternatively, to address their own real security concerns? And is the stubborn, sometimes strident character of current Russian foreign policy due to ambition or to insecurity? Is this aspect of the Russian face abroad a tool of domestic politics or is it an honest reflection of prevailing attitudes? These contrasting impressions are not entirely mutually exclusive; one can shade into another. But it matters which side of each pairing dominates, because, when added up, they recommend very different policies toward Russia.

So does a second crucial contrast. Lately it has become popular to argue that Putin's government will only accept a 'transactional relationship' with the United States and its European allies – meaning one limited to momentary forms of cooperation in specific instances where the interests of both parties happen to coincide, or in the economic and technical realms where the issue remains strictly business. Putin, they contend, has no interest in a deeper and more durable partnership with any of them, and thus it would be unrealistic for any of them to expect anything more (Aron, 2013, Ignatius, 2013, Shevtsova and Wood, 2011).

The argument is usually predicated on one of two things or, for some, on both: first, that Putin and others in the leadership eschew closer ties with Western governments, because they do not care to have partners who second-guess their repressive practices at home. And/or they find little point in making common cause with powers whose influence over global affairs they believe is waning. Putin and those around him have done much to foster this impression by treating the current economic turmoil in Europe as evidence that the Western model has lost its edge, and that the momentum is now with other rising powers (Grove, 2012).

Yet, over the first 10 years of Russian independence, US and European policy toward Russia took for granted the likelihood of achieving a deep and durable partnership with the new Russia. Indeed, in those early years Boris Yeltsin and his foreign minister, Andrei Kozyrev, formally pledged to integrate Russia into a 'democratic zone of trust, cooperation and security' stretching from 'Vancouver to Vladivostok' (The White House, 1992). As late as 2002, in the roiling wake of the September 11 attack, the US ambassador to Russia, Alexander Vershbow, described the progress in US–Russia relations as 'the beginning of a long-term security partnership – perhaps an alliance – between our two countries based on common interests' (de Nevers, 2002). Even today voices on both sides criticise an approach that is merely 'transactional' and call for a new US–Russia 'strategic dialogue' to identify where each country can be made a 'strategic asset' for the other (Graham and Trenin, 2012).

The dueling prospect of a transactional versus a strategic relationship is not far removed from the third key juxtaposition – one that centres on the question of values. The contrast in this case comes in two forms. The first closely relates to the notion of strategic partnership: must a strategic partnership be based on shared common values or can it rest only on shared national interests? Gradually, the debate along these lines has given way to a second divergence as Putin's harsher politics at home has sharpened the edges of the values question.

The Russians, including Putin and his people, have long insisted that their core values are consistent with those of the West, only adapted to Russian realities. Many in the West, however, are increasingly inclined to see these 'adaptations' as a rejection of the West's basic values. More recently the issue has veered in another direction, recast by Putin's seeming readiness to back away from the notion that, at the end of the day, common values underpin Russia's relationship with the West, and to suggest that the values that animate Western governments are debased and anaemic. Russia can do better. 'Moscow', Dmitry Trenin (2012) has written, 'is "leaving the West" mentally', having already left it strategically.

Why Care?

If British leaders wish to fashion a sturdy, broad, and coherent policy toward Russia, they should start by, at least tentatively, choosing among these contrasting perspectives. Do they believe that the basic thrust of Russian policy is to inflict damage on US and European, including British, policy, or do they see it as often troublesome, but guided by more pragmatic trade-offs between elements of cooperation and points of genuine discord? Do they believe that Russia's leaders, either because of their views or behavior, rule out anything more than a relationship limited to a narrow range of bargains in concrete instances where interests happen to overlap, or do they entertain the possibility that something more substantial could emerge? And how do they judge and weigh the matter of underlying values? Do they doubt that anything more substantial can come about, if the relationship is not buttressed by common values? And are these seen as simply missing at the moment? Worse, are they convinced that Putin's Russia is 'leaving the West mentally'? Or do they view the issue less starkly, doubting that Russia can really turn its back on European culture and values when, for more than two centuries, these have been so central to its struggle for identity? And, more immediately, might the reality be that Russians do basically accept Western political values, and the challenge is to encourage practices more in accord with them?

As noted, the choice could well be tentative, until events offer firm proof one way or the other, but it should be on the bolder, more generous side for two reasons: first, because the UK is part of economic and military alliances that are immensely stronger than is a Russia struggling to emerge from the debris of a shattered Soviet Union, it can afford to gamble on the prospect of higher-return outcomes. If at some point mounting evidence convinces British leaders that Russian policy has become essentially adversarial, unreceptive, or alien, they can safely shift course.

Second, and more important, the stakes involved warrant wagering on the more promising side of the equation. Indeed, it is the failure of both Russian and Western leadership to do justice to their stake in a healthier and more constructive relationship that, more than anything, has allowed so much damage to be inflicted on their relations. The failure in this case may not simply be a failure to articulate how crucial the relationship is or could be, but a deeper failure to persuade themselves.

The problem is that the stakes exist on two levels – one narrow and driven by the immediate issues that compel a policy response; the other more basic, distant, and critical to the shape of international politics to come. Governments on both sides have had trouble getting beyond the first, not least because addressing the second requires a longer-term strategic perspective and a readiness to work more than intermittently to achieve difficult, long-term goals.

In the British case, the immediate stakes are clear. British leaders would like to enlarge economic cooperation with Russia and its neighbours. Cameron took with him to Moscow in September 2011 a high-level British business delegation, spoke of advancing trade and investment to 'a new level', and pitched the deals done in Russia by major British firms, such as Kingfisher and Rolls Royce (Cameron, 2011). As Cameron told his university audience, 'Russia is resource rich and services light. Britain is the opposite.' A year later, Trade and Investment Minister Lord Green, with 25 British business leaders in tow, returned to Russia to push still harder on the opportunities in Britain's 'fastest growing major export market', including in financial services, life sciences, aerospace, pharmaceuticals, and railways (Sweeney, 2012).

Energy constitutes a critical component in the economic relationship, and hence serves as a second important stake for both countries. Oil and gas comprised 56 per cent of Russian exports to Britain in

2011 and Russian coal 37 per cent of Britain's imported coal. BP, as the result of the March 2013 buyout, acquired a 19.75 per cent stake in Rosneft with access to its massive oil reserves, followed a month later by Royal Dutch Shell's agreement with Gazprom to join in developing the Arctic's vast energy resources (Allen, 2012, ITAR/TASS, 2013, Select Committee, 2011, Smith, 2012).

Third, Britain, along with the United States and Russia, is a key actor in the effort to strengthen an international regime securing nuclear materials. In April 2013, representatives from the Ministry of Defence joined their colleagues from Rosatom and the US National Nuclear Security Administration in a seventh annual 'Nuclear Security Best Practices Exchange'. Focused on strengthening safeguards against the theft or seizure of nuclear material, British–Russian cooperation in this sphere closely parallels a fourth stake: fighting terrorism. Here, however, how fulsome this stake is remains unclear. British agencies cooperated with Russian counterparts in preparing for the London Olympics and have offered to do the same for the Sochi 2014 winter Olympics, but the evidence that London sees Russia as central in the broader effort to check terrorism seems thin.

Finally, British leaders in both parties stress the stake that they have in encouraging Russia to follow a path of democratic development. Why this matters to the UK is normally framed, first, as essential to Britain's fidelity to its own core values and, second, as a prerequisite permitting the economic, energy and other stakes to be realised in more handsome form. Cameron, in Moscow in 2011, sketched a grandiloquent goal of 'working together on the global stage to help create the stability and security on which our future prosperity depends', but how this has been or is to be translated into something tangible and operational remains elusive (Cameron, 2011).

Real and worthy as these interests are, they do not measure up to the larger stakes that Britain has in the relationship. Some of these are obvious, albeit far more indirect. Britain, as one of the Permanent Five (P5) in the UN Security Council, surely wishes the P5 to act as much in concert as possible, and Russian cooperation is crucial in achieving that. Britain, as a key nuclear weapons state, must care about Russia's strategic nuclear choices, not only for their impact on the general security and stability of an emerging multipolar nuclear regime, but as an architect of the nuclear matrix in which London must make its own difficult nuclear decisions. By extension, Russia is equally critical in determining the future of an endangered nuclear non-proliferation regime. It has and will continue to play an important role in the Afghan war and its aftermath, an effort for which the British have paid more than £17.4 billion and 440 lives lost. Russia is still more central to energy security in Europe, the vital core of Britain's security setting. As the world's third largest emitter of greenhouse gases, Russia's willingness to address the challenge of climate change presumably matters to a country with ambitious 2050 targets of its own. And the list goes on.

Two large, over-arching stakes, however, bring order to the entire array of British interests, and give strategic significance to the UK–Russia agenda. First, transforming the broader Euro-Atlantic region, including Russia, into a real, working security community, as British and other leaders have pledged to do since the 1990 Charter of Paris for a New Europe, would create an altogether safer Europe – one less plagued by tensions between NATO and Russia, less fixated on military balances as a source of competition, and more able to contain and resolve violence when it erupts within the region. Second, as a major power in the Euro-Atlantic region – the axis of the 20th-century international system – Britain has a basic stake in the leadership that this region, if cohesive, can provide in meeting 21st century challenges, including that of weapons of mass destructive, catastrophic terrorism, cyber warfare, health pandemics, and climate change. And, as important, it has a stake in how well the critical Euro-Atlantic axis deals with the rise of the Asia-Pacific in what will be a dual-axis system this time around.

What Is to Be Done?

Were British leaders to frame the challenge to their Russia policy in ambitious terms the task would be to reconstitute the *matryoshka* – to fit the dolls together in necessary sequence, and then help to fashion a new outer doll giving the whole doll a stronger and more auspicious construction. Embedding Britain's Russia policy in a renewed commitment to breaking down the inertia blocking the way to a more effective Euro-Atlantic security community that includes Russia will not produce results tomorrow. Nor will even the simplest steps in this direction come easily – not when tensions intervene, the Russians are unresponsive, and other immediate foreign policy pressures divert attention. Yet, minus this lode star, British policy will remain disembodied and fragmented. With it, even if difficult to follow and often unrewarded, a commitment at this level will, first, give coherence to an otherwise scattered agenda; second, create a more positive context softening the effects of tension-generating issues; and, third, produce an approach that outpaces events rather than merely fends them off.

Such an arrangement would have two essential characteristics: first, if real, it would largely eliminate the use or threatened use of force to settle conflicts among states within the community, and, second, it would unite them in defining the new priority security threats that they all face, combined with a will and a way to counter them. Nothing of the kind, however, will be possible until the legacy of mistrust that has plagued relations among key states – principally Russia with many of its neighbours – and Russia's relations with NATO is directly addressed. Nor will there be progress toward such a security community unless the impasse over the three large problems that feed this mistrust is broken: the protracted conflicts over Transdnistr, Nagorno–Karabagh, and Georgia's separatists territories; the nexus of suspicion over missile defence, non-strategic nuclear weapons, and a moribund CFE (conventional armed forces) regime; and the failure to begin the process of historical reconciliation between Russia and the Baltic states and between Turkey and Armenia.

The path forward will not be traveled on the strength of rhetorical flourishes in OSCE summit documents, or by imagining some fundamentally new institutional framework, or by waiting for the clouds to clear and new readiness to cooperate to materialise. Progress will depend on taking practical steps on concrete issues by actively working together. Such would be the case were Russia and NATO to put the quarrel over missile defence behind them by agreeing to jointly man one or more coordination centres where real-time data and information from radar and satellites could be processed and passed to the NATO/US and Russian command and control centres.[2] Such could be the case were the five littoral states to organise a cooperative approach to the many practical aspects (technical, ecological, legal, and social) of developing the vast hydrocarbon resources in the Arctic region.[3] And such should be the case were Russia and some set of European states together to intensify the pressure on the parties to the Transdniestrian and Nagorno-Karabagh conflicts to move forward.

Britain, of course, cannot alone engineer progress toward a Euro-Atlantic security community. Moreover, any effort in this direction would have to be compatible with the other objectives of Britain's Russia policy. The first reality means that pursuing the larger goal only makes sense if others put their shoulder to the wheel. Making this goal compatible with other aspects of Britain's Russian agenda – what is meant by 'fitting the dolls together in necessary sequence' – is best done by seizing on ideas that permit policy goals at different levels to work together.

For example, as proposed by a high-level expert group, national leaders would mandate senior national security officials to begin a searching, comprehensive strategic dialogue focused on all critical military dimensions – nuclear and conventional arms, non-strategic nuclear weapons, missile defence, prompt-strike weapons, cyber security, and space (Browne et al., 2013). As envisaged by these senior former officials from Russia, Europe, and the United States, to be effective this dialogue would be organised and monitored by national leaders. It would be free-ranging and designed to explore the deep sources of discord. It would not count on reaching formal agreements in treaty form, but rather concentrate on practical steps

---

[2] As proposed by senior experts on both sides. See Dvorkin (2013), EASI Working Group on Missile Defence (2012).
[3] For a more detailed illustration of what this might entail, see EASI Working Group on Energy (2012).

that could be taken unilaterally or reciprocally. And it would strive to achieve progress in stages, with different sets of actors relevant to different sets of issues concentrating on joint actions intended to build confidence and give momentum to the process.

At the end of the cold war, Britain, in cooperation with the United States, key Europe allies, and Russia, played a critical role in shaping historic events. Britain could again play an analogous role were it to take the lead in pushing for the kind of strategic dialogue urged by the expert group. In so doing it would both help to break the lethargy and paralysis that has left the Euro-Atlantic world pinned under the detritus of the cold war and foster a broader bilateral strategic dialogue between Russia and Britain that is essential if the two countries are to dismantle the barriers that prevent progress on the hard, practical issues on their agenda.

While a Euro-Atlantic security dialogue would take a comprehensive approach to the many dimensions of the military relationship, a UK–Russian strategic dialogue needs to be broader. It should encompass all aspects of the relationship; be unconstrained, permitting a frank discussion of the most neuralgic aspects in the relationship; conducted unobtrusively and at a high level, free from bureaucratic impediment; and intended to generate an action-agenda whose implementation is regularly monitored by the national leadership on both sides. Were this the over-arching charge given to the 2 + 2 'strategic dialogue' launched in March 2013, a more constructive framework would be in place when dealing with immediate issues, such as the Litvinenko case, anti-terrorist cooperation, economic ties, and the like.

For these different policy dimensions to converge synergistically, the underlying divides that cloud both the UK–Russian bilateral relationship and the EU–Russian 'doll' must be addressed deftly. No durable Euro-Atlantic security partnership, beyond short-lived collaborations, can be fashioned among states whose basic values are incompatible. But to make common values a prerequisite for starting the process guarantees its abrupt end – just as it would have had this been a requirement when forming the NATO alliance. Indeed, in the process, the more effective the enterprise becomes and the greater the identification of one with the other, the more likely all will gradually come to articulate and adhere to roughly similar values.

This does not mean that British diplomacy should avoid raising the issue of Russian human rights abuse. It does mean that, to be effective – to engage rather than simply spar with their Russian counterparts – British leaders need to stress the practical consequences of its repressive actions for the things Moscow values in its relations with the UK; do so without placing Putin and his colleagues in the public pillory; and, in particular, encourage as much consonance as possible in the message that other Euro-Atlantic leaders convey.

The values question, however, is one with ramifications, and, when dealing with it, British leaders should also be willing to take on a discussion of the conflicting values underlying issues, such as those underpinning global governance, including those related to humanitarian intervention – when, how, and by whom. Or conceivably they will need to address a newer values controversy over what Russians refer to as the 'new European values'. Russian voices warn that if Russia is expected to embrace the shifting currents in Europe over social issues, such as same-sex marriage, more damage will be done to EU–Russian relations (Pushkov, 2013).

Similarly, when thinking about what matters most in the EU–Russia relationship and how to mold a forward-looking agenda, the long-term challenge will be to find avenues by which Russia can be economically integrated *with* the EU when it cannot be integrated *into* the EU. That means, for example, working together on measures to mitigate the discrepancies between the Russian and EU energy markets. This is only likely to work if both sides set about narrowing the gap between the rules that govern their markets, rather than assuming that one market should simply be integrated into the other. It also means recognising that any Russian government will place a high priority on welding its economic ties with its immediate neighbours into more institutionalised and integrated forms. The trick will be to encourage the forms that emerge – whether a customs union or some version of the Eurasian Economic Community advocated by Putin – to be geared to the free flow of trade and investment with the EU.

The difficulty in formulating and pursuing a Russia policy this ambitious is obviously great, but, when carefully weighed, so are the stakes that make it worthwhile. At a minimum, striving to give British Russia policy a larger structure and more coherence should serve well in assisting policy-makers to deal more effectively with the issues that will come their way, including the inevitably unexpected ones. The alternative is either a policy predicated on altogether different and more menacing assumptions that largely dismisses the stakes involved or, more likely, an extemporaneous policy shifting from one urgent matter to the next, oblivious to the larger stakes involved.

CHAPTER 6

The Arab world to 2020

by Shashank Joshi

It would be trivial to observe that the Arab world is changing fast. But to grasp the pace and scale of the transformation, consider the following intellectual exercise: compare the post-war change in the political landscape of Europe on the one hand, and the Middle East on the other. In the 1950s, Europe's foremost powers were Britain, France and West Germany – joined by two interlopers, both in the continent but not of it, the United States and Russia. In the six decades since, Eastern and Central Europe have thrown off the Soviet yoke, middle powers like Greece and Italy have risen out of second-world status, and pan-European institutions have radically altered the terms of diplomatic trade. But the balance of power has not fundamentally altered. That trio of European powers and the two outsiders remain the most significant geopolitical forces on the continent, even if a unified Germany has politically and economically outmuscled its peers.

Now, perform the same exercise for the Arab world. In the 1950s, its leading actors were another trio: Egypt, Iraq and Syria. The latter two were colonial creations and the first only 30 years previously a colonial subject, yet they wielded epochal ideological and material influence. Egypt's 1952 coup brought to power a charismatic and revolutionary leader, Colonel Nasser, and with him an ideology of pan-Arabism that, though ultimately unsuccessful, would shake the region for two decades. Egypt and Syria would merge into the United Arab Republic (UAR) for three years between 1958 and 1961, and the bloc would play a pivotal role in the Arab–Israeli wars of the period (Halliday, 2005). The Gulf Arab states – including what were known then as the Trucial States – were mainly a group of underdeveloped and geopolitically irrelevant sheikhdoms under British protection. Saudi Arabia was getting to grips with its oil wealth, and locked in a cold war with the Egypt-led radical bloc (Kerr, 1971).

A Shifting Balance of Power

Fast-forward to the present, and that balance of power has been shattered (Miller, 2013). Fixed, fast-frozen relations are coming under severe stress. This is occurring while Britain's relationship to the Middle East remains wired through some of the most conservative and reactionary elements of the status quo and while that relationship is primarily articulated in a dimension of power (military) in which Britain's comparative advantage is diminishing and whose currency in the region has been devalued. These challenges to Britain are severest in the Gulf, where overt political change has been slowest, but they stretch from the Maghreb in the West to the Iran-Afghanistan border in the East.

There is, of course, much continuity. Jordan remains a fragile kingdom bound to its American and Saudi Arabian patrons, Iran's broad regional ambitions continue to cause concern to Arab powers, and the United States continues to play a key role in shaping the balance of power through arms sales and military deployments. Yet, each of those three states – Egypt, Iraq and Syria – finds itself in a condition of revolutionary or post-revolutionary disorder. Each has been brought low by endemic political violence, institutional atrophy, power-hungry elites wary of sharing power, bloated and predatory security forces, and, in the latter two cases, possible partition. This trio have become immeasurably weaker, and their decay is representative of a broader trend in the Middle East: the diffusion of power to new actors, both vertically (within states) and horizontally (across the Arab world).

We see this diffusion of power in the diplomatic activism of minnows like Qatar, in the fragmentation of al-Qaida and the resilience of its regional shards in places like the Arabian Peninsula, in the rise of a sprawling digital public sphere in absolute monarchies like Saudi Arabia, in the re-opened fissures of the Palestinian movement (Hamas-run Gaza has grown five times faster than the Fatah-run occupied West Bank), and in the growing entry (or, more accurately, re-entry) of China and India to the region's oil and gas fields and sea-lanes. This fissiparousness interacts with a series of other trends: growing sectarian enmity at every level from elite politics to street protests, intense fear of Iran's expanding nuclear programme, anxiety at the prospect of American military retrenchment, and concerns over food and water security.

Egypt, Iraq, and Syria: Political Decay

Egypt

Egypt's 2011 revolution, replacing a decades-old dictatorship that had evolved from that of Colonel Nasser, was derailed in what have been, so far, three distinct stages: first by a military junta, the Supreme Council of the Armed Forces (SCAF), jealously guarding its privileges and ruling unaccountably (during 2011–2012), then (2012–2013) by a Muslim Brotherhood-led government which ruled with increasing authoritarianism and arrogance and finally (from mid-2013) by a popular coup that saw the re-assertion of Mubarak-era elites belonging to the country's 'deep state', and the deepening of political divisions between Islamists and their adversaries.

Egypt has consequently sat on the edge of financial ruin and constitutional limbo in the years since the 2011 uprising. It shows little sign of walking back from there. It has limped on thanks to huge loans from Saudi Arabia, Qatar and Libya that have, in turn, constrained Cairo's diplomatic autonomy. The deposition of the Brotherhood represents a success for Riyadh and a setback for Doha, which had invested substantial amounts in its relationship with the Islamists. But the broad pattern of Egyptian dependence on outside actors will continue: Egypt, like Syria, is more a stage than an actor.

The dramatic fall of the Brotherhood (itself far from irreversible) leaves a mixed inheritance. The Brotherhood's heavy-handed rule tarnished the reputation of the organisation's offshoots and affiliates elsewhere – something for which rulers in the Gulf and Jordan are grateful – but also wrecked any hope that Egypt might have served as a beacon of democratic Islamism. It left the country unprecedentedly polarised and allowed the army to insert itself, with a view to semi-permanence, as the ultimate arbiter of Egyptian democracy. The brutal violence directed at pro-Brotherhood protests in the aftermath of the coup was a disturbing echo of things to come.

Much of the blame lies with President Mohammed Morsi and his political allies. Even as mass protests unfolded over June 2013, they refused to acknowledge the scale and breadth of opposition to their rule. In executing the coup, the army chief, Abdel Fattah el-Sisi, was able to marshal an impressive array of political forces to his side, including the Coptic Christian Pope, Egypt's senior-most Muslim cleric, and secular opposition leaders. There could be no better indication of Morsi's comprehensive isolation.

But had Morsi been forced into early elections rather than toppled so ignominiously, the Brotherhood would have received an electoral punishment more durable and legitimate than the arbitrary detention and violent repression of Islamists that occurred. Comparisons with 1990s Algeria – where Islamists were pre-emptively denied the fruits of an election victory, resulting in a protracted and bloody civil war – may be overblown, but there is certainly a risk of longer-term radicalisation amongst aggrieved Islamists. In truth, there are *two* competing lessons that Islamists may draw: the first is to abandon democracy if its fruits will be denied to them; but the second is that democratic participation in weak democracies will require compromise, power sharing, and moderation.

Any attempt to squeeze Islamists out of Egyptian politics altogether is both futile and dangerous. According to polls, 74 per cent of Egyptians want Sharia to be the official law of the land. Of those, 70 per cent want it to apply to non-Muslims too, 94 per cent want religious judges deciding family and property matters, and 81 per cent favour stoning as a punishment for adultery. A more recent March 2013 survey finds that Morsi's rule barely dented these figures: 58 per cent still want Egyptian laws to strictly follow the Qur'an. Indeed, the new army chief is himself an Islamist of sorts, having written his thesis at the US Army War College on the virtues of a caliphate-like system (Springborg, 2013).

It is important that Egypt's international partners, particularly the United States but also the European Union, pressure Egypt's army to allow a genuine transition to democratic *and inclusive* rule, without which political stability will continue to be elusive. Whether the restored army-led political elite can rehabilitate the Brotherhood into the latest iteration of the post-revolutionary political order will be a key test in this regard.

Iraq

Iraq is more peaceful and politically functional than the dark days of its civil war under American occupation. But it is ruled by an increasingly authoritarian and nakedly sectarian government (Dodge, 2013). The Kurds of the north revel in de facto independence, buoyed by the prospect of 45 billion barrels of oil reserves, twice the American total, and the increasing strength of their co-ethnics in northern Syria (Ajrash and Razzouk, 2013). The grievances of the country's Sunni majority have given way to a mixture of protest and escalating terrorist violence by forces loyal to al-Qaida.

The new wave of Iraqi protest after spring 2013 embodies the country's sectarian fissures. The protests are concentrated in Sunni-majority provinces. Protesters frequently excoriate Iran's influence in Iraqi politics and acclaim the Sunni-majority Free Syrian Army (FSA) fighting the neighbouring Assad regime. Sometimes, their slogans are starkly and belligerently sectarian. This naturally alienates many Iraqi Shias, who resent being associated with a foreign power and see the FSA as retrograde, Gulf-backed jihadists rather than freedom fighters. They are also likelier to see Maliki's various power-grabs as necessary steps to bring order and security to Iraq in the face of a growing regional and domestic threat from

Sunni extremists such as al-Qaida and its ideological brethren. Iraq's increasingly autonomous Kurds share some of these fears and sit in uneasy alliance with Shia political groups.

The Syrian civil war has widened these divisions and created a source of major instability. In March, around 50 Syrian soldiers who had fled into Iraq were ambushed and killed. The single most powerful Syrian rebel group, Jabhat al-Nusra, is an offshoot of al-Qaida in Iraq, and its personal and logistical networks run across the Syria-Iraq border. If Assad were to fall, this would have a catalytic effect on parts of Iraq, amplifying Sunni militancy and resulting in a flood of weapons of fighters across the border.

This does not mean that an Iraqi civil war is probable. It is important to note that while Iraq itself bleeds, the Iraqi state is relatively strong. Maliki is vulnerable in Sunni-majority areas where the Sunni militias of the al-Sahwa movement provide security, but his large and cohesive security forces serve as a buffer against wider chaos. Moreover, many Sunni groups are eager to keep the violence in check, having previously suffered greatly at the hands of al-Qaida in Iraq. It is certainly too early to talk about the country's break-up.

Yet Iraq, a country that provoked two of the largest American wars of the last quarter-century, is now a diplomatic pygmy, whose ties to Iran are viewed with suspicion and fear (Kinninmont, Sirri and Stansfield, 2013). The country is likely to avoid a return to civil war but a great deal will turn on the 2014 elections, Prime Minister Nuri al-Maliki's willingness to govern with greater sensitivity to Sunni constituencies, and the trajectory of next-door Syria.

Syria and Spillover

Syria has been laid lowest of all: a raging civil war has shattered the sectarian and ethnic mosaic, turned the Levant into the foremost destination for jihadists around the world, and transformed a once-powerful nation into the playground of its neighbours, allies, and adversaries alike. The single most powerful rebel group in Syria today is Jabhat a-Nusra (JN), an offshoot of al-Qaida in Iraq and loosely aligned to al-Qaida Core (O'Bagy, 2012). In the coming years, it would not be surprising to see Syria become a major counterterrorism concern for Arab and Western countries, much as Afghanistan became in the 1990s, and to see armed American drones flying missions over Aleppo and Homs from bases in Turkey and Jordan. The return of European fighters to their home countries, an area in which British nationals are over-represented, is also cause for longer-term concern, much as it was after the Afghan and Balkan campaigns in previous decades (Zelin, 2013). More broadly, Syria's trajectory today resembles that of Lebanon in the 1970s: a long, lingering conflict liable to result in fratricidal fighting amongst the rebels long after the regime has been toppled, and spilling forth beyond its borders (Harling and Birke, 2013).

That spillover is well underway. Syria's sectarian divisions are directly mirrored in Lebanon, where Sunni factions feel galvanised by the strength of Syria's majority Sunni uprising and chafe at the manner in which Hezbollah has come to dominate the Lebanese government over the past several years. Hezbollah, in turn, fears that the fall of Assad will fatally weaken its own position in Lebanon, and therefore participates vigorously in the fight to save Assad (Barnes-Dacey, 2013). The net effect is that Lebanon's tenuous political settlement is coming under great strain, and could give way to state collapse – for instance, in June 2013, 15 Lebanese Army soldiers were killed in clashes with a prominent anti-Assad Sunni militia leader in the town of Sidon. Pew polls show that 95 per cent of Lebanese, and 99 per cent of Lebanese Christians, worry about violence spreading to their country (Pew Research Center, 2013).

The impact on Iraq, discussed above, is self-evident: over 1,000 Iraqis were killed in violent attacks in both May and July 2013, the worst death tolls since the end of the civil war there. Jordan is more stable, but sees itself as highly vulnerable. It held deeply flawed parliamentary elections at the end of 2012. It is beset with economic difficulties, apprehensive at the rise of jihadists in the Syrian rebels' ranks, and worried about the effect of Syrian refugees on its own demography (Ryan, 2013). The scale of population displacement is such that one Jordanian refugee camp, Zaatari, is now the country's fifth largest city (Gavlak, 2013). Putting aside the truly infirm, such as Yemen, Jordan is the sick man of the

Middle East and is likely to remain so for the medium-term. Yet the country is also Britain's most important point of entry into the Middle East outside of the Gulf, given its position abutting the region's most fragile areas.

Looking over this group of countries, the contrast with Europe is apparent. Britain, France, and Germany, riven by financial woes and militarily shrunken, may be shadows of their former selves on the world stage. Yet they remain undisputed regional heavyweights. It is their choices that will shape Europe and constrain the smaller powers. Egypt, Iraq, and Syria may be at the heart of change – at the sharp end of the Arab spring – but their domestic turbulence has left them enervated on the regional stage, giving way to or, at least, competing with newer powers.

The Resurgence of Non-Arab Powers: Israel, Turkey and Iran

What is all the more remarkable is that three of the region's most important powers are now states that, linguistically and ethnically, have non-Arab majorities: Israel, Turkey, and Iran.

Israel

Israel, of course, has held a dominant regional position since 1967, and certainly since signing its peace treaty with Egypt in 1979. That year, Israel and Egypt were both promised military and economic aid in a ratio of 3 to 2 respectively, a superiority reinforced by Israel's undisputed technological edge (Brownlee, 2012). Today, Israel finds itself in the peculiar position of seeing its neighbours in a state of disorder but feeling little comfort from this. Its priority has been to insulate itself from the effects, launching repeated air strikes in Syria but avoiding any deeper involvement of the sort it so ruinously undertook in Lebanon in 1982 (Byman and Sachs, 2013). Israel's response to regional turbulence has been wary and risk-averse.

The on-going construction of settlements and long tenure of a right-wing government, supported at times by extremist parties, strongly suggests that the peace process, resumed in July 2013, is unlikely to bear fruit. Progress would require that the Palestinian factions Fatah and Hamas reconcile (or that Hamas accepts the result of a referendum), the government in Jerusalem takes radical steps to curb territorial aggrandisement, and the US president expend political capital on applying pressure. But, even then, the prospect of a two-state solution is exceedingly low (International Crisis Group 2012).

Turkey

Turkey's rise to prominence is more recent. It serves as a model, albeit one whose flaws emerged violently in the protests of May 2013, for reconciling Islam with democracy at a time when Egypt and Tunisia have struggled to do so peacefully. Its economic role in the region is growing, particularly in riskier areas neglected by Western investors. And its regional diplomacy is exceptionally ambitious. Ankara has interceded in disputes over Hamas, the Iranian nuclear programme, the Syrian crisis, and Iraq (Strauss and Gardner 2010). These efforts have been largely frustrated, but Turkish aspirations are undiminished. Within the period of one week in early 2013, Turkish Prime Minister Recep Tayyip Erdoğan managed to engineer a rapprochement with Israel and extract a ceasefire from the Kurdish PKK, rebel group, which could end a decades-old conflict. In doing so, Erdogan strengthened his ambitions to circumvent his party's term limit by modifying the constitution and assuming a beefed-up presidency (Joshi and Stein 2013).

Turkey's political and economic stability is not guaranteed. Erdoğan's use of belligerent, divisive language and violent repression of largely peaceful protests were deeply troubling signs, and they may undermine some of his domestic political objectives. Nonetheless, it is impossible to imagine regional diplomacy on a range of issues over the next decade – the future of Kurdish areas of Iraq, the relationship between competing Palestinian factions, the constitutional make-up of the post-Assad state and Western containment of Iran – without an active Turkish role. If the American commitment to NATO wanes, Turkey's military contribution to the Atlantic Alliance will become correspondingly more important.

Iran

Iran, like Turkey, has suffered diplomatic setbacks: crippling economic sanctions, the near-collapse of its sole Arab ally, Syria, and widespread regional suspicion of its intentions. Early in the Arab spring, Iran had sought to characterise the incipient uprisings as Islamic revolutions following the model of 1979. This narrative found little traction anywhere, even amongst the predominantly Shia protesters of Bahrain.

Many Bahraini Shias, like their co-sectarians elsewhere, have some theological ties to Iranian clerics. Yet there has been negligible appetite for political direction from abroad, or the adoption of a discredited Iranian political model. This runs contrary to the protestations of many Gulf Arab elites, who see Iranian interference in their affairs as pervasive and far-reaching. But it also serves as a point of some embarrassment for Iran: they have neither been able to shape the Arab spring to their advantage, nor provided succour to the disenfranchised Shia of Bahrain. Apart from the Iranian Revolutionary Guards' extensive assistance to Assad, they are bystanders.

Nonetheless, Tehran is a regional power. It is likely to remain one in spite of sanctions. It continues to project both soft and hard power into Gaza, Lebanon, Iraq and parts of Syria. The collapse of the Assad regime would weaken Tehran's ability to supply the Lebanese militant group Hezbollah, but that does not mean Iranian influence there or in Syria would evaporate. Indeed, Iran, having helped to train pro-Assad militias within Syria, and adept at operating in contested spaces, may be well placed to exploit a prolonged political vacuum there, just as it did in Iraq after the fall of Saddam Hussein. Iran is also likely to exploit the departure of US forces from Afghanistan in the years after 2014. Its influence in western Afghanistan is already substantial, and it is likely to make common cause with India and Russia in supporting anti-Taliban political factions.

Nor is Iran as unpopular as sometimes assumed. A major survey as part of the Arab Opinion Project (2012) found that, in contrast to elite Arab opinion in palaces and ministries, the vast majority of the Arab public does not believe that Iran poses a threat to the 'security of the Arab homeland'. Just 5 per cent of respondents named Iran as a source of threat, in contrast with 22 per cent and 51 per cent who named the US and Israel as threats, respectively. The largest per centage viewing Iran as a threat was reported in Lebanon and Jordan (10 per cent), and the lowest (1 per cent or less) was reported in Egypt, Tunisia, Algeria, Mauritania and Sudan. In Saudi Arabia, the state whose leadership is perhaps most fearful of Iran and most active in responding to the perceived threat posed by it, only 8 per cent believed that Iran presents a threat, far lower than that the 13 per cent who viewed the US as a threat. These numbers do not imply popularity – Iran is viewed very unfavourably in most of these countries, especially amongst Sunni respondents, and much more so since its deep involvement in supporting the Assad regime. But the intense *fear* of Iran amongst Arab rules is not echoed in the public sphere.

Why does this matter? Many Western accounts assume that Iran is on the verge of economic and political collapse, and that the ensuing regime change will bring to an end the nuclear dispute on favourable terms. But this is probably wishful thinking, and it ignores the lessons of Saddam Hussein's resilience, from 1991 to 2003, in the face of enormous military, economic, and diplomatic pressure (Gordon 2010).

Britain, a key player in the Six Powers'[1] diplomatic negotiations with Iran, ought to be open to the possibility that the Iranian nuclear dispute remains unresolved into the longer-term, with Iran neither abandoning its aspirations to uranium enrichment (as the West and the UN Security Council have demanded) nor dashing for a nuclear weapon (Joshi 2012: 56–59). The United States has set its red line at any Iranian effort to manufacture a bomb, but Iran could comfortably grow its nuclear infrastructure well shy of this point, as long as it avoided disrupting the work of IAEA inspectors (Joshi and Chalmers 2013).

---

[1] The Six Powers are also known as the P5+1 or EU3+3: Britain, France, Germany, Russia, China, and the United States.

New red lines – pertaining to Iran's enrichment capacity – might be set in due course, but it would be difficult to make these both enforceable and widely accepted by the international community. If the status quo persists, then the cumulative humanitarian impact of sanctions over time might, as in the case of Iraq in the 1990s, generate substantial international opposition to Western policy, including amongst the Arab public. Russia and China might peel away from the Six Powers negotiating with Iran, and withdraw their support for multilateral pressure. Long-term sanctions might also weaken the Iranian middle class and entrench Iranian elites, such as the Iranian Revolutionary Guard Corps (IRGC, who control smuggling routes (Wehrey et al. 2009). Although some Arab states would welcome a containment regime like this, others would consider it destabilising and unsustainable. The result would be a heightened American military presence in the region for years to come, and an embittered Iran increasingly prone to lashing out.

A resolution of the nuclear dispute is one of Britain's most profound interests in the Middle East: it would reduce regional tensions, enable a healthier relationship between Britain and its Arab allies, lower the risk of crises in the Persian Gulf, lower oil prices, and create space for Iran's political development. During the early stages of the crisis, British foreign ministers and diplomats played crucial roles in talking to Iran (Mousavian 2012). That has grown more difficult since the ransacking of the British embassy in Tehran and the tightening of sanctions. Nevertheless, one of Britain's most important tasks is to ensure that the United States does not grow impatient with the diplomatic process and revert to the application of pressure alone. The belligerence and inflexibility of the US Congress, in particular, is a major obstacle to a negotiated settlement, alongside Iran's own unwillingness to deal transparently with the International Atomic Energy Agency (IAEA). The shock election of pragmatic conservative Hassan Rowhani to the presidency in June 2013 is a highly positive development, and the appointment of a pragmatic foreign minister a good sign of his intentions, but the risk remains that the nuclear crisis becomes a permanent and festering feature of the Middle Eastern landscape.

The Gulf Cooperation Council (GCC) States and Rivalry with Iran

Iran's keenest regional rivals, the Gulf Arab states, under the de facto if tenuous leadership of Saudi Arabia, have also shown an impressive endurance. Their oil wealth, alliances with Western military powers, and (Bahrain and perhaps Kuwait aside) relative political stability has placed them in a central position to influence events, something that would have seemed puzzling to an observer of the region in the 1950s (Ulrichsen 2011: 15–30). Tiny Qatar has exerted an outsized influence on regional crises, providing arms and money to rebels in Libya and Syria, and to Islamist groups in Egypt and Tunisia. However the abdication of its Emir in June 2013 may contribute to a more inward-looking policy in the years to come. Qatar's deeply botched handling of the opening of a Taliban political office in June 2013 is a sign of its diplomatic inexperience.

Saudi Arabia has suppressed a democratic uprising in Bahrain, limited the extent of political transition in Yemen, fought to keep post-revolutionary Egypt in its strategic orbit, and attempted to corral the region's monarchies into a counter-revolutionary bloc (Kamrava 2012). This latter effort at greater Gulf Arab unity has had mixed results. We should not underestimate the extent of division within this group. The smaller of them, like Qatar and Oman, continue to maintain relatively good ties with Iran, both to hedge against Saudi Arabian power and for other reasons; Oman, for instance, was grateful for historical Iranian counter-insurgency assistance. Qatar is viewed with deep suspicion by Saudi Arabia and the UAE for its sponsorship of Islamist forces in North Africa, and notably Egypt (Roberts 2012). Saudi Arabia's sheer size, relative to its smaller neighbours, induces wariness – this explains why so many efforts at regional institution-building, such as a currency union, have come to nothing (Lynch 2011).

But what is clear is that, over the past decade, and especially since the beginning of the Arab spring, the Gulf Arab bloc has felt increasingly vulnerable. Part of the response has been internal: expanded social spending and increased wages, a greater effort to tie citizens to the public sector and thereby buy their allegiance (reversing years of efforts to expand the private sector), and greater repression. Marc Lynch (2013), Professor at George Washington University, notes that there has been 'escalating, direct public criticism of the person-alities and institutions of the monarchy', that the 'culture of public conformity has utterly disappeared' in every Gulf state, and that the ensuing repression is 'a clear sign of their diminishing power and legitimacy'. In other words, the Gulf has not been immune from the forces of the Arab Spring. This domestic insecurity is sharpest in two regards: perceived challenges from Islamists on the one hand, and Iran on the other.

The core of the GCC has deliberately and vigorously resisted what it considers to be Iranian encroachment into its strategic space. For example, Saudi Arabia sees itself combating Iranian influ-ence not just in Bahrain, but also as far afield as northern Yemen, where Iran reportedly abets the northern Houthi rebel movement in the areas abutting Saudi Arabia (Worth and Chivers, 2013); in Lebanon, where Iran-backed Hezbollah has steadily gained ground over putatively pro-Saudi Sunni factions (Prothero, 2012); in Iraq, where Saudi Arabia began to re-engage with the al-Maliki government in 2012 after years of neglect (Healy, 2012); and in Syria, where Saudi Arabia has been one of the two most significant sources of arms to the Syrian rebels (Chivers and Schmitt, 2013; Chulov and Black, 2013).

This rivalry with Iran has become increasingly sectarian in recent years. Iran is a Shia Persian state, whereas the Gulf powers are predominantly Sunni Arab states. Moreover, many Shia communities in the Arab world are socially, economically and politically margin-alised. This chimes with Shia Islam's historic perception of itself as oppressed in historical, theological, and political terms (Axworthy, 2008). In both Iraq (until Saddam's ousting) and in Bahrain, Sunni minority regimes have ruled over Shia majorities. Moreover, Shia minorities in Saudi Arabia and elsewhere remain downtrodden. Ever since 1979, then, revolutionary Iran has been a triple threat: first, because it aspired to Islamic leadership across sectarian boundaries, with an offer of a clerical model (*velayat-e-faqih*, or rule by Islamic jurists); second, because that model was a direct threat to the Saudi ideal of quietist clerics and absolute monarchs; and third, because it was thought to hold particular appeal to Shia communities within Arab states (Gause, 1994).

A reasonable working relationship between Iran and Arab states did evolve during the 1990s, and particularly after the election of a reformist Iranian president, Mohammed Khatami, in 1997. But this period of détente broke down after 2001, when an Arab narrative of a 'Shia crescent' (a term popularised by Jordan's King Abdullah) began to take shape. This supposed axis of Shia power was said to run from Iran to Iraq to Saudi Arabia's Shia-dominated oil-rich Eastern Province, and thence to Lebanon and Syria. Sunni governments fell in Afghanistan (2001) and Iraq (2003), empowering forces that were, at the very least, less hostile to Iran than their predecessors (Nasr, 2007). At their crudest, these fears portray Shia groups everywhere as Iranian fifth columnists, eager to impose radical theocratic rule and Iran's geopolitical preferences (Ulrichsen, 2011). In some aspects, the fear of Iran echoes early modern Europe's obsession with 'Popish plots' concocted by subversive Catholic minorities.

As a result, Gulf states, and wealthy individuals within those states, particularly Saudi Arabia, have, in their efforts to parry Iran, frequently sponsored intensely sectarian political and militant groups in ways that exacerbate radicalisation, embolden extremist forces, and widen divisions between communities. For example, many Saudi Arabian and Qatari weapons sent to Syria in 2012 made their way to extremist Sunni rebel groups of precisely the sort that are least likely to support a pluralistic, democratic Syria (Sanger, 2012). This is patently detrimental to Western and British, not to mention Syrian, interests.

On present trends, there is little sign that Riyadh and Tehran can reach a broader accommodation, despite the newly elected President Rowhani's promise to make this an Iranian priority. Curiously, each is convinced that the other is winning the regional struggle and that they are playing a zero-sum game. Each is also convinced that allowing democratic openings in key areas – Bahrain for Saudi Arabia and Syria for Iran – would make them greatly more vulnerable. Western policy has proven unable to arbitrate in this competition, in part because European and American states have, in nearly every respect, sided with their Gulf Arab allies against Iran.

Western Policy

This dynamic is further affected by the palpable fear in these countries that the United States, looking towards shale gas-driven energy independence and weary of two major wars in Muslim countries, is abandoning the Middle East as part of its so-called 'pivot' to Asia (Dueck, 2013).

This perception is both real and untenable. The United States has recently built a drone base in Saudi Arabia, expanded its counter-terrorism activities in the Arabian Peninsula and North Africa, dramatically upgraded arms exports to Gulf Arab states, and renewed its commitment to deterring Iranian aggression in the region (Worth, Mazzetti, and Shane 2013; Shanker, Schmitt, and Sanger, 2012). True, the Obama administration has, at the time of writing, refused to commit military forces to Syria and reduced its naval presence in the Gulf from two aircraft carriers to one (Baldor, 2013). But these are modest changes, especially when one compares the modest American regional military posture which prevailed in 2001 with the highly-militarised status quo. Contrary to popular belief, the United States is not leaving the Gulf.

Moreover, this is far from an exclusively American story. Britain and France are both more, not less, engaged in the Gulf and Jordan. In his 2012 RUSI Christmas Lecture, Britain's Chief of Defence Staff (CDS) Sir David Richards announced 'enhanced roles in Oman, Kuwait and Saudi Arabia', a greatly upgraded presence at Al Minhad airbase in Dubai (Britain also hopes to sell Eurofighter Typhoons to the country), and a greater naval commitment to the region. It is too early to call this a 'return to East of Suez' (Stansfield and Kelly, 2013), but it reflects both the importance that Britain places on the military and commercial relationships, as well as a sense of strategic drift after the drawdown of forces from Afghanistan.

This pattern of alliances associates Britain with autocratic regimes vulnerable to many of the same popular pressures as seen in Tunisia, Egypt, Libya, Syria, and Bahrain. For a variety of reasons, including oil wealth, Gulf Arab states are better placed than Ben Ali, Mubarak, Gaddafi, or Assad to resist political reform (Yom and Gause, 2012). But they are not immune. As Colin Kahl and Marc Lynch put it (2013), 'the coming years are likely to see continuing waves of popular mobilisation and political instability that could well consume even the most powerful conservative Gulf states'. What would be the implications of a larger physical British presence in the event of popular uprising or civil disorder? Would it, as British officials privately claim, produce greater leverage over allies, limit the use of violence against protesters, and help encourage reform? Or, as others warn, might it inhibit Britain from issuing criticism for fear of losing access, and retard political change by legitimating regimes that freely concede they have no interest in multiparty democracy (Davidson, 2013)?

The absence of even modest US criticism of Saudi Arabia, despite extreme human rights abuses, and the apparent US inability or unwillingness to pressure Bahrain to follow through on its promises of reform, suggests that these questions have not been adequately answered. Britain should be bolder in pressing for political reform, conditioning its arms sales and security sector assistance on such progress, and seeking American and French help in doing so as part of a relatively unified front.[2] This task will become more complicated still as the Chinese and Indian presence in the Gulf becomes more pronounced. China is already the world's largest importer of crude oil; half of its imports, and 70 per cent of India's, are from the Gulf (Jilani, 2013; Mills, 2011). Neither of these states is presently a credible substitute for European and American assistance, but that may change over the next decade.

---

[2] For an American perspective on this question, see Kahl and Lynch 2013: 54

Conclusion

The events of 2011, the erratic course of Egypt, the protracted nature of Syria's civil war all taught us, perhaps, that humility is in order when assessing how the Arab world will change over the next decade. This overview has focused on the overarching geopolitical trends: the weakening of traditional powers; the wider distribution of power across a greater range of nations and, downwards, to people previously excluded from politics; the rise of Arab–Iranian rivalry; and growing sectarianism. But it has said little of lower-order but nevertheless important issues: Yemen's political dysfunction (Johnsen, 2013), the environmental and ecological problems facing Arab states (Ulrichsen, 2011; Johnstone and Mazo, 2011), the fragmentation of al-Qaida as a global organisation into fluid, autonomous regional shards and the group's resurgence in North Africa (Pantucci, 2013), and the possible effect of falling oil prices on political stability (Arnold, 2013)

Any number of shocks are imaginable: an Israeli air strike on Iranian nuclear facilities and consequent war that engulfs Lebanon, Syria, and Western military bases in the Gulf; an earthquake that severely damages Iran's Bushehr nuclear reactor and contaminates Persian Gulf waters; a refugee crisis prompting political disorder in Jordan; Iraq's lapse back into civil war; a succession crisis in Saudi Arabia resulting from a series of royal deaths; the exclusion from power and radicalisation of Islamists in Egypt; the outbreak of al-Qaida-linked violence on Syria's periphery or even a major terrorist attack on American or European soil originating in the Levant.

Britain, with around 200,000 expatriates in the region (most in the Gulf), complex military and commercial relationships with a number of Arab governments, dependence on Gulf sea-lanes for energy supplies and on Arab intelligence services for counter-terrorism cooperation, and a stated interest in encouraging democratic reform, is deeply enmeshed in these issues (Hollis, 2010). It faces severe challenges in balancing its relationship with old and new political actors, engaging Islamists of various hues while maintaining ties to an old guard that is deeply wary of those political arrivistes (Blitz,

2013). It is deepening its role in Gulf Arab states that are becoming increasingly vulnerable to the same popular pressures that have swept away other regimes, but it cannot retrench completely without thereby undermining its ability to respond, militarily and otherwise, to that very same flux. It faces a jihadist threat that is more nebulous, local, and unpredictable than that which existed a decade ago. It faces these challenges as China, India, and others are intruding into what was once a British, and later Euro-American, sphere of influence.

What we are seeing in the Arab world at present is what Marx said of the bourgeois epoch: 'constant revolutionising [...] uninterrupted disturbance of all social conditions, everlasting uncertainty and agitation'. The Arab spring was neither teleological nor uniform, and navigating its waves will be the central task of the next decade.

SECTION 3

INSTITUTIONS

CHAPTER 7

Can the EU survive the Euro crisis?

by Charles Grant

The euro crisis is probably over: in the next few years there is not much chance of the currency breaking up, or of one of the countries in the euro falling out. The financial markets believe that eurozone governments have done and are doing just enough to hold the currency zone together, and that they will, if necessary, take whatever further steps are necessary to secure it.

What remains, however, is Europe's worst economic crisis since the 1930s. Growth is negative in much of the eurozone, which is increasing the burden of public debt in countries such as Greece, Italy, Spain and Portugal – despite the austerity they have applied. Unemployment across the eurozone averages more than 12 per cent. Current account deficits have come down in southern Europe, mainly due to low domestic demand suppressing imports. There is not much prospect of the eurozone's most indebted countries – or some others that are in the EU (European Union) but not the euro – returning to steady growth any time soon.

And as Europe stagnates, new problems are emerging, all of which are relevant to Britain's troubled relationship with the EU. Three issues, in particular, are the focus of this chapter. First, Germany has emerged as the unquestioned economic hegemon, for the first time in the EU's history. Germany's leaders are learning – slowly and sometimes with difficulty – that hegemonic countries need to act with a sense of responsibility towards their partners.

Second, the European Commission, for much of the EU's history a driving force of European integration, has been losing authority vis-à-vis the member-states. Given the Commission's crucial role in deepening and maintaining the single market, and in considering the wider European interest, this is a dangerous development. And, third, the EU is suffering from a crisis of legitimacy. The euro crisis has worsened what many perceive as a democratic deficit. Unless the EU's leaders do something to improve its legitimacy, its long-term survival cannot be assured.

None of these developments is particularly welcome for Britain's pro-Europeans. An EU dominated by Germany is not easy to sell to the British people. A malfunctioning Commission is less able to defend the single market, and to protect Britain's interests vis-à-vis the eurozone, than one that is effective. And if the EU is perceived as illegitimate or undemocratic, persuading the British to stay part of it will be harder. The chapter concludes with some thoughts on how Britain can best promote its interests within the EU.

The Problem of German Economic Hegemony

Germany's size and strength vis-à-vis its neighbours may create geopolitical imbalances in Europe. Since the second world war, German leaders have understood this problem and therefore been strongly committed to European integration as a constraint on their country's power. They still have that commitment but the problem of Germany's disproportionate power has nevertheless re-emerged over the past five years.

Never before in the history of the EU has Germany been so pre-eminent. This is partly the result of the weakness of France, Britain and the European Commission, all of which used to be more influential in the EU. And it is partly because of the relative strength of the German economy at the time of the euro crisis. Germany is the biggest contributor to bail-outs and rescue funds, and so naturally expects to set the terms for how the money is spent.

German economic power is an incontrovertible fact, and nobody can do much about it, at least in the short term. But that power alone does not explain the friction that has arisen between Germany and some other member-states. In April a draft paper from the French Socialist Party accused Chancellor Angela Merkel of selfish intransigence over her emphasis on austerity. Germanophobia has been evident in Cyprus, Greece, Italy, Portugal and Spain, all under the sway of German-directed austerity programmes. Some German politicians and commentators have hit back with unsubtle attacks on the supposed laziness of southern Europeans. In June 2013, a *Financial Times*/Harris poll found that 88 per cent of Spaniards, 82 per cent of Italians and 56 per cent of French thought German influence in the EU too strong.

Some of these tensions stem from the particular style with which Germany is exercising economic leadership. And that style in turn has been shaped by the evolution of German attitudes towards the EU over the past 20 years. When Jacques Delors ran the Commission, and Helmut Kohl ran Germany, most Germans thought that what was good for Germany was good for the EU, and vice versa. The shame of Nazism was a dark shadow hanging over Germany's leaders. At the time of German reunification, Helmut Kohl urged other heads of state and government to take the opportunity to tie Germany down through European integration. He told them that they would never get another chance.

At that time, the D-mark was the sun around which the other currencies in the Exchange Rate Mechanism (ERM) revolved. When the Bundesbank altered its interest rates, the other central banks in the ERM had to follow, immediately. François Mitterrand, Jacques Delors and other European leaders worked with Kohl to build an economic and monetary union that would constrain German economic power: the European Central Bank rather than the Bundesbank would set interest rates for the countries in the single currency. One of the ironies of the recent crisis is that, although the euro was designed to limit German power, it has ended up reinforcing German dominance of economic policy-making.

The German leaders who followed Kohl – Gerhard Schröder and Angela Merkel – do not remember the second world war and are less idealistic about the EU. Kohl thought that Germany had a special responsibility to resolve tensions within the EU, sometimes by writing cheques to other member-states. Schröder often took and Merkel has often taken a 'European' approach, but both have been readier to promote specifically German interests. For example on energy policy, Russia policy and China policy, Germany has at various times argued against or prevented the forging of common EU policies, on account of its own specific economic interests (in July 2013, for example, Germany defeated the Commission's attempt to impose anti-dumping duties on China's exports of solar panels in order to protect its bilateral commercial relationship with China).

The big EU enlargement of 2004–7 affected German attitudes. It brought in 12 relatively poor countries that made big demands on the EU budget. Many Germans realised that their interests were not the same as those of the new entrants. Since 2007, Germany has been one of the member-states most hostile to further enlargement into the Balkans.

The financial crisis that began in 2008 reinforced the Germans' worries that the rest of the EU wanted to get its hands on their money. In its early stages, France's President, Nicolas Sarkozy, proposed an EU bank bail-out fund, an idea that Germany soon killed. Germany then dragged its feet over Commission proposals to use unspent money from the EU budget for pan-European infrastructure projects that would boost investment.

This cooling towards the EU has affected German attitudes to the institutions. Most Germans remain broadly supportive of the European Parliament. The top officials in Berlin, however, have worked to ensure that MEPs do not become involved in the substance of approving eurozone bail-outs. And while the more federalist Germans still speak warmly of the Commission, the top officials and Merkel have serious doubts about its competence. They criticise it for failing to anticipate the euro crisis, for being obsessed with its own power and for its supposed inability to focus on the key issues. One sign of this changing attitude was Merkel's Bruges speech of 2010: she criticised the 'community method' (which gives the Commission and Parliament a key role in decision-making), praising instead what she called the 'Union method', according to which leaders in the European Council set the EU's agenda.

The euro crisis, which became acute in the first half of 2010, did even more to make Germans think that their interests were different to those of their partners. The German response to the euro's problems was quite simple. Profligate southerners had broken the rules and if indulged with over-generous bail-outs would have every incentive to break them again. Only budgetary austerity and structural reform would restore the South's long-term growth prospects. This response reflected the dearth of Keynesian economic thought in Germany, and the strength of 'ordo-liberalism' – a school which argues that economic policy should be rule-based and that politicians should be left with minimal discretion.

Germany has dictated the terms of rescue packages, and agreed to the minimal number of innovations required to keep the euro viable as a currency, but no more. It has accepted the European Financial Stability Facility and the European Stability Mechanism – both bail-out funds – and various European Central Bank (ECB) schemes, such as the Long-Term Refinancing Operation, which eased funding for banks, and the Outright Monetary Transactions, which would allow purchases of sovereign bonds and has calmed the bond markets. Germany has swallowed the Single Supervisory Mechanism, the first step towards a banking union.

But three years on, the medicine that Germany – together with its allies in the Commission, the International Monetary Fund (IMF) and some member-states – has forced the EU to prescribe has, in many respects, failed to work. The economies taking the medicine have shrunk, increasing the stock of public debt. Greece has needed a second bail-out and debt write-offs, while the terms of other surveillance programmes have had to be eased. The current account deficits of the problem countries have come down but bank lending has dried up and unemployment has soared.

Proponents of austerity policies are never likely to be popular, and serious Keynesians have acknowledged that the Mediterranean countries needed to get their budget deficits under control. Nevertheless the particular way in which Germany has promoted the politics of austerity has triggered high levels of hostility to the country.

First, most Germans think that their country has nothing to do with the problems in the eurozone. Few of them share the view of most of the world's leading economists, and the IMF, that Germany's massive current account surplus and its low levels of consumption have contributed to the structural imbalances, making it harder for the south of the eurozone to grow. Many Germans believe that the main cause of the crisis was southerners breaking budget rules (in fact only Greece was in significant breach of EU budget rules when the crisis began). They also argue that all member-states should emulate Germany's export-driven economic model, ignoring the fact that within the eurozone, current account surpluses have to be matched by deficits. They tend to overlook the huge exposure of German banks to southern Europe, and how the bail-outs helped those banks.

These German attitudes have fuelled a second cause of resentment: Germans tend to lecture southern Europeans with a tone of moral superiority. As Mario Monti, the former Italian prime minister, has so often observed, in Germany economics is a branch of moral philosophy. It is not irrelevant that the German word for debt, *Schuld*, is the same as the word for guilt. Many Germans believe that countries with excessive debts are guilty of unethical behaviour and that they should follow the example of their virtuous, low-borrowing German neighbours.

Third, Germany has often prevaricated over tackling problems in the eurozone, delaying decisions until the last possible moment. And sometimes it has reneged on agreements. Much of this stems from German domestic politics, which outsiders need to respect (though Germans sometimes forget that other countries have domestic politics, too). The first Greek bail-out in May 2010 was delayed because Chancellor Angela Merkel did not want it to precede the key state election in North Rhine-Westphalia. In June 2012 the EU agreed that its banking union should include direct bail-outs for banks in difficulty, in order to break the 'doom loop' of uncreditworthy sovereigns and uncreditworthy banks lending to each other. Subsequently

Germany indicated that it would not allow bail-out funds to be used in this way. And in recent months Germany has appeared reluctant to accept much progress on banking resolution regimes before its September 2013 general election.

Fourth, German leaders have not always been on top of events. Other countries' leaders have not necessarily been more clued up, but they have not been in charge. Nobody near the top of the German government seems to have had a great deal of understanding of how financial markets work. For example in October 2010, at Deauville, Merkel persuaded Nicholas Sarkozy – and subsequently the rest of the EU – that private sector bond-holders of Greek debt should take losses. Jean-Claude Trichet of the ECB, and others, warned her that such a move would spook the markets. That is exactly what happened: after Deauville, Ireland and then Portugal were frozen out of markets and slid towards requiring bail-outs.

The Cypriot bail-out in April 2013 highlighted the poor crisis management skills of the German government – and every other major actor. Germany supported the first rescue plan for Cyprus, which would have expropriated 6.7 per cent of money in bank accounts worth less than €100,000. The principle that Germany wanted to establish was that bank depositors should take a hit in bail-outs, to reduce the burden on tax-payers. This was driven by German politics: the opposition Social Democrats would only support a rescue that hit depositors – because help for the deposits of Russian oligarchs in Cypriot banks would be unpopular. But the attempt to expropriate small account holders broke EU rules on deposit guarantees and was likely to provoke a run on the banks of several member-states. Germany should not take all the blame for this foolish initiative: the Cypriot government, the IMF, the Commission and other EU capitals supported the rescue plan that was ultimately thrown out by the Cypriot parliament and abandoned. But Germany, as the eurozone's economic hegemon, took most of the criticism.

It is tough being in charge of the EU. Everybody blames you when things go wrong. But some German leaders have not yet fully understood that greater power needs to be accompanied by a greater sense of responsibility. Germany is disliked across large parts of the

EU for what is perceived as its selfish pursuit of narrow self-interest. Yet Germans tend to believe that they are blameless and treated unfairly, and that their generosity – as the largest contributor to rescue packages – goes unrecognised. They have a point. But the sometimes condescending attitude of German officials and politicians towards their partners does not help. The French, in particular, have noted a change of tone.

Given the weaknesses of France, Britain and the Commission, German economic hegemony is inevitable and probably desirable. But Germany needs to reassure its partners that this entails leadership, in the sense of acting to preserve and strengthen a system, rather than dominance, in the sense of an overbearing assertion of power.

Hegemons can have beneficial or harmful effects on the countries in their spheres of influence. Benign hegemons can encourage peace, stability and prosperity. The US's dominance of Western Europe from 1945 to 1989, and of NATO till this day, is such an example. The US has paid disproportionately for European defence but has kept the alliance together through a mixture of persuasion, soft power, example, capability, good organisation and fine diplomacy. There have been many tensions – and American mistakes – over the years, but the US has understood that leadership requires it to take others' interests into account.

Today's China has not yet learned to behave as a benign hegemon in its region. Its assertive diplomacy vis-à-vis Japan, Vietnam, the Philippines, India and other countries, notably on territorial disputes, is pushing them closer to the US. If current trends continue, China will end up surrounded by a league of hostile countries in military alliance with the US.

A comparison between Germany and China would be unfair, since Germany is a democracy that has no territorial disputes with its neighbours. The biggest difference between Europe and East Asia is that European states are embedded in the EU and NATO, which constrain their power, while the Asians lack comparable bodies. But the Germans should think about the American example. The Americans have learned that leaders attract brickbats, even from close allies, but are often wise enough not to get too angry about the criticism.

The eurozone now suffers from an alarming rift that separates 'Greater Germany' – Germany and the countries that do not question its emphasis on austerity and debt reduction, such as Estonia, Finland and the Netherlands – and the others. Worryingly for the Germans, the size of Greater Germany has shrunk since the eurozone crisis began. Austria no longer follows the German line, and even Slovakia, which had been ultra-Germanic, now calls for a softening of austerity.

By the summer of 2013 the political climate in much of the EU was shifting towards an acceptance that budgetary consolidation had been pushed to the limits of what was politically feasible: Enrico Letta's Italian government and President François Hollande in France, as well as senior figures in the European Commission and the IMF, were all calling for more emphasis on growth vis-à-vis austerity. Germany's leaders showed no signs of thinking that their economic analysis had been faulty. But some German officials acknowledged that they should have put a greater emphasis on structural reform than on spending cuts. And the country's political leaders are pragmatic enough to recognise the shifting climate. They have not complained that the Commission has given national governments more time to comply with the 3 per cent budget deficit rule.

And even if the German government remains unwilling to acknowledge a greater responsibility for the welfare of southern Europeans, some senior Germans think that it should. In May, Peer Steinbrück, the SPD's (Social Democratic Party) chancellor candidate, called for Germany to be a good neighbour and criticised Merkel for having portrayed southern Europeans in a negative light. Though not generally thought of as a Keynesian, he proposed a Marshall plan to promote stronger growth, and project bonds to mobilise private capital for investment across the EU. He is courageous to make these arguments, since they are not particularly popular with voters. Indeed, one problem in Germany is that although many politicians understand the benefits of EU membership, and that the consequences of a euro break-up would be catastrophic, they seldom make that case to the public.

One former leader who is not afraid to spell out the dangers of Germany becoming isolated is the nonagenarian Helmut Schmidt.

Speaking to an SPD Congress in December 2011, he said that 'if we Germans were to be tempted by our economic strength into claiming a leading political role in Europe, an increasing majority of our neighbours would mount effective resistance. This would cripple the EU and Germany would lapse into isolation.' He urged Germans to be sensitive to the interests of their partners and said that they should avoid advocating an extreme deflationary policy for the whole of Europe.

Germans should listen to Schmidt's wise words. The French economy is unlikely to recover its strength any time soon. Nor is the UK is likely to return to the heart of Europe. And there is virtually no chance that the Commission will recover the pivotal position that it held in the age of Jacques Delors. Therefore, for the foreseeable future, the Germans will have to wrestle with the problems that stem from their economic hegemony. They can certainly hope that France, Britain and the Commission regain some of their former strength. But German leaders will also need to soften their tone and show that they listen to the concerns of their partners. Tensions between Germany and its partners are bad for Europe and very bad for Germany.

The Problem of the European Commission's Waning Authority

The European Commission plays a key role in holding the EU together, but it is beset with difficulties. It is popular with neither governments nor voters. Twenty years ago, many people looked to the European Commission to set the EU's agenda and take the lead in managing crises. But few people expect the Commission to play that role today.

Ever since the time when Jacques Delors ran the Commission (1985–95), its authority vis-à-vis EU governments has been waning. The member-states – and especially the big ones – have sought to constrain an institution that they consider over-mighty.

The Lisbon treaty, which came into force in December 2009, created two important institutional innovations: the permanent president of the European Council, a post now occupied by Herman Van Rompuy, and the European External Action Service (EEAS), a body now led by Catherine Ashton. Both of these carry out some tasks that were formerly the job of the Commission and have contributed to its sense of insecurity.

Paradoxically, the euro crisis has led to the Commission gaining additional formal powers – on the surveillance of national economic policies – but further eroded its standing and credibility. National governments have provided the money for helping countries in trouble, so they have wanted to set the terms for bail-outs. The Commission has had to leave the high politics to the European Council, and often to a few key governments, focusing on its subordinate though important technical role.

The eurozone's travails have accelerated a long-standing shift in the nature of EU governance. The EU used to take few executive decisions that were politically salient. The Commission proposed laws and regulated, while the Council of Ministers and European Parliament passed laws. Both the Commission and the Council acted, from time to time, as an executive – for example the former blocked corporate mergers and the latter imposed sanctions on countries in other parts of the world.

But the euro crisis has led the EU to take more executive decisions that are political. The EU has forced heavily indebted counties to cut budget deficits, pass painful reforms and wind up banks. The Commission may propose such measures, but only eurozone prime ministers or finance ministers have the authority to take these decisions.

These are long-term trends, but personalities also matter. The current 'college' of commissioners contains few heavyweight politicians. Within the Commission, Barroso is a strong leader who dominates his colleagues; given the number of commissioners, he may have no choice but to rule with a firm hand. But outside the Commission, some governments complain about what they perceive as weak leadership. During Barroso's second term as president, which started in 2009, Berlin, Paris and London have become more critical of the Commission. Even some of the smaller member-states, traditionally allies of the Commission, complain about it more than they used to.

A number of governments accuse Barroso and his colleagues of failing to prioritise; or of implementing new initiatives too slowly; or of focusing insufficiently on fixing the eurozone. Some of this is unfair: the politicians who accuse the Commission of not coming up with relevant solutions to the eurozone's problems are sometimes the same ones who get annoyed when it does propose a big idea, such as eurobonds. And while the Germans have sometimes whinged about the Commission being too soft on countries under surveillance, many others believe that it has been too Germanic in its enthusiasm for budgetary discipline. Evidently, the Commission cannot please everyone.

There are two reasons, in particular, for the member-states' diminishing confidence in the Commission. First, they argue that the Commission proposes too many detailed rules, particularly in areas such as the environment, food safety and social policy. In May 2013, for example, Polish ministers complained about Commission attempts to regulate the shale gas industry and to ban menthol cigarettes – both of which are popular in Poland. In the same month the Commission proposed banning olive oil in re-usable bottles, but then climbed down after a storm of protest. Earlier in the year, German politicians sharply criticised a Commission proposal to set quotas for women on company boards.

Some senior Commission officials acknowledge that the institution can be over-active. But they blame the increasing sway of the Parliament over the Commission. And that is the second reason why some national capitals have turned against the Commission.

The Parliament has exerted more influence over the second Barroso Commission than the first, and not only because the Lisbon treaty gave it more power. Lobbyists and non-governmental organisations (NGOs) have their own pet projects for new EU rules and find it relatively easy to influence MEPs. The Parliament then puts pressure on commissioners to come up with new directives. They are loath to annoy MEPs, since the Parliament can cause trouble for them. Another reason why commissioners like to propose new rules is to justify their existence. The Commission's secretariat-general works hard to cull what it regards as superfluous legislative proposals, but does not always win the argument with commissioners.

None of this is to say that that the Commission should ignore the Parliament. That body is better placed than any other to vet the work of commissioners and, working with the Court of Auditors, to criticise their mistakes. Before the appointment of the last two Commissions, the Parliament played an admirable role in questioning sub-standard commissioners-designate and forcing them to withdraw. Given the Parliament's powers of co-decision over new laws, the Commission cannot and should not ignore it.

The problem is that over the past four years the Commission has become much closer to the Parliament than to the Council on many issues. The Commission should be accountable to both – it is appointed by governments and approved by the Parliament. But it should also be independent of both.

The politicisation of the Commission is a problem. There has always been some ambiguity over its contradictory roles: it is a political body that initiates legislation and brokers compromises among the member-states; a technical body that evaluates the performance of member-state economies; a quasi-judicial authority that polices markets and rules; and also a negotiator on behalf of the member-states. During the euro crisis the Commission's technical role has grown, which makes the ambiguity more problematic. When it pronounces, say, that France may be given two further years in which to meet the 3 per cent budget rule, is that the result of objective economic analysis or a reflection of the shifting political climate in national capitals? This ambiguity gives governments and others an excuse to criticise the Commission.

Politicisation can mean favouring political parties. Some socialist politicians claim that the Commission has been over-indulgent of Viktor Orban, the Hungarian prime minister accused of curtailing political pluralism, because he is in the European People's Party, which is the leading force in the Commission. There is not much evidence for this particular claim, but if the Commission becomes too party-political, its ability to carry out technical functions effectively may well be compromised.

Next year's European elections could accelerate the Commission's politicisation. Most of the pan-European political parties say they will each designate a candidate for Commission president, ahead of the elections. Their idea is that the European Council should propose as president the candidate of the party with the most MEPs – and that the Parliament should then invest him or her. Were the European Council to propose any other name, MEPs would reject it.

If it works, this procedure would be unlikely to do much for the legitimacy of the Commission: the competing Commissioners are likely to be unknown to most voters. But it is far from certain that the political parties and the European Council will, in the end, play this game. If they do allow the Parliament to appoint Barroso's successor, the Commission is likely to become more beholden to the Parliament – and the leading party within it – than is currently the case.

Such an outcome would be alarming, because the EU needs a strong and independent Commission – to consider the wider European interest, draw governments' attention to long-term trends, propose solutions to pressing problems (whether in the wider EU or the eurozone), work doggedly to achieve a deeper single market, and perform its monitoring role in eurozone governance. As the eurozone integrates, one key task will be to ensure a smooth relationship between the countries inside the euro and those outside it. Decisions made by the eurozone should not damage or fragment the single market.

So what can be done to strengthen this flagging but crucial institution? The most important step requires not a treaty amendment or an institutional reform, but simply an agreement among heads of government. They should decide to reinforce the Commission's independence by appointing strong figures as commissioners, and above all by ensuring that a heavyweight politician takes on the presidency.

The member-states should mandate the new president and his team to maintain their independence from the European Parliament, and support them in their efforts to do so. After the last European elections the Commission and the Parliament reached an 'inter-institutional agreement', covering future legislation and procedures, which gave the Parliament several things that it wanted. The Council of Ministers spurned the opportunity to make this a tripartite arrangement; if it had done, it could have balanced the legislative activism of the Parliament and pulled the Commission closer to it. After the next European elections the three main EU institutions should seek a tripartite accord on the EU's work programme.

As for reform of the Commission itself, the problem of too many commissioners needs to be tackled. There are not enough important jobs for 28 commissioners to do, and with so many people around the table, substantive discussions are almost impossible. The one-commissioner-per-country rule encourages both governments and those they appoint to the Commission to assume – in breach of the treaties – that the job of commissioners is to represent their homeland.

So the next president should divide his or her commissioners into seniors – who could become vice presidents – and juniors. There should be an informal understanding that, though all commissioners are of equal legal status, the senior ones will coordinate the work of the juniors in their particular areas of responsibility. In the longer run, when the treaties are re-opened, the EU should adopt a system whereby big countries would always have a commissioner (though not necessarily one of the top jobs) and smaller countries would take it in turns.

Another useful treaty change would be to give the European Council the right to sack the Commission. The Parliament has that power and by threatening to use it forced the resignation of the Santer Commission in 1999. If the treaties said that either body could sack the Commission, its equidistance between governments and MEPs would be reinforced. And that would help to give the EU the strong and independent Commission that it needs.

The Problem of the EU's Poor Legitimacy

The EU has long had a problem of legitimacy, but the euro crisis has made it worse. According to Eurobarometer, 72 per cent of Spaniards do not trust the EU. The Pew Research Center finds that 75 per cent of Italians think European economic integration has been bad for their country, as do 77 per cent of the French and 78 per cent of the Greeks.

For more than 60 years, the EU has been built and managed by technocrats, hidden from the public gaze – or so it has seemed. In fact national governments have taken most of the key decisions, but public scrutiny has been insufficient. This model cannot endure, because the EU has started to intrude – particularly in the euro countries – into politically sensitive areas of policy-making.

Political institutions can gain legitimacy from either 'outputs' or 'inputs'. The outputs are the benefits that institutions are seen to deliver. The inputs are the elections through which those exercising power are held to account. The euro crisis has weakened both sorts of legitimacy.

The outputs are hardly impressive. Economies are shrinking in many member-states, credit is in short supply in southern Europe, unemployment in the eurozone is over 12 per cent, and youth unemployment in Spain and Greece is above 50 per cent. Neither the EU nor the euro appears to be delivering much in the way of benefits – whether to Greeks who blame Germans for austerity, or to Germans who resent contributing to Greek bail-outs.

Input legitimacy has also suffered. Given the complexity of decision-making, with power shared among many institutions, lines of accountability in the EU have never been easy to follow. But the perception that power is unaccountable is growing, especially in the heavily indebted eurozone countries.

Power over economic policy has flowed away from national parliaments and governments to financial markets and to unelected institutions. Having mismanaged their economies, Greece, Portugal, Ireland and Cyprus have had to negotiate programmes of deficit reduction and structural reform with the 'troika' of the European Commission, European Central Bank and International Monetary Fund. Other countries, such as Italy, Spain and Slovenia, have avoided full bail-out programmes but had to follow the Commission's budgetary prescriptions in order to avoid reprimands and possible disciplinary proceedings. Decisions on bail-outs, and the conditionality that applies to them, have been taken by euro-zone finance ministers and heads of government. It is not at all clear where and how such decisions can be held to account, as became evident during the messy rescue of Cyprus in March.

There is no silver bullet that can suddenly make the EU respected, admired or even popular among many Europeans. Its institutions are geographically distant, hard to understand and often deal with obscure technicalities. However, unless the EU becomes more legitimate and credible in the eyes of voters, parts of it could start to unravel. For example, at some point eurozone governments may seek to strengthen their currency by taking major steps towards a more integrated system of economic policy-making. But then a general election, a referendum or a parliamentary vote could block those steps and so threaten the euro's future.

The best way to improve the EU's standing would be to improve its 'outputs'. If European leaders moved quickly to establish a banking union to strengthen the EU's financial system; if Germany did more to stimulate demand, thereby helping southern European economies to grow; if structural reform started to restore the competiveness of those economies; and if unemployment started to fall – then EU leaders would look competent, and support for eurosceptics and populists would wane. For the most part such outcomes require not new institutions, but better policies.

Nevertheless EU governance is in bad need of an overhaul. For many federalists, the answer to perceptions of a democratic deficit is simple: when decisions take place at EU level, the European Parliament should exercise democratic control (alongside the Council of Ministers). And if more decisions are being taken at EU level, the powers of the Parliament over them should grow.

However, these arguments face both practical and theoretical difficulties. The practical problem is that the Parliament has serious shortcomings as an institution. Since its first direct elections in 1979, four major treaties have boosted its powers. MEPs now have consid-erable sway over the EU's laws, budget and international agreements. Yet in every European election, the turn-out has declined – from 63 per cent in 1979 to just 43 per cent in 2009.

MEPs do a good job in some areas. In recent years they have, for example, improved the directive on hedge funds and private equity, and helped to reform the Common Fisheries Policy. But few voters are aware of the Parliament's good work and many of them are sceptical that MEPs represent their interests; a lot of MEPs have little connection to national political systems.

Much of the time, the Parliament's priority appears to be more power for itself. Since the 2009 European elections, MEPs have – as described in the previous section – increased their hold over the Commission. The Parliament always wants 'more Europe' – a bigger budget and a larger role for the EU – but there is little evidence that most voters think the same way.

There are also theoretical objections to the Parliament becoming the main body for democratic oversight of the eurozone. In the EU's usual law-making procedures – known as the 'community method' – the Parliament plays an important role. Thus in the last few years it has amended and approved new laws on eurozone budgetary discipline. And it is probably the best-placed body to question the Commission on its monitoring of member-state economies.

However, the money that rescues heavily indebted member-states has to be voted by national parliaments. The EU budget is not involved to a significant degree, so the European Parliament plays only a minimal role in bail-outs. Decisions on bail-outs and the conditionality that applies to them are taken at EU level by eurozone finance ministers and heads of government. But these decisions have to be implemented by national parliaments: the German Bundestag had to vote money for Cyprus, while the Cypriot parliament had to approve the winding up of Cypriot banks.

These are reasons to increase the involvement of national parliamentarians in eurozone governance – and in the EU more broadly. Critics of their involvement argue that most of them focus on national issues and have little understanding of the wider European interest. Those are valid points. Any attempt to enhance the role of members of parliament (MPs) therefore needs to encourage them to 'think European'. The European Council has helped heads of government to do so. The prime ministers who attend wear two hats – as national political leaders and members of the EU's supreme authority. As Luuk van Middelaar, an adviser to Herman Van Rompuy, demonstrates in his excellent new book *The Passage to Europe*, when national leaders attend the European Council, they start to consider the European interest – sometimes to their own surprise.

So how can MPs play a bigger role in scrutinising the EU? There are increasing numbers of 'inter-parliamentary' bodies that bring together MPs and MEPs. These range from the general Conference of European Scrutiny Committees (COSAC) to more specialised groups for foreign policy and Europol. And the recent fiscal stability treaty set up a 'conference' that will gather together MPs and MEPs to scrutinise the operation of the treaty and discuss wider economic issues. However, these bodies – though useful – are merely consultative. They do not give MPs a sufficient stake in the EU.

Accountability should start at home. Some parliaments, such as that of Denmark, have good systems for holding ministers to account, before and after they attend the Council of Ministers. Others, including that of Britain, scrutinise draft laws but do not follow Council meetings closely. National parliaments could improve their systems by emulating best practice across the Union.

The links between national parliaments should be strengthened. The Lisbon treaty created the 'yellow-card' procedure, whereby if a third or more of national parliaments believe that a Commission proposal breaches subsidiarity – the principle that decisions should be taken at the lowest level compatible with efficiency – they may ask that it be withdrawn. The Commission must then do so or justify why it intends to proceed. So far this procedure has been used just once, when the Commission withdrew a measure that would have enhanced trade union rights. A small treaty change could turn the yellow-card procedure into a red-card procedure, so that, say, half the national parliaments could force the Commission to withdraw a proposal. A similar system could enable national parliaments to club together to make the Commission propose the withdrawal of a redundant or unnecessary EU law.

A more fundamental reform would be to implement the long-discussed idea of establishing a forum for national parliamentarians in Brussels. The forum's workload should be modest, so that the best and brightest MPs want to participate. It should not duplicate the legislative work of the European Parliament. Rather, the forum should ask questions about, and write reports on, those aspects of EU and eurozone governance that involve unanimous decision-making and in which the Parliament plays no significant role.

This forum could become a check on the European Council. It could challenge EU actions and decisions that concern foreign and defence policy, or cooperation on policing and counter-terrorism. On eurozone matters the new body could – meeting in reduced format, without MPs from non-euro countries – question the euro group president and give opinions on bail-out packages. The forum could start work as an informal body and, if it proved useful, be endowed with formal powers – such as electing the euro group president – through a new treaty.

Hopefully, the forum would encourage MPs to think European. Sceptics and cynics will rightly argue that a new institution cannot on its own make the EU accountable. But in the long run, MPs will have to become more involved in the workings of the EU. Because MPs are usually closer to their constituents than MEPs, and because they are elected on a higher turn-out, they stand a better chance of ameliorating the EU's crisis of legitimacy.

How Can Britain Influence the EU?

As the EU tries to sort out these and other problems, the British will be debating whether to stay in or leave. One of the key questions for the UK will be the relationship of the euro countries to those that stay out of the single currency. An unholy alliance of British eurosceptics and some European federalists is now arguing that the countries in the euro and those that plan to join it will set the agenda for the EU as a whole. They argue that these governments will meet together frequently, caucus and pre-cook decisions for the wider EU, including those on single market rules. The conclusion of these eurosceptics and federalists is that Britain might as well leave the EU.

That is the view of Lord Lawson, a former Conservative chancellor, who wrote in *The Times* in May 2013 that the British 'will be increasingly marginalised as we are doomed to being consistently outvoted by the eurozone bloc.' As for the pledge by British prime minister David Cameron to reform the EU, Lord Lawson is sceptical. Any changes that Britain could achieve would be 'inconsequential', he predicted. He therefore says he would vote no in the referendum on EU membership that Cameron has promised in 2017.

Wolfgang Münchau, an influential *Financial Times* columnist but – unlike Lord Lawson – a federalist, has similarly argued that if Britain stays in the EU it will have very little influence on the rules. 'Faced with the combined development of a eurozone economic union and a transatlantic free trade zone, the added benefits of EU membership lose their appeal if most of the benefit can be had outside,' he wrote in January 2013. 'If one is absolutely certain that one will never join the eurozone, there is really not much point in being a member of the EU.'

But this analysis is too pessimistic. A British government that plays its cards well can still shape EU decision-making. To be sure, the decision of Britain's Conservatives to leave the European People's Party, the dominant group in the European Parliament, has not helped (this left the UK in a weak position to oppose moves in the Parliament to limit bankers' bonuses). Nor did Cameron's big speech on Europe in January 2013, which said that Britain might leave the EU after a referendum. As the European Council president, Herman Van Rompuy, responded: 'How do you convince a room when you have one hand on the door handle?'

But the UK is still capable of fighting its corner in the EU. For one thing, the euro countries disagree on many policies. Eleven of them plan a financial transaction tax among themselves (though they are finding it very hard to agree on the design), while others, including Ireland, the Netherlands and Luxembourg, will stay out of that. Countries such as Finland, the Netherlands and (sometimes) Germany want to deepen the single market, while the southern members of the euro are reluctant to do so.

For another, the media's understandable focus on the euro's ills has obscured the many things the EU does that are nothing to do with the single currency. The EU is busy with the single market, competition, trade, energy, transport, climate, the environment, farming, fishing, regional development, overseas aid, foreign policy, defence, enlargement and justice and home affairs. The UK has influence in some of these areas, like foreign and defence policy, but would have more clout if it followed certain precepts.

First, the UK needs to improve its lacklustre economic performance. Governments that run countries with strong economies are always listened to with respect.

Second, the UK should strive to maintain the authority of the European Commission. This will not come naturally to the British, especially since that body can be over-eager to defend its own prerogatives. But the Commission has an interest in preventing the fragmentation of the single market and in ensuring that its rules are made by all the member-states. It opposes the French idea for the eurozone to have its own secretariat – an innovation that could foster caucusing on wider EU business.

Third, the UK needs to do a better job of making friends in the EU. For many years, British ministers and officials have failed to invest in relationships with like-minded governments such as the Nordics and the Irish. When the Central Europeans joined the EU in 2004, many of them looked to the UK as a natural friend. They were subsequently hurt that the British ignored them while the French and Germans courted them. The current British government has made efforts with Germans and the Dutch but needs to do better.

Fourth, the UK needs to understand that clubs have mores as well as rules. The EU's mores include a commitment to compromise. When the UK respects this principle, as did in the recent negotiations on the EU's budget, and on banking supervision, it may achieve good results. But threats to wield a veto diminish the UK's authority. David Cameron's refusal to accept the 'fiscal compact' on budgetary discipline in December 2011, despite the fact that it would not have affected the British, lost his government much good will.

Fifth, the UK should take the initiative and show leadership where it has expertise, in areas such as foreign policy and defence, energy and climate, or trade and the single market. Countries that take the lead earn good will. A lot of other member-states, including some in the euro, would respond positively to a UK that was pro-active rather than passive.

Many of the UK's partners value its economic liberalism, Atlanticism and global outlook. They would welcome British proposals for reform. But British political leaders – from all the main parties – need to emphasise that they want Britain to stay in the EU and expect it to do so. And they need to find the courage to take on Lord Lawson and others who argue for British withdrawal. Then the British government and its ideas for reform will be taken seriously.

A more influential Britain would help the EU to cope with the problems this chapter has focused on. The problem of German hegemony would be moderated by a UK that took initiatives and had many friends. A strong Britain could help the Commission to stand up to protectionist pressure or bullying by the Parliament, and to be an institution that champions EU reform. And the more that the UK engages with the EU, the more influence it would have in promoting the role of national parliaments in EU governance. On the other hand, a British exit would reinforce Germany hegemony, weaken the Commission's economic liberalism and remove a potential champion of greater accountability.

CHAPTER 8

Is NATO sliding toward irrelevance?

by Kori Schake

No, it is not.

The great NATO chronicler Stan Sloan used to say that the most reliable cliche in the West was 'NATO is in crisis' (Sloan, 2008). For it has been true throughout the entire history of the North Atlantic alliance, and it will remain true. That it was and is true is actually the proof that NATO remains relevant: because if it were fading quietly away there would be nothing to fight about among allies. We would have the placidity of disuse. But instead, we have perennial concerns about whether the institution will prove resilient enough for application to the new challenges facing us. Allies keep finding it useful as new dangers crop up, and those require new tools and new ways of working that we thrash out together.

It is easy to lose perspective on the extraordinary transition this alliance has made. It successfully adapted to the end of the cold war, members determining that even without the Warsaw Pact threat, our common defence was worth continuing. It embraced new members from its former adversaries, helping stabilise their transitions to democracy. It rose to the challenge of intervening in the Balkan wars, learning stability operations as a core competence. It figured out how to work with other institutions because that was essential to many NATO members. It went to war in Kosovo to prevent ethnic cleansing. It invoked Article 5 for the first time and patrolled American skies after the September 11 attacks. It has managed to hold together through 12 years of fighting in Afghanistan. It went to war in Libya to prevent the Gaddafi government carrying out its threats against its own citizens. And it currently has military forces deployed in Turkey to protect that ally against further provocations by the Assad government in Syria.

All while bickering about burden-sharing, levels of defence spending, 'the right of first refusal,' and whether the United States is disengaging from Europe. All while Europeans have been for two decades deeply engaged in the project of building the European Union. All while some allies were fighting in Iraq, a war vehemently opposed by many others. All while a rising China began to draw concern from US defence planners. It's actually an extraordinary record of achievement.

Moreover, the basic bargain that brought NATO allies together is likely to keep them together. NATO ensures that the United States is enmeshed in European security concerns, and that Europeans work collectively to build security in Europe. Other, later additions, such as projecting power beyond Europe, have strengthened the value of the institution.

The Arguments Supporting Irrelevance

Given NATO's record of succeeding despite frequent reports of its imminent demise, the burden of proof ought really to be on those who believe the 28 countries that have entangled themselves together in NATO will now decide to allow it to atrophy. What would be their rationales? There are several lines of argument: first might be that the allies – or at least some allies – have better options than continuing to work with each other; second, friction among allies makes continued cooperation impossible; third and finally, that collective defence just isn't necessary any longer.

Better Alternatives
NATO could become irrelevant if its members found other ways to meet their security needs. An alliance of 28 members in Europe

and North America isn't the optimal grouping for addressing the contemporary security needs of those countries. To some outsiders NATO looks too rich, too safe, too white, too Christian for ease in intervening in many parts of the world; the colonial legacies of many of its members add concern about its motives. NATO excludes countries like Australia, Japan and South Korea that are active and important contributors in its current operations; and includes some countries that are reluctant and stingy participants in the common defence.

The United States longs to have a non-NATO option. My country gets weary of pulling defence capability initiatives out of its hat, a new one every NATO summit just about, to jolt European allies into spending more. Increasing European defence spending has long since become another illustration of Samuel Johnson's description of second marriages, the triumph of hope over experience. Europeans are often sanctimonious and condescending toward us, 'Athens to your Rome,' exasperating given the share of the common defence we shoulder and the number of international problems American policy-makers are required to address simultaneously.

It is easy for Americans to overlook that European demands of us spring from the belief that we are different and better than other strong countries – that, in fact, we are not Rome. Our NATO allies expect more of us and hold us to account; frustrating as that can be, it is a contribution to American foreign policy and a reminder that expedient choices diminish us.

Still, Americans long for allies that are less trouble and more help, and periodically we set out looking for them. But we always keep being pulled back to Europe by the fact that we have no better allies to trade Europeans in for – others countries turn out to be just as much trouble and even less help.

Where would the United States find better allies? A rising Asia might produce them, except that our long-standing Asian allies cannot seem to put their second world war grievances to rest in the way Europe masterfully did, which inhibits multilateral cooperation and the military capabilities of potentially formidable allies, especially Japan. Asian countries remain understandably rooted in the security conflicts of their neighbourhood, limiting their potential contributions elsewhere.

India provides an illustration of the difficulty of finding major allies outside the NATO context. There was hope in the run up to the 2003 Iraq war that India might be a major force contributor: it was a rising power, democratic, with a solid military and a government desirous of showing itself a major international player. But India, like most rising powers, has urgent domestic needs that make most international problems of secondary importance. Like most developing countries, it has challenges of governmental capacity that make it more difficult working together, especially by contrast to the known patterns of working together among NATO governments.

Mexico, the country with the closest alignment of interest with the US, is likewise consumed with the important transformations and problems of pulling itself forward. Brazil has a fundamentally different view of the international order than does the United States, as witnessed by their efforts to negotiate with Iran. China may become a country that views its interests as aligned with the United States, but at the moment we are hedging against their actions and potential. Russia is declining rather than rising, and defines its security interests in contravention to the United States, even with hopeful 'resets' of the relationship by every new American administration. South Africa, the newest addition to the club, has little vision beyond Africa and a patchy record even there. Even if the BRIC states continue to rise – by no means assured on the basis of recent economic performance – their perspective on international security issues, their willingness to be contributors to broader international security, their potential military contributions, and the ability of their governments to carry out policies all make for less than meets the eye as potential substitutions for NATO Europe.

Europeans' frustrations with the United States surely likewise militate for exploration of alternatives. The US is overbearing, dismissive of Europeans' considerable strength and contributions, insistent that our choices are superior. We stampede to address the problem of the moment with little perspective on either the historical underpinnings or the long-term involvement necessary for enduring success.

Where would Europeans get an alternative to American entanglement? From each other, of course. That would remove 80 per cent of NATO combat power, however (NATO Parliamentary Assemby, 2013). Whatever one thinks of the aggravations of being an American ally, it is a country influential in international institutions, engaged in much of the world. It comes with a military that (even in these spending-constrained days) constitutes 42 per cent of global defence spending, much of it technological innovation, and a country more willing than most to put its sons and daughters in harm's way. Getting away from NATO wouldn't prevent Europeans having to deal with the US, but it would delink Europe from American military power and the patterns of cooperation and influence NATO provides.

Moreover, the US is not unique in producing frustrations; 20 years of intensive work building a common foreign and security policy in the European Union has revealed similar concerns by some governments about their fellow Europeans. While the European Union has done some very good work in defence policy, the dilemmas of pooling assets, sharing risk, building consensus, and buying weapons bedevil it as much as they bedevil NATO – perhaps all the more so for the narcissism of small differences.

Europe, too, could try to turn the kaleidoscope and build a new set of allies. The problems that inhibit American success may be less of an impediment for Europeans. It may be easier for Europeans to accept the constraints of international institutions and policy compromises; they may work more easily in large coalitions without a central hub; their moral authority may be superior without American ballast. But even then, the practical difficulties of constructing coalitions for a fight or institutions and practices for extended interaction would be significant disincentives.

For most Europeans, NATO remains the place where they have the greatest influence over American defence choices. The war in Afghanistan was a surprise for many European governments, who had assumed that European involvement would mean NATO leadership and were sorely disappointed to find themselves in a trailer park in Tampa with other countries contributing forces and without the policy and military planning influence they were accustomed to in NATO.

The SACEUR (Supreme Allied Commander Europe) is Europe's advocate in the American defence constellation; other commanders aren't knowledgeable of European capabilities simply because their responsibility is working with the partners in the area of their geographic responsibility. They may welcome European participation in operations, but NATO remains Europe's best bet for influencing American decisions. The exception is, of course, Britain, which has the ability to achieve those things bilaterally with or without NATO.

Moreover, the patterns of cooperation in NATO have created a bias in favour of assistance and a relatively efficient means of organising that assistance. One of the lessons of the Iraq war was how difficult it actually was for NATO allies to deny other NATO allies assistance to fight a war they deeply disapproved of. The German government, staunchly opposed to the war, not only provided essential support to the US deployments, but used their influence with Belgium to prevent closing of its ports to US military transshipments. Most new NATO members sent troop contingents.

Turkey was the main outlier to the pattern, surprising the United States by denying us transit and stationing for the launch into Iraq. But the reticence of Prime Minister Erdogan to take an unpopular choice in the midst of a difficult transition to assert civilian control of the country, and his principled position that the government needed approval of the Turkish Parliament, are not dispositive. A democratic Turkey – especially if it can succeed without continuing its assault on journalists and politicising the courts – would be an important strategic asset as well as a triumph of 'western' values. Turkey's foreign and defence policy choices more recently are trending in ways more collusive for the alliance (if not for the European Union).

Overwhelmingly, the problems associated with replacing NATO with a better set of allies, for both Europe and the United States, give strong incentives for making do with what is already at hand.

If it continues to make strategic sense for NATO allies to sustain the organisation, might there still be or emerge impediments that prevent it? There could be. Two categories of difficulties could overwhelm the common desire to prevent NATO's irrelevance: issues that become so dominant and intractable they fray the organisation beyond repair, and Europe or the United States simply becoming disengaged from each others' concerns.

Insurmountable Differences

History is replete with instances of states making choices that squander strategic advantage; NATO could certainly run up against new issues, or run aground on old issues, that fracture the comity on which continued engagement relies. Aspirations by some Europeans for the European Union often seemed, at least to Americans, to have that potential in the 1990s; the failure of the European project – whether through the collapse of the monetary union, British withdrawal, or public rejection from either debtor or lender countries – could yet pose such an existential threat.

Nuclear strategy is often cited as an example (principally by advocates of changing it) of an issue so divisive, and on which allies have such incompatible interests, that it could tear the alliance apart. This is a more difficult case to make, given that NATO leaders have so often threaded this needle. An alliance pliable enough to hit upon the 'dual track' strategy of deploying a new generation of nuclear weapons while committing to negotiate their withdrawal is likely able to contort itself to a common approach, whatever the dictates of substance.

NATO's Alliance Strategic Concept, agreed at the 2012 NATO summit, is a stronger statement of commitment to nuclear weapons as an essential element of NATO defence than had been made since the end of the cold war (NATO, 2010). Questioning from German quarters set in motion a process of consensus building that actually built a strong foundation for continuity in nuclear policy, including by the German government.

The role of allies ordinarily not much engaged in nuclear issues also gives the debate an interesting new dynamic. Norway, for example took a leadership role working with the Dutch and Belgian governments and produced a rule that any changes to current nuclear strategy or forces requires consensus among allies. This dramatically reduces the prospect of a single government, or small collective of governments, upending the policy by objecting; they must now persuade all allies to produce a change.

Divergent militaries are a perennial problem in NATO, but the issue has grown in salience with recent years. It used to be that the battlefield could be sectioned, nations assigned different areas on the map with the purpose of deconflicting activity – preventing us from harming each other, but leaving each force to its own fight. The advance of joint operations (air, sea, and land power used integrally) in our military thinking and capabilities has given NATO an enormous advantage over many other militaries because we are able to work multinationally in this way, while many other countries struggle to operate jointly. Technological advances of the past 20 years have further integrated military operations and increased their reliance on information technologies to increase the range, precision, synthesis of data, and communication. This 'transformation' makes more difficult the ad hoc piecing together of coalitions and greatly advantages militaries that have standing cooperation and interoperable equipment.

But the wars of the past decade have introduced differential rates of innovation in our militaries. Most prominently, the US has pressed forward with numerous adaptations to the conditions faced by our forces fighting in Iraq and Afghanistan, producing up-armored vehicles, drones that give persistent surveillance and attack targets, unmanned supply helicopters, energy breakthroughs in batteries and alternatives, 'blue force' tags to identify friendly militaries. These new technologies drive new operating concepts and generate further innovation. They save lives in combat and create new opportunities for the forces that buy and adopt them.

Not all NATO militaries – in fact very few NATO military forces – are adopting the suite of capabilities that have percolated into the US (Rasmussen, 2012a). The gap between forces is widening, and in ways that will be difficult to overcome. NATO's attempt to bridge the gap, creating a peer of the SACEUR responsible for transformation and linked to the long-term budgeting by nations, has been successful to some extent, but important chasms are opening that could become determinative, making working together more detrimental, outweighing the advantages accrued by fighting in coalition.

Important as these changes are, my sense is they are unlikely to develop into an issue that threatens the alliance. The gap seems currently less important than it was a decade ago, when US transformation had leapt the transom into networked operations but most allied forces had not. The hubris evident in both civilian and military US circles about our combat prowess diminished with our difficulties in winning the wars in Iraq and Afghanistan; we are happier to have allies present even if they cause operational difficulties, and more willing to tailor operations to tasks allies can succeed at. Friction remains, certainly, as Secretary Gates' abrasive description of European operational shortcomings attests (*Wall Street Journal*, 2011). But that simply takes us back to the American problem of not having better allies to trade the Europeans in for.

Lastly, the alliance could become irrelevant because its constituent governments simply get tired of hearing it from each other. Exasperation has ended many a marriage, and NATO allies have been arguing over the same issues for 64 years. Perhaps the phenomenon of gray divorce will extend from baby boomer couples to the transatlantic couple. This, too, seems unlikely. For better or worse, the NATO alliance keeps finding new security needs, expanding the aperture of its activity. Even though the arguments are familiar – burden-sharing, risk sharing – the circumstances change. Arguments about caveats took on different casts in Afghanistan, where the US was the demanding party, to Libya, where the US wanted to shield itself from European claims on its forces.

Peace in Our Time

A final genus of issue that could make NATO irrelevant is having the security agendas of its members pulled in different directions. The Obama administration loudly and proudly announced a 'pivot to Asia.' That this has amounted to little more than trying to diversify our basing options beyond Japan, rotating a few thousand Marines through Australia and hopefully other countries, increasing by 2020 from 50 per cent of the Navy in the Pacific to 60 per cent, and picking up the trade agenda of the previous administration has not diminished the administration's insistence that a rising Asia is the strategic focus of the United States (Stuster, 2013).

The department of the US government most responsive to political direction and capable of strategic planning is the Pentagon. Changes in strategy actually do result in changes to funding allocation and force structure. The 'rebalancing' to Asia is prioritising forces and operations for that theater. As spending constraints begin to bite – they have not yet; despite sequestration, we are still only talking about reductions to planned increases in defence spending, not actually reducing our spending – naval and air assets will be prioritised, basing infrastructure in the Pacific will be given attention and assets in Europe brought under intense scrutiny for their contribution. The US Army is already replacing permanent stationing in Europe with rotational forces, and pressure on the (badly managed) Army budget will likely force the rotations to be reduced in frequency and duration. The services will seek to consolidate forces and infrastructure in the territorial US, and they will have ardent allies in the US Congress for that. Even training opportunities will become less frequent and more focused on Asian allies as the 'pivot' progresses.

Still, as Norwegian Foreign Minister Espen Barth Eide (2012) rightly puts it, 'China is not just rising for the United States, China is rising for Europe, too.' America's emphasis on sorting out the pressing security problems in Asia need not force a divergence between the US and Europe. In fact, many of China's choices, such as theft of intellectual property and cyber-crime, are common cause across the Atlantic. If China's economy moves up the value chain, such that it challenges German primacy in heavy machinery or other European economic interests, security interest could follow. The values agenda inherent in European engagement is an enormous benefit to the US in Asia, as would be greater political and military involvement of Europe to help manage a disparate collection of American allies in Asia.

Strategic divergence could also emanate from Europe, in the form of a groundswell that Europe is largely safe, and safer if it declines to be militarily involved beyond Europe. Al-Qaida successfully intimidated Spain out of the coalition fighting in Iraq by threatening to bring home to Spanish territory the violence al-Qaida imposes elsewhere; parties to the conflict in Syria have brought violence to Turkey in retribution for its support of rebels fighting the Assad government. European governments, especially those with large populations of unassimilated immigrants, could decide their security interests lie in a policy of non-alignment, so to speak.

It is also possible that Europeans could be consumed with rising insecurity in Europe – a revanchist Russia, erosion of democratic institutions in Hungary, creeping authoritarianism in countries mired in dire economic circumstances with little hope of improvement. It is also possible that the US, consumed with more pressing problems posed by North Korea, Iran and others, might take little interest in Europe's concerns, or would consider them easily manageable by Europe alone. Slowly and through inattention, the Atlantic could widen.

It seems unlikely, though. Russia, especially, remains a central preoccupation of the Obama administration, and Americans debate whether our policy should continue engagement of the Putin regime, but there is no faction arguing that a Russia making the choices this Russian government is – and with public support within Russia for many of the policies we find most egregiously concerning – is not dangerous or that our policies wouldn't be strengthened by transatlantic consensus.

While potential fault lines do exist, none of them currently seem of a magnitude such that they could rend a breach in the transatlantic alliance.

After Afghanistan

The latest round of questions about NATO's future arise from the fact its mission in Afghanistan will draw to a close in 2014 or thereafter. There is always a fear in NATO that unless the alliance has a grand concept, a new direction, it will become obsolete. The metaphor often used is of a bicycle: unless it is going forward, it will topple over (Rasmussen, 2012b).

The bicycle metaphor has never fit well with the strength of the basic NATO bargain, but the time when it had the greatest credence was probably the end of the cold war. Germany yearned so for unification that many in the Kohl government were willing to leave NATO to achieve it. The Soviets loudly argued amidst the crumbling of the Warsaw Pact that NATO should likewise be disbanded. The euphoria of a changed Europe indulged an awful lot of wishful thinking. Former Soviet 'allies' overtly sought protection from the West for their new-found freedom, while most NATO allies were concerned about provoking Russia or thought the way to ensure Poland's security was a new kind of positive relationship with Moscow. In those circumstances, it made sense for the alliance to undertake major new activities to assist the transition of former Warsaw Pact or Soviet states, and to consider expanding its membership on a decelerated timetable.

With the Balkan wars raging, advocates of an activist NATO argued it needed to go 'out of area or out of business.' The argument was unpersuasive in motivating governments to intervene; NATO was driven into the former Yugoslavia by outrage at the barbarity of its civil war, the press of refugees into European countries, and fear of 'war happening again in Europe'. As with the end of the cold war, new security problems drove the adaptation of the institution. And so it has been with September 11 and Afghanistan: NATO takes on new missions because its members are pressed by new problems, and would prefer to run those risks collectively.

This time really is different. With austerity biting all our countries, there is little public enthusiasm for an activist foreign policy and (relatively) little money to pursue it. NATO is likely to be seen as a cost-efficient way to provide for our defence, which would be more expensive without collective action. Any pressure for a bold new mission for the alliance will be understandably derided and surely ineffective. But that does not mean NATO will lack important undertakings or missions that keep it central to the security agendas of its members.

As the alliance moves into the future, three challenges will rear up again and need to be addressed. That they are old challenges – spending, nuclear issues, and the extent to which we must address security beyond our borders in order to be secure – only proves Stan Sloan's adage.

As Always, Spending

It is a fact universally acknowledged, as Jane Austen put it, that all of the NATO governments are strapped for cash. Some have solvency problems, nearly all have liquidity problems. The crippling austerity imposed on Greece, Spain, and Portugal may yet need to be administered to Italy, France, and others. In this landscape, it will be amazing if governments can keep defence spending from settling into a much lower priority in their budgets. With direct threats to all of our countries at historically low levels, defence will be toward the front of the line for the chopping block – and it should be.

Properly handled, the coming time of austerity could actually benefit NATO cohesion. The past decade has seen reductions in most European defence budgets and substantial increases in American spending. The disparity has been much attended to, and as the Gates speech exemplified, derided by Americans. Now that we, too, are facing a decade of defence austerity due to our unsustainable debt and our sustainable political gridlock, the US will have less reason to criticise Europeans. It is probably too much to expect my country to acknowledge that our European allies have a much better record of producing security cost-effectively by means we should study and learn from – but at least the stentorian lectures about Europe's growing ineffectualness are likely to abate.

That alone would be a welcome boost to transatlantic relations. The United States' harangues are both untrue and enfeebling. Untrue because Europeans constitute many of the world's best militaries. Enfeebling because we are persuading our closest friends in the world they are incapable of doing anything of value without us or by any means different than we would. It is simply untrue that Europeans are militarily weak. They could fight and win against any military in the world except the US. They would fight differently than the US does with all its spiffy, expensive equipment. But by emphasising the difference between us and them, the US has gone a long way to convince them to do nothing.

The austerity about to hit the US military will create incentives for fixing the drivers of our expensive defence: force structure not aligned to strategy; exorbitant procurement practices that produce too few weapons at too high a cost and too late to field; and exploding personnel costs that are crowding out operational funding (Roughead and Schake, 2013). These changes could produce incentives for more commonly developed weapons (although the experience of the Joint Strike Fighter is discouraging), more access to the American market for non-American defence competitors (price will become more salient in service selection), and more need for cost-sharing with others.

NATO could really help nations by moving more fully into defence planning, helping nations identify capabilities gaps and fostering cooperation either alliance-wide or bilaterally and in smaller collectives where trust is especially high and assets can be shared. We missed most of the opportunities of the past decade for using the NATO defence planning mechanism to help as European budgets contracted; we can help ourselves by putting it to better use now.

Sustaining the Nuclear Bargain

One of the most telling indicators of NATO's resilience has been its debate on nuclear strategy and nuclear forces. Another round of debate will be engendered by the need to replace German dual-capable aircraft. Advocates of a nuclear-free NATO Europe (for Russia seems to be making no effort to denuclearise its forces) argue that Germany opting out of the nuclear mission should precipitate a broader reconsideration. Britain, too, will have expensive choices to make about the form of its nuclear deterrent. There is a concern that those national choices will precipitate reconsideration, and greater shifting of the burden to US strategic forces in ways that will call into question extended deterrence.

While the Chicago summit will make any fundamental change to the NATO nuclear posture difficult, the cost of maintaining the status quo will weigh heavily in nations' policy debates, and those national decisions will have effects on the alliance. Many alternatives exist to strict continuation of existing practices, though. Preserving wide participation in the nuclear endeavor is more important that the exact terms of that participation. In fact, budget-driven choices about delivery systems could be used to expand participation – many NATO nations, including new members who are not currently assigned operational roles, have delivery systems that could be deployed to allied countries and included in the missions.

Beyond Europe

The Arab awakening will take at least a decade before its trajectory is fully revealed. If parallels to the European revolutions of 1848 have any merit, it could be decades before the consequences of publics demanding greater political rights and economic opportunities play out. Globalisation's ease of movement for people, money, and ideas will bring aspects of those struggles into our societies. How we choose to deal with them, and many other pressing security developments, will have far-reaching effects on allied countries.

After September 11, the George W. Bush administration came to believe that America could not be safe without assertive involvement in the rest of the world. The Obama administration has reconsidered the proposition, especially where the use of military force is concerned. That reconsideration has actually brought American and European attitudes into closer alignment. We agree that hard work needs to be done in the international order for us to remain safe at home and to sustain the kind of international order in which our societies and economies prosper. The US is less convinced of the value of military interventions, Europeans perhaps a little more so. As with so many other NATO debates, it is both perennial and shows that while we still have much to fight about among ourselves, we continue to believe we are better off working together to protect our countries and advance our interests.

CHAPTER 9

Challenges for the United Nations

by Michael C. Williams

Dag Hammarskjöld, perhaps the most successful Secretary-General of the United Nations (1952–61) famously said 'the UN is not here to take us to heaven, but to prevent us from going to hell' (Weiss and D.Z. Kalbacher, 2013). On that criterion alone the UN can claim some considerable success. Nearly 70 years since the creation of the United Nations, while there have been far too many wars since 1945, there has never been a war between the major powers. For that the UN can claim considerable responsibility. By contrast, barely 20 years after the establishment of the League of Nations in 1919 Europe was again at war and within a short period the whole world with it. Many countries left the League in the 1930s, including Germany, Italy, the USSR, Japan, Hungary and Spain. Unlike the ill-fated League, no country other than Indonesia in 1965, and then only briefly, has ever left the UN. On the contrary, every newly declared state has rushed to seek membership, from Afghanistan in 1946, one of the first Asian members, to South Sudan in 2011.

In this regard one of the most impressive spectacles of the UN is its annual General Assembly in New York when, in the space of three weeks, every head of state or government in the world journeys to Manhattan, often facing the ire of New Yorkers and the anger of Congressmen, seeing foes of the United States from Fidel Castro to Yasser Arafat, complete with gun-toting holster, to Hugo Chávez and Mahmoud Ahmedinejad in recent times. Tempers may be raised in

Congress but an important principle is honoured each autumn as the US recognises the importance of the UN and the reality that a part of the East River is international territory. Every year, the President of the United States, including George W. Bush, journey to New York not only to address the General Assembly but also to hold a reception which, while bringing gridlock to Manhattan, invites all the world's leaders to an event hosted by the US President.

In doing so the UN underlines a universality which was never present in the League of Nations. Unlike the League it boasts not only a large Secretariat but also a Security Council and a General Assembly that can, *in extremis*, be called into session any day of the year as the situation demands. And unlike the League the UN is a forum of continuous discussion. With regard to international peace and security the founders of the UN drew on the failures of the League and were, thankfully, able to rectify many of its shortcomings.

Through the decades the United Nations has promoted and facilitated cooperation in areas from international security to economic development, human rights to education, world health to peacekeeping and climate change. At its founding in 1945 the UN had 51 Member States; by 2013 that had risen almost four fold to 193. That very universality, literally encompassing the entire globe, is one of the reasons why it has not only survived but continues to be indispensable to the management of international peace and security and much else. For the United Kingdom, as its global reach shrinks, the importance of the United Nations in our foreign policy could, and should, increase in the coming years. After the traumas of Iraq and Afghanistan, when the failures of military operations outside the UN have become self-evident, Britain must renew its commitment to the United Nations, not least to fully earn its occupancy of a permanent seat on the Security Council.

Reform of the Security Council

Governance issues continue to haunt the UN. On the one hand the General Assembly encompasses the entire world with all

193 states having one vote, from the smallest to the largest, and continually growing. On the other, the Security Council has not changed substantially since its establishment in 1945. Indeed the only change, marginal at that, was in 1965 when the number of non-permanent members of the Security Council was increased from six to ten.

It is often forgotten that the very first meeting of the United Nations Security Council took place in London on 17 January 1946 at Church House, Westminster, the headquarters of the Church of England. Appropriately perhaps the General Assembly met in the nearby Methodist Central Hall. Both buildings lay just a stone's throw from the two houses of the British parliament.

Then, as now nearly 70 years on, the Security Council had five permanent members – the United States, Russia, China, Great Britain and France. Then these countries were the major political, economic and military powers in the world, with the British economy being second only to that of the United States. Today it is the seventh, with three countries with larger economies – Japan, Germany and Brazil – all pushing hard for Security Council membership.

Increasingly this is a problem, with whole continents like Latin America and Africa disenfranchised. India, the world's second most populous state and largest democracy, is excluded as is Europe's largest economy, Germany. Not to mention the fact that Japan, whose financial contribution to the UN is second only to that of the United States, is also excluded. With the passage of time the absence of meaningful reform for almost seven decades inevitably undermines the legitimacy and authority of the UN. An especially heavy burden in this regard falls on Britain and France, whose original occupancy of permanent seats in 1945 stemmed not only from the fact that they were among the victors at the end of the second world war, but also that they administered vast colonial territories and peoples in Africa and Asia. Palpably this is no longer the case.

For the United Kingdom permanent membership of the Security Council has been hugely important for successive British governments, enabling them to influence global policy on every aspect of international security.

It has become a feature of the Security Council that P5 (Permanent 5) unanimity, upon which so much rests, is harder and harder to obtain except on thematic matters and often these are of small import. The nature of the bipolar world until the collapse of the Soviet Union in 1991, and to an extent thereafter, was ultimately determined in Washington and Moscow. Nevertheless, the end of the cold war led to a transformation of the UN Secretariat and of the post of Secretary-General. This was particularly striking during the tenures of Boutros Boutros-Ghali (1992–96) and Kofi Annan (1997– 2006). The Security Council in the 1990s was freed of the straitjacket of the cold war and, when Iraq invaded Kuwait in 1991, it was able to move into action on the same day. By this time too none of the P5, with the possible exception of France, had strong interests in Africa, leaving it open to the Security Council freed of the vestiges of colonialism to launch several new operations in that continent.

The urgency of reform is apparent to all, or almost all. Everyone agrees that the present structure is flawed but a consensus on how to change it remains out of reach. Without it the democratic legitimacy and responsibility of the Security Council and of the United Nations itself risks being eroded. In their current chastened economic circumstances the United Kingdom and France, in particular, need not to retreat behind the ramparts but, on the contrary, to be in the forefront of efforts to reform the UN, including the Security Council. A consensus for change has eluded previous attempts at reform but, absent progress, problems are being stored up for future generations to handle. Prominent among them is the absence of any permanent voice from Africa or Latin America in the inner sanctum of the Security Council, let alone India, which by 2030 will almost certainly be the world's third economy after China and the United States. It was an axiom of the UN's founding fathers that Great Powers had to be given special privileges to prevent them blocking or leaving the international system as Germany, Italy and the Soviet Union had done in the 1930s. By virtue of its population, its economy and its decades-long commitment to democracy, India cannot be denied that privilege for much longer.

Karl Marx in his analysis of 19th-century capitalism was fond of pointing out the contradictions and tensions between base and superstructure. The substance of global power is changing, and rapidly so since 2000. By contrast the superstructure, and above all the Security Council of the United Nations, remain frozen in time. With the acceleration of economic change in particular, the Security Council, the apex of the international system, is increasingly looking untenable and anachronistic.

In recent years the most salient reform proposal was that advanced by Kofi Annan when he was Secretary-General. He put forward two proposals in 2005, both increasing the number of seats on the Security Council from 15 to 24. His first suggestion was to add six permanent seats, but without vetoes, and three additional rotating seats. The second suggestion would have added a new category of eight semi-permanent seats, to be held for four years with one new rotating seat. The timing of his proposal was unfortunate, coming as it did only months after the US/UK invasion of Iraq, with both countries unwilling to be seen as accommodating Security Council changes (Annan, 2012)

Peacekeeping, Past and Future

For many years one of the most visible and critical contributions of the United Nations to international security has been peace-keeping. Yet there is no mention of the term in the UN Charter of 1945 and it was not until 11 years later, in 1956, that the first real peacekeeping force was established. Indeed, this was one of the major achievements of Dag Hammarskjöld as Secretary-General. Following the British and French invasion of Egypt over the Suez Canal crisis and the outbreak of war between Egypt and Israel, the Security Council, in Resolution 998 of 4 November 956 established UNEF (United Nations Emergency Force), not as a small observer mission as had happened before, but as a force inter-posed between the antagonists. For the first time the world saw the blue helmets.

Within a few years, in 1960, the first major UN peacekeeping force was established in the Congo (ONUC), set up in the midst of a disastrous Belgian withdrawal from the country. For all the problems the Congo has to this day, it probably would not exist as a country had it not been for the United Nations' continuing contribution to the modern Democratic Republic of Congo (DRC). Historically, where peacekeeping missions were given clear mandates, and empowered to use force if necessary, they fared better than when they did not. In this respect the responsibilities of the Security Council are heavy and the need for clear mandates is imperative. Alas, that was not the case with UNPROFOR in Bosnia, leading to the tragedy in Srebrenica in 1995 when the Security Council paid too much attention to the European members of the Security Council, the United Kingdom and France.

Today the majority of UN peacekeeping operations are in Africa and the states that commit troops are either African or South Asian (Indian, Pakistani and Bangladeshi). A striking figure in this regard is that the total number of European peacekeepers serving in Africa in 2011 was less than 100. In part this reflects a war wariness following the Iraq and Afghanistan wars and the subsequent budgetary pressures, but also an unspoken sentiment to leave African conflicts to Africans. This paltry number of European peacekeepers is in stark contrast to the fact that three of the five permanent seats if Russia is included on the Security Council are occupied by European countries. There are European troops in other UN missions, for example, UNIFIL in Lebanon, although they are there to a considerable extent because of Israeli unwillingness to tolerate a mission dominated by non-European troops. But even taking this into consideration Europeans constitute a mere 8 per cent of UN peacekeepers globally while African countries contribute 38 per cent.

Nor is Europe's poor performance confined to its military contributions. It fares little better with regard to contributions to UN police forces. In 2008 it contributed 17 per cent of UN police units, a figure which had dropped to a mere 5 per cent by 2011. In large part this was due to the drawdown of the UN mission in Kosovo but it reinforces the obvious conclusion that Europe is not pulling its weight with regard to police or military contributions to peacekeeping. As permanent members of the Security Council the United Kingdom and France need to pay particular heed and be aware of their responsibilities. There are many areas where they can and should make available more assistance.

A striking example is the UN's critical need for enabling assets such as helicopters, engineers and military hospitals. While countries like India have these, other contributors, such as most African states, do not have these assets. Most European countries do. The author of this chapter first served in a UN peacekeeping mission in Cambodia (UNTAC) in 1992/3. At that time Germany provided a military hospital and France, Netherlands and Sweden all provided troops and helicopters. Those days are sadly gone. Now UN missions in Africa, often in large countries like the Congo (MONUSCO) and Sudan (UNAMID), where helicopters are desperately needed, cope without European contributions. This is a situation which cannot last for ever without doing considerable damage to European global influence and especially that of the two European members of the Security Council, the United Kingdom and France.

Cooperation with Regional Organisations

The authors of the United Nations Charter showed considerable foresight in the provision it makes for cooperation with regional organisations in Chapter VIII, and this at a time when regional groups hardly existed. Cooperation with regional organisations has long been a touchstone of the work of the United Nations, as recognised in the Charter and numerous resolutions of the General Assembly and the Security Council. In many ways, the United Nations and regional organisations have unique and complementary capacities that, when properly coordinated, can contribute decisively to the prevention and management of armed conflict.

In recent years, these relationships have strengthened and deepened across a wide spectrum of activities, including peacemaking and crisis mediation, peacekeeping, and humanitarian assistance. In support of this growing cooperation in the field the Secretary-General has convened over the years a number of high-level meetings and retreats with the heads of regional organisations to ensure coordination and mutual understanding on operational imperatives as well as broader strategic issues facing the United Nations and its partners.

In its core work in conflict prevention, preventive diplomacy and mediation, the UN is in permanent contact with its counterparts in regional organisations to ensure information-sharing and cooperation on a country, as well as regional issues of mutual concern. In a growing number of instances in which regional or sub-regional organisations take the leading role in peacemaking or crisis diplomacy in their neighbourhoods, the United Nations is frequently present as a partner, providing support and advice as required. This is frequently the case in Africa.

At the UN the Department of Political Affairs (DPA) has also developed with partner organisations a series of regular 'desk-to-desk' dialogues, which are designed to improve mutual understanding of each others' structure and organisation, review and improve channels of cooperation, and develop recommendations in that regard. Such 'desk-to-desk' dialogues, as well as regular communication and consultation, are on-going between the DPA and organisations including the African Union (AU), the European Union (EU) and the Organization of American States (OAS). The DPA also holds a similar annual staff-level meeting with relevant officers of the Organization for Security and Co-operation in Europe (OSCE).

The UN also assists in building regional capacity, either through projects exclusively focused on mediation, or as part of more comprehensive capacity-building assistance programmes. This includes the 10-Year Capacity-Building Programme for the AU, launched in 2006. Under that programme, the UN has been working with the AU to address its needs in the area of political and security affairs, including conflict prevention and mediation support, electoral assistance and support to AU policy organs. In order to improve knowledge and understanding in the field of conflict prevention and mediation, the UN regularly offers joint training programmes for staff from regional organisations.

This cooperation is very welcome, especially with groupings like the AU, whose budget is very limited compared to European organisations like the EU or the OSCE, or even for that matter to the OAS. One of its most concrete current manifestations is UNAMID, the joint AU/UN hybrid mission in the Darfur province of Sudan, currently the largest peacekeeping mission in the world. Welcome though this is in developing the capabilities of the AU, it also masks the unwillingness of the European countries to contribute to peace-keeping, in stark contrast to their efforts in the 1990s following the end of the cold war.

If cooperation with regional organisations like the AU has gone reasonably well, it has been more difficult with self-selecting groups like the G8 and the now the G20. Unlike the AU, EU, ASEAN, the League of Arab States and the OAS, the G8 and G20 have no formal structures. Moreover, many of their critics believe that they partly exist to give countries like Germany and Japan, Brazil and India some recognition and standing, thereby delaying reform of the UN, and above all the Security Council, further. Furthermore, although the EU is present in these groupings, the UN is not.

While the British Prime Minister David Cameron has suggested that G8 meetings should be held at the same time as the annual UN General Assembly, his motivation in doing so seems to stem from narrow housekeeping concerns rather than any attempt to link the two. But hitherto neither the G8 nor the G20 has invited the United Nations to its summits and there seems to be no intention to do so now, especially as the proposal has not met with approval from other G8 members. By and large discussion of the global financial crisis after 2008 has been within the confines of the G20 excluding the vast majority of UN members whose people have been most affected.

The lack of legitimacy of both organisations has been openly questioned, among others, by Jonas Gahr Store, the Norwegian Foreign Minister:

The G20 is a self-appointed group. Its composition is determined by the major countries and powers. It may be more
representative than the G7 or the G8, in which only the richest

countries are represented, but it is still arbitrary. We no longer live in the 19th century, a time when the major powers met and redrew the map of the world. No one needs a new Congress of Vienna. (*Der Spiegel*, 2012)

UN reform is not an event but a process. The UN has achieved a great deal but is traditionally poor at noting its own success. There is a great hunger to make the system better for the people it aims to serve and to be more justifiable in the current fiscal climate. It is the responsibility of Member States, as well as the organisation, to take forward reform, and there are many fora to encourage different ways of participating in, and contributing to, change. The key themes which emerged across all areas of discussion centre round the multi-directional trust deficit, lack of coherence and variable impact/accountability.

The trust deficit is evident within the UN system, between the organisation and Member States, and between the Security Council and the General Assembly to take two examples. Partnerships need to be rebuilt in all these areas. Member States should stop referring to the UN in the third person and accept responsibility for leading and enabling change. Donors need to trust the UN to deliver through a funding framework that maximises ownership of responsibility, and accountability through measurement of impact achieved rather than funds spent or activities carried out. They should empower UN managers by restraining tendencies to micro-manage and instead focusing on strategic outcomes. In return, UN managers need to take ownership in their areas and be prepared to ensure proper control of resources and to account for their activities through measurable monitoring and evaluation of results. Member States should not intervene in routine staffing and structural issues. In return, the UN should operate a merit-based system, combining competence and experience, and using the performance appraisal system properly as a tool for helping staff development, rewarding good performance and identifying and dealing effectively with under-performance.

Lack of coherence is an obstacle to both reform and effective delivery across the UN system. Coherence of vision and strategic goals are lacking in many areas, reflecting the fragmentation of the organisation, numerous governing bodies, multiple delivery objectives (for example for funds and agencies), poor mechanisms for prioritisation, and so forth. The multiple change initiatives which have grown up risk dissipating resources, energy and patience (of both staff and Member States). Bringing coherence to the change agenda would pay dividends. At the country level, there is often resistance to coordination of strategies and an assumption that bringing coherence to the UN's efforts must mean a loss of individual branding or control. The immense difficulty of integrating all the existing structures across the UN system is often cited as reason for not making efforts to bring about greater coherence. But both these symptoms could be tackled by integrating thinking, not institutions, starting with a common vision and strategic goals cross-sector, for which the delivery levels should then have the flexibility to design their contributions according to shared analysis of the needs. This would enable coordinated (not combined) planning and programming, and coordinated measurement, analysis, evaluation and lesson learning.

At the delivery level, there would be real gains from greater practical coherence across the system – for example, consolidated support functions; integrated business centres; HQ integration of those working on a geographical issue (for example country desk officers in the DPA and DPKO [Department of Peacekeeping Operations]). Giving the Secretary-General (and the Secretariat) flexibility in moving resources without micro-management by Member States would enable greater planning and structural coherence across the organisation.

But important though all these managerial and organisational reforms are, they cannot mask the fact that it is above all reform of the governance of the United Nations which cannot be delayed much longer.

At the end of the day the United Nations remains the only international institution that enjoys global legitimacy. Indeed this legitimacy has grown over the decades since 1945. At its birth only Ethiopia and Liberia were independent countries in Africa and, amazingly, only China, Thailand and Afghanistan in Asia. Now every country in the world is represented, from the United States to Iran, from Switzerland to North Korea, Australia to Cuba, from the most populous state – China (1.4 billion) to the least populous – Tuvalu (10,000).

A UN Case Study: Conflict in the Middle East – The Limits of Power

The Middle East has in some ways shaped the United Nations. The establishment of the State of Israel in 1948 occurred only a few years after the establishment of the United Nations. No issue has been on the agenda of the Security Council or the General Assembly so long. From Gaza to Iraq the UN has been active over seven decades.

Often the UN's missions have taken place in the midst of considerable violence. Indeed, two of its senior envoys have been assassinated in the region, Count Folke Bernadotte in 1948 and Sergio Vieira de Mello in 2003. The Security Council has been almost continuously active addressing acute crises and establishing observer missions and major peacekeeping missions such as UNIFIL in Lebanon. At the same time as the UN has sought to address the effects of conflict, it has been unable to play a decisive role as the Security Council has often been divided and key members, especially the US, have preferred to operate outside the UN. Too often the UN has been asked to address the consequences of conflict initiated by Security Council members themselves such as the UK/French invasion of Egypt in 1956 and the US/UK invasion of Iraq in 2003. In both cases the UN was left struggling with the consequences of these invasions. Many would argue that the primary modus vivendi of the UN has been to preserve fragile ceasefires and temporary arrangements in the absence of a consensus to resolve underlying conflict. To this day Israel's borders with Lebanon and Syria are policed by UNIFIL, established in 1978, and UNDOF, established in 1967.

The UN has sometimes presided over critical moments in Middle Eastern history. The fundamental principle of 'land for peace' for example was established by Security Council resolution 242 in

November 1967. Again in 2002/3 the Security Council created the Quartet and the 'road map' to try to implement a two-state solution for Israel and Palestine. It is not the fault of the UN that progress has not been made in that regard. On his retirement as Secretary-General in December 2006 Kofi Annan spoke of the need 'to match professions of concern with a concerted effort to make a strategic difference' in the Middle East. And, as the Syrian crisis grows, even those missions like UNIFIL and UNDOF that have preserved stability on Israel's borders are increasingly under threat as the international community struggles to deal with one of the most savage and dangerous wars of the 21st century.

GLOBAL CHALLENGES

CHAPTER 10

How fragile is the global nuclear order?[1]

by Graham Allison

How fragile is the global nuclear order? Could the web of agreements, institutions, and actions that has constrained the proliferation and use of nuclear weapons be as tenuous today as the political landscape of the Middle East was in December 2010 – when most intelligence agencies, investors, and experts expected the decade ahead to be more or less like the decade that had preceded it? Could it be as fragile as the euro is today?

Judgments about systemic stability are notoriously unreliable – and almost always less certain than we imagine them to be. Recall the assurances by authorities prior to 2008 that global financial markets were sound, stable, and resilient. Recognising that judgments about the global nuclear order should include an asterisk to remind us of the substantial uncertainties, this chapter nonetheless presents my best judgments in the hope of stimulating debate.

First, the global nuclear order is at greater risk today than is generally recognised.[2] Indeed, if one recalls the cold war mantra in

---

[1] For suggestions that helped strengthen the argument, I want to express thanks to Matthew Bunn, Shai Feldman, Martin Malin, Steven Miller, Joseph Nye, Gary Samore, James Sebenius, and William Tobey.

[2] The global nuclear order includes the entire web of agreements (Non-Proliferation Treaty, arms-control treaties, and security guarantees), institutions (IAEA, NATO, Nuclear Suppliers Group, and others), and actions (reassurance, threats, and attacks like Israel's destruction of reactors in Iraq and Syria) that constrains the spread and use (either by terrorists or states) of nuclear weapons.

which risk equals probability times consequences, the risk of unraveling is unacceptably high. As President Barack Obama (2009b) has warned, 'just one nuclear weapon exploded in a city ... would destabilise our very way of life.'

Second, unquestionably, thousands of able and committed individuals have been working harder over the past decade than earlier. Nonetheless, the inconvenient truth is that we are paddling upstream against a mighty river. While our more vigorous efforts propel us forward, ever more powerful currents push us in the opposite direction. Paradoxical as it seems, the fact that we are working harder and smarter to strengthen the global nuclear order does not mean we are not falling further behind (Graham and Talent, 2008: xv).

Third, avoiding the spread of nuclear weapons, a successful nuclear terrorist attack, or even nuclear war, will demand substantially more than the sum of what is being done today. As four of the most distinguished American statesmen have warned, 'the accelerating spread of nuclear weapons, nuclear know-how, and nuclear material has brought us to a nuclear tipping point. The world is now on the precipice of a new and dangerous nuclear era' (Shultz et al., 2007, 2008). Greater success will require a surge of strategic imagination and determination as extraordinary as the leap President John F. Kennedy and others took in the aftermath of the Cuban Missile Crisis in 1962 to create the nuclear arms control regime and the Non-Proliferation Treaty (NPT).

Forces for Order and Disorder

An optimist's assessment of the global nuclear order would begin with two remarkable facts. First, since 1945, no nuclear bomb has been exploded in anger. Second, since the end of the cold war, the prospect of a nuclear Armageddon has become almost unthinkable.

Moreover, the spread of atomic weapons has slowed. In 1963, when four nations had nuclear weapons, President Kennedy envisioned 'the possibility in the 1970s of the President of the United States having to face a world in which 15 or 20 or 25 nations may have these weapons' (Schlesinger, 2002: 897). Thanks to the success of the NPT and other initiatives, however, today there are just nine.[3] Most countries have pledged in the NPT 'not to manufacture or otherwise acquire nuclear weapons,' including more than 40 nations that have the technical capability to construct their own arsenal quickly (UN Office for Disarmament Affairs, 2013).[4]

The optimist would acknowledge that vulnerabilities remain. As President Obama has noted, 'in a strange turn of history, the threat of global nuclear war has gone down, but the risk of a nuclear attack has gone up.' President Obama and Prime Minister David Cameron have underlined two real and present dangers: nuclear terrorism and the possibility of a 'second nuclear age' (Bracken, 2012).[5]

To counter these threats, in Prague in 2009, President Obama announced a bold vision for 'a world without nuclear weapons.' In 2010, his administration signed the New START Treaty with Russia, substantially reducing the number of deployed strategic nuclear warheads. Obama also hosted the world's first Nuclear Security Summit in 2010, the largest gathering of heads of state at the invitation of an American president since the conference in San Francisco in October 1945 that created the United Nations. That meeting was followed in 2012 by the Nuclear Security Summit in Seoul that focused the minds of leaders and governments on a critical issue: locking up all nuclear weapons and materials beyond the reach

---

[3] United States, Russia, United Kingdom, France, China, Israel, India, Pakistan, and North Korea. Four additional countries had nuclear weapons but have now eliminated them – South Africa, Ukraine, Kazakhstan, and Belarus.

[4] Furthermore, as my colleague Matt Bunn has argued, the non-proliferation regime has demonstrated the capability to learn from experience and adapt to changing realities. Due in part to this flexibility, today there is only one state actively advancing along the path towards nuclear weapons, fewer than in any previous decade since the 1940s.

[5] Obama (2009) called nuclear terrorism 'the most immediate and extreme threat to global security.' The UK's National Counter Proliferation Strategy (UK Foreign and Commonwealth Office, 2012) argued that: 'without continued global efforts to reduce vulnerabilities in the security of material and information, there is a *significant likelihood* that terrorists will at some point acquire CBRN capability' (emphasis added).

of terrorists or thieves. In the past decade, a considerable 'ground game' has persuaded state after state to improve the security of fissile material, tighten export controls, implement counter-trafficking measures, and comply with safeguard agreements.

Nonetheless, these efforts represent only one side of the equation. On the other side is an array of actors and factors that threaten to undermine the current global nuclear landscape. For purposes of assessment, consider ten major trendlines:[6]

- the relentless advance of science and technology and accelerating diffusion of nuclear know-how;
- the growing specter of 'megaterrorism';
- North Korea's expanding nuclear weapons programme;
- Iran's success in crossing successive red lines as it develops its nuclear weapons options;
- Pakistan's ticking nuclear time bomb;
- eroding confidence in the non-proliferation regime;
- mounting evidence for those who believe nuclear weapons enhance their security;
- the continued risk of 'loose nukes': weapons and materials;
- a potential 'renaissance' in nuclear energy production; and
- wildcards: failure to imagine 'unknown unknowns.'

21st-century Realities

The bomb the United States dropped on Hiroshima in 1945 was never tested. Manhattan Project scientists were so confident in their 'gun-type' design that they agreed with military authorities that the first use would be the test. Scientific accounts released in the years that followed revealed just how simple it was to duplicate this weapon. As American bomb designer John Foster wrote in 1973: if enough highly-enriched uranium (HEU) or separated plutonium

---

[6] Technically, several of these trendlines can more precisely be described as 'factors.'

is at hand, 'it is possible to make an atomic bomb using information that is available in the open literature.' Four decades later, the computational capacity available to a would-be bomb designer with an iPad is more than five billion times greater than the capacity of the supercomputer used for developing the hydrogen bomb.

The relentless advance of science and technology and diffusion of knowledge have been the major drivers of improvements in human well-being in the past century. Typically, however, these advances are two-edged swords, empowering evil as well as good. Improvements in computational capacity, machine tools, transportation, communication, and the spread of information make it easier for groups around the world to produce nuclear weapons. When manufacturing parts for a centrifuge or a bomb, advances in computer-assisted manufacturing tools now allow a precision that previously required a master craftsman. The current UK foreign secretary has underlined this reality, noting that 'the global spread of nuclear technology and materials threatens a new age of nuclear insecurity involving a rash of new nuclear weapons states or even the acquisition of nuclear weapons by terrorists' (Hague, 2009).

The infrastructure we celebrate as 'globalisation' allowed the celebrated 'father' of Pakistan's nuclear programme to become the world's first full-service nuclear black-marketeer. In 2004, A.Q. Khan was exposed for selling bomb designs and nuclear weapons technology to Iran, Libya, and North Korea. Then-IAEA (International Atomic Energy Agency) Director General Mohamed El Baradei called Khan's network the 'Wal-Mart of private-sector proliferation.' His complex global supply chain built centrifuge parts in Malaysia, repackaged them in Dubai, and distributed them through agents in Europe (Broad et al., 2004).[7] The multinational enterprise included partners and buyers in more than 15 countries. A decade after Khan's network was exposed, continuing advances in science and technology provide unintended but undeniable enablers for future nuclear black-market dealers.

---

[7] Khan lives and travels freely in Pakistan today, still treated as a national hero and the mastermind behind the country's nuclear arsenal.

Reductions in barriers to information, communication, and transportation also enhance the means for mass-casualty terrorism. On September 11, 2001, 19 unskilled terrorist hijackers executed a large-scale terrorist attack more operationally challenging than detonating a nuclear weapon. This assault killed more people than the Japanese attack on Pearl Harbor that brought the United States into the second world war. On September 11, al-Qaida demonstrated that a small group could kill on a scale previously the exclusive domain of states, introducing the world to an era of 'megaterrorism' (Allison, 2012).

Over the past decade, the United States, United Kingdom, and others have pushed al-Qaida's central leadership to the brink of 'strategic defeat.' Osama bin Laden was killed in May 2011. But Ayman al-Zawahiri, al-Qaida's new leader, remains alive, active, and desperate to retaliate, and two of the group's top chemical, biological, radiological, and nuclear weapons (CBRN) experts – Saif al-Adel and Abdel Aziz al-Masri – are still on the loose.[8]

Al-Qaida's CBRN ambitions are only the tip of the iceberg. The present era of megaterrorism is defined not by actors but by the underlying *condition* that makes mass-casualty attacks possible: advances in science and technology have superempowered smaller and smaller groups to kill larger and larger numbers of people. Consider, for example, Bruce Ivins, the US government microbiologist responsible for the anthrax attacks that killed five Americans in 2001. Had Ivins distributed the supply of pathogens he made with sprayers he could have purchased off the shelf, tens of thousands of Americans could have died. Ordinary graduates of nuclear engineering programs with as little as 16 kilograms of HEU could build and detonate a crude nuclear device capable of killing hundreds of thousands (Allison, 2004: 221).

---

[8] For more on the al-Qaida threat, see http://belfercenter.ksg.harvard.edu/files/al-Qaida-wmd-threat.pdf.

A Dangerous Trio:
North Korea, Iran, and Pakistan

While the realities of technological change and megaterrorism are inescapable, three urgent challenges pit the United States, United Kingdom, and others against North Korea, Iran, and Pakistan.

Defying five rounds of UN sanctions and explicit demands by the United States and China, North Korea has demonstrated that even the smallest, poorest, and most isolated nations on Earth can build a nuclear arsenal. However unacceptable, what that says about the balance between the guardians of order and the forces of disorder cannot be denied.

At the turn of the century, Pyongyang had two bombs' worth of plutonium, a warehouse with 8,000 spent fuel rods containing enough plutonium (after reprocessing) for another six, and a moth-balled reactor at Yongbyon. The storage facility was fully inspected by the IAEA, which operated round-the-clock camera surveillance. Since 2003, Pyongyang has withdrawn from the NPT, expelled IAEA inspectors, reprocessed the spent fuel for six bombs' worth of plutonium, conducted three nuclear tests, and developed missiles capable of reaching Japan or American bases in Guam.[9] It now also has at least one uranium enrichment facility capable of producing several more bombs' worth of HEU each year.

The role of extortionist-in-chief has fallen to the young and inexperienced Kim Jong-un. His rhetoric about attacking South Korea or the United States with nuclear weapons follows North Korea's well-worn script that uses bluster and risk-taking to extract petty payoffs. But North Korea's expanding nuclear arsenal poses at

---

[9] In April 2013, the US Defense Intelligence Agency assessed 'with moderate confidence' that North Korea 'has nuclear weapons capable of delivery by ballistic missiles; however the reliability will be low.' Director of National Intelligence James Clapper walked back this claim, stating that 'North Korea has not yet demonstrated the full range of capabilities necessary for a nuclear armed missile.' See http://www.nytimes.com/2013/04/12/world/asia/north-korea-may-have-nuclear-missile-capability-us-agency-says.html?pagewanted=all&_r=0.

least two larger dangers. First, failure to halt Pyongyang encourages nuclear ambitions among others in North-east Asia. Despite a credible American nuclear umbrella that shields South Korea and Japan, as North Korea's belligerence grows, both countries have clearly been reassessing their options. Polls conducted after Pyongyang's third nuclear test in February 2013 indicated that more than 60 per cent of South Koreans support having their own nuclear weapons (Dalton and Yoon, 2013). A prominent South Korean politician, Chung Moon-joon, called for precisely this solution during a visit to Washington in April (Sanger, 2013). Moreover, Japan has long had enough weapons-grade plutonium and HEU for thousands of nuclear warheads.[10] While the Japanese political establishment remains opposed to nuclear weapons,[11] mounting concerns over North Korea and a rising China could change that calculus. If it decides it needs the bomb, Japan has the capacity to quickly become a nuclear weapons state.

North Korea's third nuclear test, probably using uranium, sent an unspoken but decidedly dangerous message to the world: nukes may be for sale. Could Kim Jong-un imagine that he could sell a nuclear weapon or HEU to a state like Iran or even a terrorist group like al-Qaida – and get away with it? Incredible as it might seem, if past is precedent, the answer is unquestionably yes. His father, Kim Jong-il, did sell Syria a plutonium-producing reactor that would have by now produced enough plutonium for Syria's first nuclear bomb, had it not been destroyed by an Israeli airstrike in 2007. Not only did he go unpunished, but he got paid. As former US Secretary of Defense Bob Gates (2010) has warned: North Korea is willing to 'sell anything they have to anybody who has the cash to buy it.'

Meanwhile, newspaper headlines on Iran highlight sanctions, sabotage, and Iran's decision to divert some of its uranium stockpile for conversion into research reactor fuel. Nonetheless, Iran's

---

[10] Japan has 45,000 kilograms of weapons-grade plutonium and more than 1,000 kilograms of HEU. See Von Hippel and Takubo (2012) and International Panel on Fissile Materials (2010).

[11] See http://belfercenter.hks.harvard.edu/files/veto_players.pdf.

advance towards the bomb continues. Over the past decade, Iran has methodically crossed successive Israeli and American 'red lines' in pursuit of nuclear weapons. In 2001, Tehran had zero centrifuge cascades producing zero enriched uranium. By Obama's Prague speech in 2009, Iran was spinning 4,000 centrifuges and possessed enough low-enriched uranium (LEU), after further enrichment, for its first nuclear weapon. Today, Ayatollah Khamenei's regime has more than 10,000 centrifuges operating and is installing another 3,000 advanced IR-2 centrifuges that will function at three times the rate of the current model. Iran now has enough LEU, after further enrichment, for six bombs and is producing enough for an additional bomb every five months. It has also stockpiled almost a bomb's worth of medium-enriched uranium (IAEA, 2013b).

Western intelligence agencies are confident that they would detect an Iranian attempt to 'breakout' to its first nuclear weapon if Tehran used material from declared facilities at Natanz and Qom. But if Iran has constructed other, undiscovered covert enrichment plants, it could 'sneak out' to surprise the world.[12]

If Iran continues advancing towards the bomb, the international community will in the not-too-distant future face a choice between two ugly options: attack or acquiesce. Both Obama and Cameron have affirmed their determination to 'do everything we can to stop' Khamenei from obtaining nuclear weapons (Hope, 2012). But unless a bolder and more imaginative diplomatic initiative can produce an agreement that stops Iran short of a bomb, doing so may require Israel or the United States to conduct airstrikes on Iranian nuclear facilities. In response, most analysts foresee that Iran would launch ballistic missiles at Israel and unleash surrogates – including Hamas and Hezbollah – against Western bases, interests, and individuals across the region and beyond.

If instead the international community acquiesces, Iran is not likely to be the last state in the neighbourhood that goes nuclear. The decade that follows could see a cascade of proliferation across

---

[12] See http://www.scientificamerican.com/article.cfm?id=how-close-iran-first-nuclear-bomb.

the Middle East. As General James Mattis, commander of US Central Command, testified in March, 'at least one other nation has told me' it would also obtain a nuclear weapon if Iran develops the bomb (Martinez and Ferran, 2013). The most obvious candidate is Saudi Arabia, whose long-time head of intelligence, Prince Turki al-Faisal, has stated publicly that if Iran obtains weapons of mass destruction (WMD), 'we must, as a duty to our country and people, look into all options we are given, including obtaining these weapons ourselves' (Reuters, 2011). Some in the intelligence community suspect Pakistan has already agreed to provide the House of Saud with its first nuclear weapon in the event of an Iranian bomb. Turkey, Iran's neighbour with growing regional and international ambitions, may decide to follow. Egypt, as the self-declared leader of the Sunni Arab world and sensitive to changes in Israeli posture inevitable after an Iranian nuclear test, could also seek its own bomb.

An increasingly unstable Pakistan poses an even more acute near-term danger. In December 2008, the US Commission on the Prevention of WMD Proliferation and Terrorism (of which I was a member) concluded: 'Were one to map terrorism and weapons of mass destruction today, all roads would intersect in Pakistan' (Graham and Talent, 2008: xxiii). Pakistan has the fastest growing nuclear arsenal in the world, having quadrupled its stockpile of nuclear weapons since 2001. Over this same decade, a burgeoning Islamic insurgency, demoralised army, precarious nuclear posture towards India, and paranoia about American intentions to neuter their bomb have increased the risk that Pakistan's weapons could be stolen.

Active miniaturisation of battlefield weapons that will be deployed under looser command and control will worsen an already dangerous posture that leans heavily on nuclear warheads to deter India's over-whelming superiority in conventional arms.[13] This strategy also makes it more likely that nuclear weapons could fall into the hands of

---

[13] See http://belfercenter.ksg.harvard.edu/files/Narang.pdf.

terrorist groups like Lashkar-e-Taiba, which conducted the Mumbai attacks that killed 166 people in 2008.[14]

There is an even more troubling scenario. What would happen to the country's 100 nuclear weapons if Pakistan were to lose partial or full control over its territory? The army, custodian of Pakistan's atomic bombs, largely dismisses international concerns about the security of their nuclear weapons. Recent experience, however, offers little comfort. As a reality check, consider this question: could Pakistan's army and intelligence leaders have been *unaware* that Osama bin Laden lived within its borders for six years, moved five times with three wives, and fathered four children? Incredible as it seems – after having combed through the treasure trove of computer files, hard drives, and notebooks captured in the raid on bin Laden's compound in May 2011 – that is the American intelligence community's current best judgment.

Non-proliferation Regime Fatigue

Eroding confidence in the non-proliferation regime also threatens to undermine the global nuclear order. In exchange for voluntarily agreeing under the NPT 'not to manufacture or otherwise acquire nuclear weapons,' the 184 non-nuclear weapons states expected the five declared nuclear weapons states to fulfill two principal obligations: to demonstrate progress towards global disarmament and to ensure the right for all signatories to obtain nuclear equipment and technology for peaceful use (UN Office for Disarmament Affairs, 2013). In 1995, to win support for permanent extension of the NPT, nuclear weapons states made an additional promise to convene a meeting of the nations in the Middle East to discuss a regional 'WMD-free zone.'

---

[14] While India displayed extraordinary restraint in its muted response to the Mumbai attacks, Prime Minister Singh has warned unambiguously that the next major terrorist attack on Indian soil would trigger a sharp military response. An Indian conventional attack on Pakistan could quickly escalate into a nuclear war.

While nuclear weapons states continue to preach non-proliferation, they have, in the view of many non-nuclear weapons states, turned their back on their own commitments.[15] Disarmament has been sluggish and uneven, and progress on essential measures like the Fissile Material Cut-off Treaty and Comprehensive Test Ban Treaty has stalled. Despite more than 300 rounds of discussion, the WMD-free zone conference promised nearly two decades ago has still not taken place. In fact, it has been postponed indefinitely, largely due to Israeli objections backed by the United States.[16]

Moreover, nuclear weapons states have attempted to constrain national development of nuclear fuel enrichment and reprocessing, reinforcing the view that the NPT sustains discrimination between nuclear 'haves' and nuclear 'have-nots.' That resentment was reflected in the unanimous August 2012 decision by 120 members of the 'Non-Aligned Movement' to back Iran's right to a full nuclear fuel cycle (Erdbrink, 2012).

In fact, the United States and Russia have slashed their nuclear arsenals by more than 85 per cent since their cold war heights. The United Kingdom has nearly halved its stockpile since the end of the cold war, from 400 to 225 (Norris and Kristensen, 2006, 2011, 2013a, 2013b). These same states, however, continue to modernise their nuclear forces and rely upon nuclear deterrence for their security. While the Obama administration repeats the President's vision of a nuclear weapons-free world, its 2010 Nuclear Posture Review affirms that: 'as long as nuclear weapons exist, the United States will sustain safe, secure, and effective nuclear forces,' essential for 'deterring potential adversaries and reassuring allies' (US Department of Defense, 2010). Prime Minister Cameron (2013) has called Britain's nuclear deterrent 'an insurance policy that the

---

[15] For a thoughtful discussion of strengths and weaknesses of the NPT regime, see http://www.amacad.org/pdfs/nonproliferation.pdf; http://belfercenter.hks.harvard.edu/files/miller_athens.pdf; and the 2013 spring issue of *Washington Quarterly*.

[16] For more on the WMD-free zone, see http://belfercenter.ksg.harvard.edu/files/WMDFZ_PDF.pdf.

United Kingdom cannot do without.' The French government also advertises its nuclear deterrent as 'the ultimate guarantee of our sovereignty' (Présidence de la République, 2013). Israel, which maintains a thinly veiled nuclear weapons programme, has mastered the art of changing the subject whenever the issue arises.

More importantly, recent experience in the Middle East has provided evidence for those who argue that nuclear weapons offer protection from attack. Westerners mostly talk and listen to each other, rarely putting ourselves in the shoes of potential adversaries. But reflecting on the lessons recent Western actions have taught others, President George W. Bush's former Undersecretary of Defense Eric Edelman offers a sobering quip. In his words: if you are like Iraq and do not have nuclear weapons, you get invaded; if you are like Libya and give up your nuclear programme, you only get bombed.

And, indeed, others in the region have noticed. As the Western intervention in Libya was beginning in March 2011, Iran's Supreme Leader noted that, in a 2003 agreement with the United States, Muammar Gaddafi 'wrapped up all his nuclear facilities, packed them on a ship and delivered them to the West.' Khamenei recommended that others 'look in what position they are now' (Risen, 2012). North Korea's official newspaper agreed: 'Let the American imperialists and their followers know! We are not a pushover like Iraq or Libya' (Choe and Sanger, 2013).[17] For Pyongyang, nuclear weapons are 'an all-powerful sword for protecting the sovereignty and security of the country' (Korea News Service, 2013).[18]

---

[17] Whether North Korea is right to draw this conclusion is a legitimate question. Even prior to 1994, Pyongyang was able to deter Western aggression without nuclear weapons (by placing 15,000 conventional artillery tubes on the South Korean border).

[18] Even the Pentagon, in a recent report to Congress, takes note: 'In North Korea's view, the destruction of regimes such as Ceausescu, Hussain, and Qadhafi was not an inevitable consequence of repressive governments, but rather a failure to secure the necessary capabilities to defend their respective autocratic regime's survival.' See http://info.publicintelligence.net/DoD-DPRK-2012.pdf.

The Good News

Taken together, the first seven trendlines paint a darkening picture of the past decade as well as prospects for the next one. There are, however, several modest silver linings.

Responsible nations have made significant progress in locking down nuclear weapons and materials. After the discovery of A.Q. Khan's network, the UN Security Council adopted Resolution 1540, requiring countries to pass and enforce national legislation to prevent non-state actors from obtaining nuclear, biological, or chemical weapons. Other initiatives have followed, including a UN convention on nuclear terrorism and global efforts to down-blend, consolidate, and eliminate nuclear material stocks.[19]

At the first Nuclear Security Summit in 2010, participants pledged to secure all vulnerable nuclear material within four years. While this goal will not be met, it has nonetheless helped spur governments to act. In the past four years, 11 countries have entirely eliminated their stockpiles of HEU and separated plutonium, making them fissile material-free. In addition to nuclear weapons states, this leaves only 17 countries with more than 1 kilogram of weapons-usable nuclear material (Nuclear Threat Initiative, 2013).

Meanwhile, the vaunted 'renaissance' in civilian nuclear energy production has stalled. Prior to 2011, rising concerns about green-house gas emissions and high oil prices stimulated a renewed interest in nuclear energy as a clean and reliable alternative. But a resurgence in national nuclear energy programs also increased risks that these could provide an excuse for national development of nuclear fuel cycles (including enrichment and reprocessing). The same production line of centrifuges that enriches uranium to 4 per cent to fuel a reactor can also enrich uranium to 90 per cent (HEU) for use in a nuclear bomb.

---

[19] As of January 2013, the global stockpile of HEU was estimated to be 1,390 metric tons, a 15 per cent decrease since mid-2009. The estimated stockpile of separated plutonium was estimated at 490 tons, a 2 per cent decrease. See http://fissilematerials.org/.

The Fukushima meltdown in 2011, however, sent a chilling message to countries with nuclear energy ambitions: these programmes pose significant risks and can bring substantial unforeseen costs. Since the incident, 20 nuclear power plants worldwide, including three-quarters of Germany's entire fleet, have been permanently shut down. At this point, only two of Japan's nuclear reactors are producing electricity. Except for the United Arab Emirates, no country that did not previously have a nuclear power plant has begun construction of a reactor since 2011 (IAEA, 2013a). Apart from Iran, no additional states are actively pursuing a full nuclear fuel cycle.

In short, public skepticism, increasing costs, and cheaper energy alternatives have sapped many nations' interest in moving forward with nuclear energy projects. If China follows through on its plan to develop a 'plutonium economy,' however, talk of a nuclear 'renaissance' may return.

Wildcards

The nine trendlines discussed above are identifiable, even if difficult to assess. An attempt to assess the relative stability of a system, however, must also recognise potential 'wildcards.' After the terrorist attacks of September 11, 2001, National Security Adviser Condoleezza Rice testified to the 9/11 Commission: 'No one could have imagined them taking a plane, slamming it into the Pentagon ... into the World Trade Center, using planes as a missile' (CNN, 2004). Obviously, al-Qaida did. Rice's colleague, US Defense Secretary Donald Rumsfeld (2002) earned a footnote for his contribution to epistemology by distinguishing between: 'known knowns,' 'known unknowns,' and 'unknown unknowns.'

Among the known unknowns, is it possible that Iran has already purchased fissile material for several bombs from North Korea or from the former Soviet arsenal? Could a technological breakthrough make it possible to generate enough fissile material for a bomb within days or months? Could remnants of al-Qaida, including two of its top nuclear experts (mentioned above), be about to execute a nuclear September 11? And beyond these known unknowns, what about the unknown unknowns?

Conclusion

After facing the existential threat of nuclear war during the Cuban Missile Crisis, John F. Kennedy and Nikita Khrushchev determined: never again. Their conviction spurred a surge of diplomatic initiatives: a hotline between Washington and Moscow, a unilateral moratorium on atmospheric nuclear testing, and a ban on nuclear weapons in outer space. Kennedy's nightmare of a 'world in which 15 or 20 or 25 nations' had nuclear weapons helped awaken leaders to the unacceptable dangers of unconstrained proliferation. Refusing to accept this future, the international community responded with an array of creative responses, the centrepiece of which remains the NPT.

These decades-old efforts laid the foundation for the global nuclear order we live in today. While applauding the extraordinary work of leaders and governments over the past decade to strengthen that order, it is impossible to ignore powerful currents pushing us in the opposite direction. On the current trajectory, my bet remains that we are more likely than not to see an act of nuclear terrorism that devastates the heart of a major city, or even a nuclear war.[20]

The current UK foreign secretary has correctly identified preventing nuclear terrorism and uncontrollable nuclear proliferation as 'a top foreign policy priority of any British government' (Hague, 2010). An important member of the nuclear club, the United Kingdom should now match words with deeds. Efforts to declassify the size and nature of its nuclear deterrent, collaborate with allies on technical verification, and lead European actions to isolate Iran and North Korea are a fine start, but more can be done.

First, as I have argued elsewhere, the United States should communicate an unambiguous warning to North Korea: if a nuclear bomb of North Korean origin explodes on American soil or that of

---

[20] See Graham Allison, *Nuclear Terrorism* (2004).

an ally, it will be treated as a direct attack from Pyongyang and be met with a full retaliatory response (Allison, 2013). If Iran builds nuclear weapons, it should receive an identical warning. Accurate attribution is a prerequisite for a policy of strict accountability. The United Kingdom has significant expertise in nuclear forensics – the capacity to identify the source of fissile material used in a bomb – and British investments in this arena should be expanded. Second, with the 2014 Nuclear Security Summit on the horizon, the United Kingdom has an opportunity to announce plans to significantly reduce its stockpile of civilian weapons-usable plutonium, the largest in the world.[21] This would require Britain to convert this plutonium into mixed oxide form or immobilise it in a glass or ceramic mixture (Royal Society, 2007). Finally, the United Kingdom should consider declaring a moratorium on civilian plutonium production and challenging other plutonium-producing states, such as France and Japan, to do the same.

As the success of the decades since the 1960s demonstrates, the uncontrollable proliferation or use of nuclear weapons is not inevitable. Bending the trendlines discussed above, however, will require far more ambitious and imaginative steps, including options outside of the current agenda. As Henry Kissinger (2006: vi) has argued, 'the great powers should recognise that, after the explosion of just one nuclear bomb in one of their great cities, their publics will demand an extreme form of preventive diplomacy to assure that this can never happen again.' In former US Senator Sam Nunn's (2005) oft-quoted words: 'the day after a nuclear terrorist attack, what would we wish we had done? Why aren't we doing it now?'

---

[21] As of January 2013, Britain had an estimated 91 tons of civilian separated plutonium. See International Panel on Fissile Materials (2013).

CHAPTER 11

Climate conflict: How will global warming threaten our world?

by Jeffrey Mazo

The 21st century will be dominated by global climate change. It is already probably too late to avoid exceeding global warming of 2°C since pre-industrial times, a level widely accepted as 'dangerous'. Warming of 4°C, which could be considered catastrophic, is possible by the end of this century, with 6°C posing an existential threat to civilisation in the next. The world has already warmed by 0.7°C since pre-industrial times, and is bound to see at least a further 0.6°C rise simply from emissions already in the atmosphere. While the precise trajectory of warming will depend on political, economic and social developments, it is clear that global warming, and the resulting climate change, will have direct and indirect security impacts as well as creating a radically new environment in which more traditional security concerns will play out.

The impacts of climate change include rising sea levels and population displacement; increasing severity of typhoons and hurricanes and both increased frequency and severity of other extreme weather events; droughts, floods and disruption of water resources; extinctions and other ecological disruption, wildfires, severe disease outbreaks, and declining crop yields and food stocks (IPCC, 2007a). Many of these problems affect one another: flooding and water stress damage agriculture, malnutrition increases the susceptibility of a population to epidemics and chronic illness, and so on. The world is already beginning to experience the first fruits of climate change, as ecological zones move, and extreme weather events become increasingly common (IISS, 2011a).

Dangerous Climate Change

In 1992 the United Nations Framework Convention on Climate Change (UNFCCC) was open for signature at the Rio Earth Summit. Its stated objective was the 'stabilisation of greenhouse-gas concentrations in the atmosphere at a level that would prevent dangerous anthropogenic interference with the climate system' (UNFCCC, 1992: Art. 2). 'Dangerous' was not defined in the convention, but over the following two decades a consensus emerged around 2°C of warming above pre-industrial levels as the threshold for dangerous climate change. This level was formalised at the 2009 Copenhagen climate summit (UNFCCC, 2009). But the figure of 2°C is essentially arbitrary: some scientists have argued for a threshold at 1.5°C; some countries pushed for this to be adopted in Copenhagen, and the issue will be revisited in light of the pending 5th Assessment Report of the Intergovernmental Panel on Climate Change (IPCC) in the negotiations towards a new global accord based on the Durban Platform (UNFCCC, 2011).

Moreover, 2°C was chosen in part because it is a nice round number. It was first mooted in the IPCC's Third Assessment Report in 2001, based on what became known as the 'burning embers' diagram, in which the severity of impacts were represented impressionistically in five 'Reasons for Concern' by a continuous spectrum from yellow to orange to red as the risk in each category increased with temperature (IPCC, 2001: Fig. SPM-2). The diagram was updated based on new data in the 4th Assessment Report, yet was not included in that report because of political objections by a number of countries (Smith et al., 2009). The level of impact that was considered dangerous in 2001, at 2°C, is now expected to occur at 1.5°C, or 1°C, or in some categories even the current level of 0.6°C and, given that the cut-off point for inclusion of studies in the 4th report was 2005, there is a significant body of further research that improves our confidence and degree of understanding of the impacts, and suggests more severe impacts in many categories, particularly agriculture and food security (Good et al., 2010).

In May 2012, the world passed a symbolic threshold of 400 parts per million of carbon dioxide (CO_2) in the atmosphere, a level not seen for at least 800,000 years (NOAA, 2013). While this level is still low enough to avoid exceeding the 2°C threshold, or even 1.5°C, greenhouse-gas emissions continue to rise. They would have to peak by 2020, and decline steeply thereafter, to have a likely chance of keeping eventual warming below 2°C (UNEP, 2012). This is technically possible, but politically unlikely. And depending on the scenario, the threshold could be crossed before mid century (IPCC, 2007b: 14).

In evaluating the potential foreign policy and security impli-cations of global warming, it is important to clearly differentiate between short-, medium- and long-term climate change. In the short term – 10 to 20 years – climate change will be slower and less severe, and will be to some extent obscured by natural variability in the climate system. In the long term, by the end of the century, climate change could be quite severe, but the exact path is unpredict-able and the time scales are beyond the planning horizon for effective policymaking, other than in the area of mitigation measures such as emissions reduction to avoid the worst outcomes. In the medium term, on the scale of decades, uncertainty in projections is minimised (Hawkins and Sutton, 2009) and policies can begin to be put in place now to deal with the challenges.

It is also important to consider the rate of expected warming as well as the absolute amount. We are already experiencing both climate change and its security impacts (see below). But these have been subtle, and are not unambiguous. They stem from a relatively modest rate and amount of warming: some 0.7°C since the 18th century, but the bulk of it in the last 50 years. The current rate of warming is around 0.2°C per decade, and is likely to accelerate. Mitigation efforts that do not succeed in keeping warming below a

2°C, 4°C or 6°C threshold may nevertheless slow the warming down, making adaptation easier. Moreover, although there is some evidence that the rate of surface temperature increase over land has slowed somewhat over the last decade or so (Otto et al., 2013), overall global warming continues unabated, with much of the heat going into the deep oceans. This not only enhances sea-level rise, it means that the temporary slowdown in land surface heating is at the expense of greater, earlier long-term warming (Balmaseda et al., 2013).

Finally, it is important to note that the scientific understanding of expected climate change on a regional basis is much less robust and granular than for the globe as a whole, in terms of rate, severity and even, in the case of rainfall patterns in some regions, whether there will be an increase or decrease.

Climate Change Impacts

The security threats from warming-induced climate change include territorial boundary disputes and conflicts over resources. As sea levels rise, coastlines change and low-lying islands disappear; this will affect the legal basis of some maritime territorial claims. The thinning and shrinking summer ice in the Arctic is making potentially huge resources, especially oil and gas, accessible for the first time, and will soon open new shipping routes. This will lead to shifts in the geo-strategic and geo-economic balance. Most importantly, through its impacts on the availability of clean water and food, the geographical pattern of disease vectors, and the stability of communities and shelter, climate change has the potential to exacerbate human insecurity and contribute directly or indirectly to political or violent conflict in weak and failing states. This means that the types of threats to international stability emanating from such states, such as transnational organised crime, terrorism, migration and so on, will be enhanced.

Climate change will thus act as a 'threat multiplier' or 'accelerant' of conflict and instability, although for the human security of those directly affected, it may be better described as a 'risk multiplier'.[1] For example, climate change is one of four broad and interrelated trends threatening global food security (IISS, 2011b). The dynamics of food security are complex, but climate (or weather), as both a chronic problem and through sudden shocks, is commonly mentioned as influencing food security in household surveys in the developing world. And the other trends – water scarcity, competition for land and high energy prices – are all also driven or enhanced by climate change. Reduced crop yields and crop failures due to reduced rainfall or availability of irrigation water are only part of the story. Some effects of climate change, such as longer growing seasons, may be positive in the short term in some regions, and there might even be a net positive effect with modest global temperature increases. But the regions worst affected will tend to be those already experiencing high levels of food insecurity and least able to compensate or adapt. Fisheries and aquaculture will be affected by ocean warming and acidification and destruction of coral reefs, while sea-level rise can result in salinisation of coastal soils and aquifers. Crop pathogens, such as wheat stem rust, are spreading more widely and more quickly as winters become wetter and warmer. With regard to energy, the principal threat comes from sea-level rise and increasingly frequent and severe storm surges affecting low-lying coastal or off-shore infrastructure. Water availability influences all aspects of energy production, from hydrocarbon extraction and refining to nuclear power plant cooling to hydroelectric generation to biofuel production.

Climate change has already had a direct impact on food production and prices (IISS, 2011a), and is affecting human security in other ways. As early as 2000, it has been calculated, 154,000 deaths and 5.5 million disability-adjusted life years (years lost to illness, disability or premature death), or 0.3 per cent and 0.4 per cent of the global total respectively, could be attributed to the warming that had occurred between 1961 and 1990 (WHO, 2008). Between 2000

---

[1] This concept was introduced in CNA Corporation (2006), and was taken up among others by Solana (2008) and USDoD (2010). For more detailed discussion see Mazo (2011).

and 2004, nearly 5 per cent of people in developing countries were affected by climate-related disasters (UNDP, 2007). Fewer than 1 per cent of people in the developed world were so affected, a reflection of both the geographical focus of the threat and the greater resilience that comes with wealth. By 2009, climate change was already causing, on average, more than 300,000 deaths and economic losses of $125bn and 'seriously affecting' 325 million people every year (Global Humanitarian Forum, 2009). Over the preceding five years, weather-related disasters had caused anywhere between $50bn and $300bn losses in a given year. Estimates and projections for the numbers of people who will experience food or water insecurity over the course of the century due to climate change strongly depend on scenario, but could be an order of magnitude greater than what is happening now.

In the short to medium term, the human security and economic stresses generated or exacerbated by climate change are likely to lead to increased social fragility, conflict and state failure in the developing world, not just in already fragile states but affecting more stable nations as well (Mazo, 2010). The link between climate change (and indeed other environmental stresses) and conflict is contested (Tertrais, 2011). Some empirical studies show a strong link, while others show no link at all, or suggest that historically the problem has been a cooling rather than warming climate. Even if there is a clear link, it is less clear that, given the uncertainties of projecting climate change, it can be of any real use to policy-makers. Yet the very lack of consistency in such studies, and their high sensitivity to the choice of data sets, time frames and definitions of violence and conflict, suggest that this methodological approach to the question is flawed, and that case-based analysis is a better way to consider the problem. An interesting parallel is provided by climate science itself. The current consensus on anthropogenic global warming, is firmly grounded in a consilience of method, evidence and theory (Oreskes, 2007). More specifically, although climate models differ from one another and in different runs of the same model in their specific, detailed projections, they agree, within the limits of experimental error, on the overall warming trend; projections of climate change, broadly considered, are relatively insensitive to the choice of model or variables. Environmental conflict studies, on the other hand, are highly sensitive to such choices. In any case, if climate change is more a threat multiplier than a direct driver of conflict, and just one of many variables in a highly complex and multiple causal system, it is unlikely that empirical studies will be able to control sufficiently for other variables to distinguish its real contribution.[2]

The risk of inter-state conflict over increasingly scarce resources, or newly accessible resources, in the face of climate change is another question. In the Arctic, most of the putative resources that are expected to become accessible as the ice melts lie in undisputed national waters or exclusive economic zones (EEZs), and the countries with Arctic coastlines have all agreed to use existing international law and UN mechanisms to resolve disputes over potential overlapping claims to extended EEZs. Elsewhere, the historical record shows that violent conflict between states over scarce water resources is rare to non-existent, and that in fact management of transboundary resources is an area where otherwise antagonistic nations tend to cooperate. A meta-analysis of research on the nexus between environment and conflict from a range of methodological approaches concluded that there is no evidence that environmental problems have been a direct cause of inter-state warfare. Conflicts involving environmental factors occur predominantly within states, and where they do transcend state borders they tend to be sub-national rather than classic inter-state conflicts (Schubert et al., 2008: 30). Under extreme climate change this may change, but in those conditions other impacts will be so severe that the question is essentially moot. The same study concluded that environmental factors are only one, and rarely the decisive, contribution to a complex interaction of other political, social and economic factors underlying conflict. The adaptive and problem-solving capacity of a state or society is perhaps the most critical factor affecting whether environmental crises will lead to conflict.

---

[2] For a more detailed discussion of these issues see Mazo (2010). More recent studies not covered in that discussion include Hsiang et al. (2011), Zhang et al. (2011), Scheffran et al. (2012) and some 16 papers in a special 2012 issue of the *Journal of Peace Research*, 49(1).

The conclusion of the Pentagon's 2010 Quadrennial Defense Review on the security implications of climate change thus seems robust:

> Climate change could have significant geopolitical impacts around the world, contributing to poverty, environmental degradation, and the further weakening of fragile govern-ments. Climate change will contribute to food and water scarcity, will increase the spread of disease, and may spur or exacerbate mass migration. While climate change alone does not cause conflict, it may act as an accelerant of instability or conflict, placing a burden to respond on civilian institutions and militaries around the world. In addition, extreme weather events may lead to increased demands for defense support to civil authorities for humanitarian assistance or disaster response. (USDoD, 2010)

Case Studies

Two case studies illustrate in greater detail and specificity not only how climate change functions in a web of complex causation as a contributor to instability and conflict, but also illuminate the diffi-culty of using such a framework for prediction and policymaking.[3]

Darfur

For example, the violence in the Darfur region of Sudan in the last decade was in some respects simply a continuation of a low-grade conflict dating back to the 1980s, with its origins in tribal conflicts over access to water and grazing land (ACD, no date). Between 2003, when major fighting broke out, and 2007, between 200,000 and 500,000 were killed (UNEP, 2007: 75). By the end of 2008, there were 2.7 million internally displaced persons, and over 250,000

---

[3] Material for the Darfur case is taken from Mazo (2010); for the Arab spring, from Johnstone and Mazo (2011, 2013).

refugees had fled to neighbouring countries (USAID, 2010). Large-scale fighting was for the most part over by this time, but low-grade conflict has continued to the present. As early as 2006–2007, leaders such as former US Vice President Al Gore, UN Secretary-General Ban Ki-moon and the UK's Special Representative for Climate Change John Ashton were arguing that human-induced climate change was a major contributing factor to the violence (Gore, 2006; Ban Ki-moon, 2007; Reynolds, 2007). While other factors were certainly at work, especially bad governance, ethnic antagonisms and despotism, these leaders were almost certainly right in describing Darfur as the first modern climate-change conflict.

Darfur's complex ethnic mosaic (Prunier, 2005) is less important than the contrast between agriculturalists and pastoralists, whose relationship is governed by competition for land and water resources. Historically the two lifestyles coexisted symbiotically, but population growth, together with declining productivity of agricultural land, necessitated the expansion of land under cultivation. A simultaneous deterioration of pastureland meant that pastoralists needed more area to support a growing animal population (Brooks, 2006). Of the 40 violent local conflicts in Darfur between independence in 1956 and 1970, 29 involved grazing and water rights (UNEP, 2007). Until 1970, such conflicts were mostly resolved locally through established structures, but legal reforms destroyed such mechanisms without providing a viable alternative (Mohamed, 2006; O'Fahey, 2006). Movement of pastoralists from Chad, who did not respect the traditional conflict-resolution mechanisms, was also a factor. These developments weakened the ability of society to cope with the stresses placed upon it by a more arid climate. There was an extended period of desiccation in the Sahel from the 1960s to the 1990s, with severe drought in the 1970s and early to mid 1980s. Darfur, in particular, experienced a very severe drought in 1980–1984 and again in 1990. Although there was a wetter trend beginning in the 1990s, rainfall in the region remains below long-term norms (Webersik, 2008).

The rebel Sudanese People's Liberation Army/Movement (SPLA/M) was founded in 1983 in largely Christian southern Sudan in response to the introduction of sharia law and retraction of the south's limited autonomy. But the 1980–1984 drought culminated in the famine of 1984–1985, causing widespread displacement of peoples, conflict between pastoralists and farmers, and 95,000 deaths. In 1987 the Khartoum government began arming Arabic-speaking Muslim pastoralists in southern Darfur against the putative threat from the SPLA/M (ACD, no date). Following the 1990 famine, the SPLA/M made incursions into Darfur, where it was defeated by government forces and local Arab militias (precursors of the modern Janjaweed) in 1991–1992. The militias then turned against a number of non-Arab tribes, who reacted by forming armed militias of their own (ACD, no date). Low-intensity conflict continued until 1999, and there were sporadic outbreaks of political violence up to the resumption of major conflict in February 2003 (Prunier, 2005). The Darfur rebel groups blamed the Islamist and Arab-centric regime of President Omar al-Bashir, which came to power in a coup in 1989, for oppressing and displacing African farmers in favour of Arab pastoralists. The government responded to the 2003 attacks by training and arming defence militias and sending troops for counter-insurgency. Fighting between militia groups, and between the rebels and government forces, spread, and there were widespread reports of atrocities against civilians.

To many observers, the coincidence of drought and conflict make the causal contribution of climate change self-evident. Empirical studies of the link in this particular case are contradictory (Kevane and Gray, 2008; Burke et al., 2009). But simple correlation is not the whole story; climate is a threat multiplier, not a prime mover. The report which introduced the concept of climate change as a threat multiplier in 2006 argued that 'Darfur provides a case study of how existing marginal situations can be exacerbated beyond the tipping point by climate-related factors' (CNA Corporation, 2006: 16). Some scholars have been harshly critical of the conclusion that climate change caused the Darfur conflict, but their arguments are based on either moral issues (the belief that such attribution absolves leaders of culpability for their actions, including genocide) or on an assumption that multiple causes are linear and additive rather than complex, interactive and multiplicative. There is no real disagreement that the Darfur conflict is in some sense an environmental conflict, merely a difference of emphasis and perspective. Climate change was neither a necessary nor a sufficient condition for the violence, but by that standard, none of the other drivers were either. Climate change was simply one element in a complex causal web.[4]

The Arab spring

The suggestion that climate change may have been the factor that pushed Darfur past a 'tipping point' is thus misleading, as it follows the same assumption that causation is linear and additive. But the Arab spring provides a case where extreme weather events linked to climate change have a stronger case for being such a trigger. Here, too, the causal factors are complex and interrelated, and neither climate nor weather were either necessary or sufficient triggers for the wave of unrest that spread throughout the Arab world in late 2010 and early 2011. But a proximate factor behind the unrest was a spike in global food prices partly due to extreme weather in many parts of the world in 2010–2011. This was not enough on its own to trigger regime change – food-price spikes and food riots have happened before – but it is unlikely that the Arab spring would have happened when it did without it.

In February 2011 wheat was trading at $8.50–$9 a bushel, compared to about $4 in July 2010. Excessive rainfall in Canada cut that country's 2010 harvest by nearly a quarter. Drought and wild-fires in Russia cut the wheat harvest by around 40 per cent, leading to an export ban. Extreme weather also affected harvests in Ukraine, the United States, Australia and China (Johnstone and Mazo, 2013; Sternberg, 2013). Sugar prices hit a 30-year high in 2011 as adverse weather in Australia, Brazil and Pakistan affected production.

The Middle East and North Africa is particularly sensitive to such spikes. The world's top nine wheat importers are all in the region, and seven of them experienced civilian deaths during polit-ical protests in 2011 (Sternberg, 2013). Rioting in Algeria in early January 2011 was a direct response to high unemployment and

---

[4] For a fuller exploration of these issues see Mazo (2010: 79–86).

higher prices for staple foods (*Al-Arabiya*, 2011). Demonstrators waved baguettes on the streets of Tunisia, Jordan and Yemen. As protests spread to Egypt, they were principally aimed at the Mubarak regime, but Egyptian families were spending 40 per cent of their income on food, and food-price inflation was 20 per cent (Curtis et al., 2011; Lowrey, 2011).

While individual weather events can never be unambiguously attributed to climate change, the severe weather of 2010–2011 is exactly what is expected to happen with increasing frequency as the globe warms. Moreover, where it has been possible to analyse specific events statistically in sufficient detail, such as the UK floods of 2000, the European heat wave of 2003 and the Russian heat wave of 2000, there are indications that global warming has made comparable events anywhere between twice and eight times as likely to occur in a given year. There is an 80 per cent chance that the July 2010 heat record in Moscow would not have happened in the absence of such warming (Rahmstorf and Coumou, 2011; Coumou and Rahmstorf, 2012).

The Arab spring was thus a textbook case of climate change as a threat multiplier. Social, political and economic conditions all appear, in retrospect, to have made the region ripe for unrest. The indirect influence of climate change was again neither a necessary nor a sufficient factor – a different Arab spring might have broken out in any case, with a different trigger, but it was a necessary factor in the specific chain of circumstances that led to the actual events of 2010–2011. Moreover, it was not just the proximate effect of the food-price spike; prolonged drought in many countries of the region over the preceding decade led to water stress, migration from rural to urban areas and transnational migration. These issues were particular acute in Syria (Femia and Werrell, 2013; Werz and Hoffman, 2013).

To be sure, the outcome of the Arab spring varied from country to country. Some nations, particularly some of the wealthy Gulf monarchies, were scarcely affected. Others saw relatively peaceful regime change and a transition to democracy. Yet others saw large-scale repression and civil war. Again, in the short and medium term the link between climate change and insecurity, within nations and in the international system, is not straightforward. It appears to have little predictive value other than in general terms. It may be possible to identify regions of the world at greatest risk, but almost impossible to quantify the relative risks. The next strategic shock may be entirely unanticipated, as the Arab spring was. What we can expect as the world warms is an overall increase in such shocks.

Policy Responses

What, then, should the UK be doing about climate change in terms of foreign policy? This question has to be approached from four perspectives: short or medium term versus long term, and prevention versus adaptation.

In the long term, climate change could lead to inter-state conflict and pose an existential threat to nations, even to modern civilisation. To be sure, such catastrophic effects lie at the extreme end of projections, based on the most pessimistic assumptions and outer edges of the uncertainty ranges. (It is important to remember, however, that the so-called 'worst-case scenarios' do not represent the worst that could happen; they are only the worst of the set of illustrative scenarios chosen by the IPCC to ensure consistency and comparability across various studies. The reality could be even worse than the worst-case projections, or conversely, better than the best-case projections.) Such catastrophic consequences will also manifest only on the order of a century or more in the future, and are entirely unpredictable in timing or scope. Only the general magnitude of the threat can be assessed. There is therefore little that can be done, beyond support of continued basic research, in terms of immediate policy responses to cope with the effects.

The need here is to minimise the chances of such extreme climate change, and this can only be done through early and radical reductions in global greenhouse-gas emissions. The UK should continue to lead, within the European Union (EU) and as part of a unified EU approach in international negotiations within the UNFCCC process, to achieve an effective and enforceable global agreement per the Durban Platform by 2015, to take effect in 2020. And it should lead by example, avoiding watering down the process and goals of the 2008 Climate Change Act in the face of the immediate economic situation. Outside the UNFCCC and parallel processes such as the G20 and the Major Economies Forum, the UK should continue efforts to keep the security implications of climate change on the UN Security Council agenda, as it did in 2007 and 2013 (a similar debate was convened in 2011 under the German presidency). Not only does this give the issue an essential high profile, the Security Council is also one of the only institutions that can legally authorise collective action by the international community of the sort that may be increasingly necessary in a warming world. There is some resistance to this approach: two permanent members of the Security Council, Russia and China, argue that other UN bodies such as the UNEP and UNFCCC are the appropriate places to discuss the issue, and many developing countries agree. But there has been progress. In 2007, Pakistan led the G77 objections to the first UK-inspired debate; in 2013, Pakistan, holding the Council presidency, joined with UK to stimulate the third debate. Because of objections from Russia and China, however, it had to be held as an informal 'Arria-Formula' meeting.[5]

These are thus short-term policy recommendations for the longest-term problems posed by climate change. In the medium term, the UK, in the context of the Responsibility to Protect and its own national interests, should be prepared to support an increasing number of interventions and peacekeeping operations under the aegis of the Security Council, the EU Common Security and Defence Policy structures, NATO and ad hoc coalitions. It is precisely those conditions that have led to such interventions in the past that will be exacerbated by climate change in the next few decades. Peace-building and state-building missions require as much a civilian as a military component and UK capabilities in this regard should continue to be strengthened. Climate change projections, global and regional, need to be taken into account in developing the UK's civilian and military force structure and capabilities, and

[5] For a detailed discussion of the role of the Security Council in debating climate change, see Holland and Vagg (2013); for a contrary view, see Jayaram (2013).

in developing joint capabilities with EU partners. These issues are likely to be explored in some detail in the next Strategic Defence and Security Review (SDSR), and any conclusions and recommendations need to be robustly implemented. The 2010 recommended that the Foreign and Commonwealth Office (FCO) take the lead on coordinating work on the security implications of climate change and resource competition (Cabinet Office, 2010: 52, 66). Similarly, the next SDSR is likely to offer a clarification of UK interests in the Arctic and recommendations for new capabilities to protect them, and these should be given priority.

These essentially reactive responses to the short- and medium-term impacts of global warming should be paralleled by an increased and re-oriented focus on assistance to developing countries to adapt to climate-change. As part of the UN's Post-2015 Development Framework, intended to replace the Millennium Development Goals upon their expiry in two years' time, the UK should continue to work towards the inclusion of the consideration of conflict, fragility and security as a prerequisite for sustainable development in its own right, as well as ensuring that climate-change projections are taken into account across the board. This should build on the May 2013 report of the Secretary-General's High-Level Panel (HLP), co-chaired by the Prime Minister, which identified climate change as the one trend that will, above all, determine whether the international community can achieve its ambitions (HLP, 2013: vii–viii). The UK, and particularly DFID (Department for International Development), should make climate change projections and expected impacts central to determinations of most effective targeting of limited official development aid, and ODA (official development assistance) should be coordinated with climate adaptation funding provided through international mechanisms to ensure maximum efficiency. Such adaptation efforts themselves should not be conceived of in isolation, but as parts of an overall development approach to fragile states.[6] Without changing the overall goals and

---

[6] For discussions of the problems of and frameworks for development in fragile states, see Zoellick (2008).

ethos of UK overseas aid, this could entail a shift of resources from the most fragile states to those that have developed to a point where they no longer need aid under current criteria, but are at particular risk from climate change, and especially those where a regression into fragility and conflict would be most dangerous for their neighbours and the rest of the world. This might also entail changing the sectoral emphasis of aid.

Just as the UK's Climate Change Act and unilateral targets for both emissions reduction and adaptation lend it soft power and moral leadership that could help catalyse international solutions to climate change, a refocus of the UK's ODA around climate change, modest as it might be in a global context, could offer a model for global efforts and achieve results far beyond its direct effects. Finally, if there was ever a case for 'joined-up government' – for policy coordination cutting across all areas of policymaking – climate change is it. The effects of climate change, even the most direct, are still relatively minor, but over the next few decades, as the world continues to warm and the impacts become increasingly severe, they will come to affect, as a threat or risk multiplier, many if not most of the challenges and trends discussed in other chapters in this volume.

CHAPTER 12

What hope for the bottom billion – and what role for Britain?

by Paul Collier

Economists have an impressive record of being wrong. Writing in 1961, Nobel Laureate James Meade explained why Mauritius would never develop: it is now Africa's richest economy. Writing in 1966, Nobel Laureate Gunnar Myrdal explained why Indonesia was doomed to stagnation: its take-off is now dated to 1967 (Myrdal, 1966). In *The Bottom Billion*, published in 2007, I analysed why 60 small countries, mostly in Africa, had not developed: most of them are now growing. Superficially, at least, I share the fate of Meade and Myrdal, if not their distinction. But in fact I think that the analysis and message of *The Bottom Billion* remains valid.

The Bottom Billion had two rallying cries, the reasons for which are now more apparent than when I proposed them. One was that the international community should focus its aid more narrowly on these countries rather than distribute it widely wherever poor people were to be found. The other was that we should broaden our policy instruments: aid was not enough, we needed to bring laws, trade policy and security support into play as well.

Since 2007 the old category of 'developing countries' has become yet more inappropriate. Emerging market economies have continued to diverge from the countries of the bottom billion and it has become increasingly evident that aid for these countries is not appropriate. Not only is it a drop in the ocean of their budgets, but they are middle-income economies increasingly able to meet their remaining poverty problems from internal redistribution. Further, aid is about the long term. All the emerging market economies now offer credible hope that the next generation will escape poverty. Only the countries of the bottom billion do not yet provide this hope and that, for me, remains the ultimate rationale for aid.

But it is also more apparent that aid is not enough. With the commodity booms many poor countries have the potential for transformation by harnessing their own natural assets. Whether this happens depends on economic governance. As I will discuss, our laws are far more powerful instruments than our aid in this struggle. Our trade policy can make it easier or harder for poor countries to break into job-intensive manufacturing, the surest route out of poverty. For years the European Commission has been pursuing a strategy of 'Economic Partnership Agreements' with Africa, to no effect. The attempt to force reciprocal trade liberalisation on African governments has predictably been met by angry resistance. It is high time to move on to a more viable strategy. Europe's model for Africa should not be to require Africa to liberalise in favour of Europe, but to encourage African countries to liberalise in favour of each other. We should be using enhanced market access to Europe as an incentive for Africa to follow the successful European model. That is indeed what the African Union and the ACP (African, Caribbean and Pacific) countries have asked us to do. To date it is a missed opportunity. Africa continues to be insecure, and we continue to be inconsistent in our assistance. The latest dramatic last-minute military intervention by France to save Mali from being overrun by invading Islamic militants underlines both Africa's fragility and our lack of foresight.

The traps that I discussed – poor governance, natural resources, conflict and isolation – remain critical guides to how appropriate global policies can help the world's poorest countries. I will organise my discussion around them.

Poor Governance

Many poor countries are badly governed and this is a major cause of their continued poverty. But it is important for Britain to recognise that the struggle for decent governance is primarily domestic. In all such countries there are brave people, some of them inside the government itself, trying to achieve change. It is their struggle, not ours, and clumsy international pressure can backfire, discrediting the reformers by their apparent association with foreign powers. We have a role to play, but it is a modest one of trying to keep the public finances as clean as possible.

Exploitative elites depend for their political power on maintaining patronage systems: the distribution of largesse to supporters. To sustain these systems they need to resort to corruption, either misappropriating public funds or extorting bribes for favours. This provides several points for international intervention. One of these is aid: in most of the poorly governed, low-income countries, aid is a substantial proportion of the budget. While we should categorically avoid telling recipient governments on what they should spend this money, we should insist that it is spent accountably. We can never identify what public money is used for what purpose: in technical language, aid is 'fungible'. Hence, the only way we can ensure that aid is not being misappropriated is if the entire budget is properly scrutinised. Of course, in the process of being accountable to donors, budgets will also become accountable to citizens.

While looting the public purse is one key route by which crooked politicians fund their patronage systems, the other is to extort bribes. It is extremely difficult for honest leaders in poor countries to tackle bribery because they lack the skilled investigative teams necessary to secure convictions. In contrast, all the OECD (Organisation for Economic Co-operation and Development) countries have them. We simply need to use them to crack down on foreign bribery. As a result of the Bribery Act, Britain now has exemplary legislation, but laws only become effective once supported by investigations. The record of investigations around the OECD is highly variable: America routinely mounts hundreds of investigations; France and

Italy have conducted none at all. After a decade of inertia, Britain is at last becoming more active. As part of global standards against bribery, all OECD governments should commit to a minimum annual rate of investigations.

But the easiest point at which to disrupt bribery is to prevent the money being laundered into untraceable foreign bank accounts. The 2013 Report of Kofi Annan's Africa Progress Panel estimates that Africa loses around $25bn in illicit financial outflows, almost as much as it receives in aid (Africa Progress Panel, 2013).

The lawyers who facilitate these transactions are not based in Lagos; they are in London. African governments are impotent to address money laundering, but we could close it down. Fake companies, known as 'shell companies', are the vehicle for bribes. A World Bank study of 150 cases of grand corruption found that shell companies were important in 70 per cent of them. A shell company conceals its true owners and it is astoundingly easy to establish one. A recent experimental study sent 7,000 emails to law firms around the world requesting one to be set up. In some emails a premium on normal fees was offered for secrecy. The emails attracted a 40 per cent positive response, higher for those with this incriminating offer. Britain was high in the global league table of the legal lackeys of embezzlement.

Compliance with anti-money laundering procedures has degenerated into box-ticking. For the true ownership of companies to become a matter of public record a new approach is needed, combining tighter responsibility for reporting, increased investigative effort, tougher penalties, and automatic exchange of information. Corporate opacity is not inadvertent: it is the cumulative achievement of some of the most brilliant professional minds on the planet, who have been royally rewarded for selling their souls. Here, more specifically, is what is needed to close it down.

First, the true 'beneficial' ownership of a company must be provided when the company is registered. To make this a reality, the lawyers who register companies must themselves be licensed, and must provide their own identity as part of the process of registration. The lawyer who registers the company must then be held liable for the accuracy of the information provided. Since lawyers can be presumed to be adept at obfuscating true ownership while providing viable defences that they followed any due diligence procedures that might be required, the only viable form of liability is 'strict liability'. In plain English this means that if the information is false, no defence is accepted: we apply it for the pollution of water, and we should also apply it for the far more damaging pollution of information. In turn, strict liability is only as powerful as the penalties that enforce it. If the penalty is a fine then lawyers will perform the calculation: the probability of detection times the cost of the fine, and simply build this into their fees. Hence, the penalty has to be something that cannot be passed on. The effective penalty is therefore an automatic jail sentence. Lest you think this is wildly unreasonable, the Isle of Man sets this standard already. As a result, lawyers based in the Isle of Man probably take rather more care in establishing beneficial ownership than those in London.

As well as this base, the identity of the beneficial owner must include his unique tax identification number (TIN). Names and addresses are not sufficient: they are neither unique nor readily automated. The resulting data must be automatically exchangeable with other authorities internationally, and must use a machine-readable system which is internationally compatible.

Finally, the system has to be effectively global. This means that the current secrecy havens must either be opened or isolated. Isolation is remarkably easy to impose: the international community already has the model from tackling terrorist finance. All that is needed is a list of non-compliant jurisdictions combined with a banking rule which prevents banks in compliant jurisdictions from conducting any transactions with those in non-compliant ones. The threat of isolation is so severe that it would not need to be implemented: once mooted, havens would rush into pre-emptive compliance.

This package will fix money laundering. It will take some years of international cooperation to achieve: it will be undoing the intent of legal structures laboriously and ingeniously built over many years by some of the most brilliant legal minds on earth. But the 2013 British G8 has already launched it; we just need to see it through.

Natural Resources

The economies of the bottom billion have grown in the past decade primarily because of the global boom in commodities. African exports are dominated by commodities and so the continent bene-fited from a large improvement in its terms of trade. The commodity super-cycle is over: the global recession has softened prices, but fortunately Africa's own commodity boom will continue. Although Africa is thought of as resource-rich, as of the millennium its known natural resources were far less per square mile than the rich world of the OECD. This was not due to geology but to a lack of prospect-ing. The rise in commodity prices triggered prospecting and Africa and other previously neglected regions were the obvious places for search. Valuable resources have been discovered in many countries that were not previously considered resource-rich. For example, oil has been found in Ghana, Kenya and Uganda; gas in Mozambique and Tanzania; gold in Burkina Faso; copper in Mongolia. Over the coming decade these discoveries will come on stream.

The many billions of dollars of natural resources that will be exported by the bottom billion constitute the biggest single oppor-tunity these countries have ever had. Poor societies can have the finance to transform themselves with their own money. But the history of resource extraction in such countries has most commonly been of plunder rather than development (Collier, 2010; Collier and Venables, 2011). Africa has been parted from its resource wealth for a small fraction of its true value. Mining in frontier condi-tions is a risky business and so returns should be commensurate. But economics makes a key analytic distinction between profits and rents: whereas profits are a return on capital, rents are unearned. Although the distinction is lost on accountants who wash rents into profits, it is fundamental to resource extraction. Unlike purely productive activities, resource extraction generates rents as well as profits, as inherently valuable assets are lifted from the ground. If dot.com companies take big risks, they will sometimes legitimately make profits that are spectacular. But resource extraction companies are given custody of the natural wealth of others: they are analogous to banks, not to dot.com companies. Spectacular 'profits' from resource extraction are in reality likely to be rent-seeking: companies snaffling the natural assets of poor people. Such behaviour demonstrates not exceptionally high business talent but exceptionally low corporate ethics. As with banks, since resource extraction companies are the custodians of other people's assets, they need to be regulated more tightly than companies that do not have such a responsibility. Over the past half-century the international community has built a global system of bank regulation, led by the Bank for International Settlements and the International Monetary Fund. Even so, periodically we have found that regulation has been inadequate. In contrast, until very recently resource extraction companies have been operating without any specific global regulation. Such limited corporate scrutiny as has been provided has come from the better-regulated stock exchanges. But many resource extraction companies are listed only on weakly regulated exchanges or, worse, are privately held. Such companies are currently unlikely to be fit for the role of custodians of natural assets.

Africa and other poor regions have reaped the consequences. Companies have used their massive advantage over governments in respect of knowledge and capacity to negotiate deals that are unfair. Once a deal has been agreed, companies then avoid paying the taxes due by means of transfer pricing. Finally, even those revenues that are paid by companies often fail to enter the official budget process and so their use cannot be properly scrutinised by citizens or officials. Each of these we can do something about: I take them in turn.

The Africa Progress Panel describes recent transactions in the Democratic Republic of Congo (DRC) in which natural resources appear to have been sold for $725m below their true value. This reflects both excessive the secrecy of the negotiation process, and the gross asymmetries of information and capacities between companies and governments. The space for negotiation can be shrunk by drawing up codes of mining taxation which apply to all companies. Governments need expert assistance in designing such codes. Once concluded, contracts can be published: this is a new voluntary standard of the Extractive Industries Transparency Initiative. DRC has belatedly placed all its contracts on the web. Asymmetries of information can be reduced by gathering public geological information prior to selling prospecting rights. With modern technology relatively cheap aerial surveys can reveal a lot. By making geological information a public good, governments can induce greater competition in prospecting and, have a better idea of what rights are worth. Belatedly, some donors are now beginning to finance the costs of such surveys. Prospecting rights can also be sold through auctions, flushing out information about true value through competition between well-informed companies. The international agencies could offer standard services for conducting such auctions. Finally, donor agencies can address the gulf in capacities, paying for the lawyers needed by governments to ensure that agreements are reasonable. The African Development Bank is now establishing such a fund.

Even once deals have been agreed, companies can still avoid their obligations through tax avoidance. In Africa the standard method of such tax avoidance has been 'transfer pricing', by which companies set up subsidiaries in Africa which sell their output to other subsidiaries registered in tax havens, at prices below true value. As a result, the African subsidiary does not make profits and so is not subject to taxation. The profits duly show up in tax havens where, as companies are keen to assert, all tax due is properly paid. That due tax is approximately zero is a happy corollary of the hard work of an astute and appropriately rewarded lawyer. The Report of the Africa Progress Panel estimates that Africa loses around $35bn each year from transfer pricing, around $5bn more than it receives in aid. To tackle transfer pricing, the OECD is currently proposing to establish a central unit that would produce guideline prices for transactions between subsidiaries of the same company. In preparing their accounts, companies would be required either to use these benchmark prices or to justify why they had not done so. This needs to be complemented by building capacity in African tax authorities. To date, Norway is one of the few donors sufficiently far-sighted to realise that aid spent on strengthening tax authorities has far greater benefits than aid that directly meets human needs, even though it is less photogenic. The OECD endorses the Norwegian approach and goes further. It proposes a 'tax inspectors without borders' programme in which tax officials from OECD countries would spend some months in African tax authorities demonstrating how these benchmark data can be used to curtail transfer pricing. A few years ago, in an opinion survey of who young French women regarded as most eligible, 'doctors without borders' came top. Perhaps 'tax inspectors without borders' might find recruitment surprisingly easy.

The above measures are designed to increase the revenues paid by resource extraction companies. A complementary process is then needed to ensure that these payments actually reach properly scrutinised budgetary processes. This has been the remit of the Extractive Industries Transparency Initiative, which Britain and France have belatedly joined. The days of preaching what we do not practise are thankfully over. Public reporting by companies of their payments became mandatory in the USA in 2010 and has just become mandatory in the European Union. It should now rapidly become a global standard.

Conflict

Many African countries remain fragile. In the first three months of 2013 Mali was overrun by Islamist rebels before being saved by last-minute French military intervention and the government of the Central African Republic was overthrown by rebels from Chad despite the presence of South African peacekeeping troops. What these events demonstrate is that many African countries lack the military capacity to secure their territory, and the region has not yet managed to coordinate adequate collective security. Anachronistically, security continues to depend upon the willingness and capacity of former colonial powers to intervene militarily. Sierra Leone, Ivory Coast and Liberia are now at peace because of British, French and US-supported UN military interventions a decade ago. Nobody regards this as a satisfactory state of affairs.

In the face of state failure, the international community has a long history of oscillating between pusillanimous passivity and gung-ho intervention. Kuwait in 1991 was gung-ho; Somalia in 1993 was gung-ho until the 'Black Hawk down' incident swung opinion into fearful passivity. The result was the abandonment of Somalia to two decades of conflict, followed by the catastrophic pusillanimity in Rwanda in 1994, leading to genocide, and in Ivory Coast in 1999, leading to a spiral into civil war. By 2002 we were back to gung-ho, with a spectacularly successful British intervention in Sierra Leone. The momentum of gung-ho carried on into Iraq and Afghanistan, the manifest failures of which swung us back to pusillanimity as currently displayed in Syria. Pusillanimity almost led to Mali becoming another Somalia. For example, the American standing military force devoted to Africa, AFRICOM, was left to stand and watch as the country was overrun by a small force of Islamic rebels: a strategy somewhat flattered by the description 'leading from behind'. Only the panicked last-minute intervention by France averted catastrophe.

Can we find a middle way? I suggest two complementary approaches.

The Sahel region is fundamentally fragile in a straightforward sense. Being fragmented into many small economies, no government has the military capacity properly to exert a monopoly of force over its territory. While rebellions may superficially seem to be heroic resistance struggles against repression, in post-colonial Africa they are usually catastrophes for their societies, paving the way not for liberation but for deepened poverty (Collier, 2009). The African Union has recently estimated that Kony's Lord's Resistance Army, which has ranged across national borders in its long-lasting destruction, has been responsible for over 100,000 deaths. Similarly, the rebel forces that caused the collapse of Mali's government led to the replacement of one of Africa's most democratic governments by military rule.

West Africa, and perhaps Africa as a whole, needs a common standing military force that can be deployed against rebellions. This cannot be a blanket guarantee of military protection to incumbent governments regardless of conduct and below I will suggest the limits to such security. But here I want to focus on how Africa could get the common force that would provide security under normal circumstances. Africa already has a rudimentary pan-African force, but it lacks finance and logistics. In effect, Africa needs the equivalent of NATO. Britain, France and the USA in partnership with South Africa, can provide the sustained finance, logistics and diplomacy that can over the next decade build an African NATO. It will unfortunately be needed for many years.

Not all regimes should be protected by this international security. Two recent cases in which support for regime security would have been unwarranted were Ivory Coast in 2010 and Libya in 2011. Each of these transitions was rather well-managed by the international community and we should learn from these rare successes. In each case an incumbent regime unambiguously crossed a clear red line. In Ivory Coast the incumbent lost an election which he had invited the United Nations to supervise. The UN declared the opponent the victor but the incumbent president clung onto power. At this point the international community cut off all finance to the regime. Fortuitously, Ivory Coast was in the Franc Zone and so the government was even unable to access its accounts in the regional central bank, the winner of the election being declared the legal signatory for the accounts. Once it was evident who had the money, the large government army melted away, enabling the small opposition forces to take over the country virtually unopposed. In Libya the red line was Gaddafi's murderous radio threats to hunt down opponents: 'we will find you in your cupboards'. The international community found the gumption to cut the money flow, froze his assets, put up a no-fly zone, and provide limited military support for scratch rebel forces. As in the Ivory Coast, once it became apparent that Gaddafi would not be able to finance his military despite its overwhelming superiority, it gradually melted away.

In Syria Assad managed for a long time to avoid crossing any red lines. Once he did so, the international community still failed to act sufficiently decisively to send a clear signal to his military. Assad's money flow has been reduced but his assets have not been frozen. There has been no attempt at a no-fly zone, although Turkey may well be in a position to impose one. It has been left to Qatar to intervene, but it has lacked the power to induce the army to abandon Assad.

Military fragility is such a sensitive issue that it may be impossible to formulate a coherent strategy: we may be condemned to continue blundering between pusillanimity and gung-ho. But between them the approach of building an African NATO and setting down some red lines which would trigger a financial freeze and possibly a no-fly zone, may offer a viable alternative.

Isolation

Many of the countries of the bottom billion are small, isolated economies. Developing such economies other than through natural resource extraction is extremely difficult (Collier, 2013). Small and isolated is not beautiful. Self-sufficiency may appear desirable, but it is romantic nonsense. Small and isolated condemns a society to poverty because it condemns people to being unproductive. The sources of high productivity – the sort of productivity that the average British person achieves at work each day – are not mysterious. Ever since Adam Smith they have been recognised as scale and specialisation. Large organisations enable workers to reap economies of scale. Specialisation enables a worker to acquire skills instead of being a jack-of-all-trades. With specialisation comes trade: to a first approximation, everything depends upon everything else. Small, isolated economies cannot combine scale with specialisation: if they have sufficient specialised firms to span the range of activities that a modern productive economy needs they will all be too small to reap scale economies.

The conclusion from this is that small, isolated economies need to become integrated into the global market. Only this way can they specialise, and so reap scale economies without having to produce everything that they need. But breaking out of isolation is costly and also often requires diplomacy. South Sudan is the ultimate small, isolated economy. Its only access to the sea runs north through Sudan, with which it has been at war. The southern route to the sea lacks even a single paved road and requires passage through at least two other countries. South Sudan desperately needs politically reliable rail access to the coast, as does Rwanda which is currently dependent upon a long and inadequate road. However, there is no necessary reason why such a railway would be a viable commercial investment. The market solution might well be to leave small isolated economies to rot. Nor can such poor economies necessarily find the finance to make a huge and low-yielding investment. The cost of achieving integration should therefore be borne by the international community. Abandoning these societies to continued poverty is not acceptable: social objectives are not coincident with commercial objectives. In the 1990s donors such as the World Bank wound down their infrastructure funding, on the false premise that private finance would fill the need. The private sector is highly unlikely to perform this function for small, isolated economies. Since it is vital, it should be a future priority for aid budgets.

Conclusion

The countries of the bottom billion are making progress. They weathered the 2009 global crisis remarkably well, reflecting a decade of quietly putting in place prudent fiscal and exchange rate policies. Many are beginning to harness the huge opportunity of resource extraction. Investors are beginning to take Africa seriously, both as a site for production and as a market. So, there is now much hope for the bottom billion.

But these opportunities are no more than that: they may be seized, or they may be missed. The coming decade will see a critical struggle within each of these societies between people trying to harness the opportunities and those wanting to revert to plunder. This is not our struggle: Africans, not us, will determine whether and when they converge on an increasingly global prosperity. But it is both in Europe's interest as Africa's neighbour and major trading partner, and a matter of human concern to anyone who finds poverty in the midst of plenty intolerable, that Africans should win their struggle. We should therefore design our international policies with the intelligence and consistency that these intractable challenges demand.

CHAPTER 13

Humanitarian intervention: What future for the responsibility to protect?

by Simon Adams[1]

Although the primary motivation for the establishment of the United Nations (UN) in 1945 was for the victorious powers to construct an international system that would prevent a third World War, the baleful shadow of Auschwitz also loomed over proceedings. This helps explain the resulting ideological and moral tension between the reinforcement of national sovereignty and the promotion of universal human rights. It is a tension that dominated the UN's first five decades, despite a growing acceptance of shared humanitarian ideals.

Meanwhile, Polish Jewish refugee Raphael Lemkin had to invent a whole new word – 'genocide' – to explain the magnitude of the Nazi's murderous campaign against the Jews of Europe. His post-war pursuit of a Genocide Convention was due in part to the fact that Lemkin regarded it as obscene that while there were established international conventions prohibiting piracy or the traffic of narcotics, state-sanctioned mass murder was traditionally viewed as an issue of domestic policy. As Lemkin argued: 'It seems inconsistent with our concepts of civilisation that selling a drug to an individual is a matter of worldly concern, while gassing millions of human beings might be a problem of internal concern' (Power, 2007: 48).

---

[1] This chapter was written with the research assistance of Nadira Khudayberdieva.

Despite the adoption of the Genocide Convention in 1948, every time the UN was faced with the actual reality of genocide over the following half century it faltered. It failed to stop the Khmer Rouge's 'killing fields' in Cambodia during the 1970s and to confront the genocide in Rwanda in 1994. It took 50 years and the end of the cold war, but accumulated shame and repetitive failure eventually provoked progress.

Kofi Annan was elected UN Secretary-General in 1997. Haunted by the genocides in Rwanda and the Bosnian town of Srebrenica, Annan was also dealing with the political detritus of a decade of so-called 'humanitarian intervention' where western powers asserted that they had a right to militarily intervene in another country's affairs if they felt there was sufficient moral justification to do so. To many ex-colonies in the global South this appeared a little too much like a case of 'civilizing mission' redux – only this time with a rifle in one hand and a copy of the relevant extracts from the Universal Declaration of Human Rights in the other.

A key turning point was Kosovo. There is no doubt that the Yugoslav government targeted Kosovar Albanians for 'ethnic cleansing' in 1999 and that there was need for an international response to their plight. However, NATO-led protective military action in Kosovo took place without UN Security Council authorisation. As has been widely argued since, NATO's intervention in Kosovo was therefore morally justifiable but illegal under international law. After Kosovo and with the start of a new millennium, Annan posed the resulting dilemma very sharply: 'if humanitarian intervention is, indeed, an unacceptable assault on sovereignty, how should we respond to a Rwanda, to a Srebrenica – to gross and systematic violations of human rights that offend every precept of our common humanity?' (Annan, 2000: 48).

The UN is built around the principle of sovereign equality – the idea that all states have the right to determine their own affairs within their own borders. Furthermore, they have a right to territorial integrity (i.e. not to be invaded) as enshrined in Article 2(7) of the UN Charter. But UN scholars will point out that the Charter also includes Article 39, giving the Security Council powers to intervene in any situation that threatens international peace and security. Annan recognised that mass atrocities, by their very nature, pose a grave threat to international peace and security.

Annan's comment was also a tacit acknowledgement that while the UN was established to stop conflicts between states, most conflicts now take place within national borders. Worldwide, between 1989 and 2009 governments were responsible for 83 per cent of deaths from 'one-sided violence' (Human Security Research Group, 2012: 204). All too often civilians remain the primary focus of armed forces whose intent is to terrorise or destroy specific groups or communities.

The Responsibility to Protect

Prompted by Annan and funded by the Canadian government, in 2001 the International Commission on Intervention and State Sovereignty (ICISS), led by international diplomats Gareth Evans and Mohammad Sahnoun, confronted these questions and developed the concept of the 'Responsibility to Protect' (R2P). The Responsibility to Protect does not seek to be a panacea for all the evil – from poverty to piracy – that plagues our world. Instead it is focused exclusively on four mass atrocity crimes and three operational pillars.

The four international crimes are ethnic cleansing, genocide, war crimes and crimes against humanity, with the latter three clearly defined by the Rome Statute of the International Criminal Court. The three pillars for implementing R2P include an explicit acknowledgement of the primary sovereign responsibility of every state to protect its populations from these crimes (pillar 1); the responsibility of the international community to assist states in meeting that responsibility (pillar 2); and finally, an acceptance that if a state is manifestly failing or unwilling to uphold its responsibility to protect then the international community must be prepared to take appropriate action in a timely and decisive manner in accordance with the UN Charter (pillar 3).

The Responsibility to Protect was unanimously adopted at the 2005 UN World Summit, the largest assembly of heads of state and government in history, while the three pillars concept was first introduced in the UN Secretary-General's 2009 report on R2P. However, much of the initial political momentum around R2P was created in Africa. When the African Union proclaimed its Constitutive Act in July 2000, Article 4(H) boldly proclaimed that the new organisation would defend:

> the right of the Union to intervene in a Member State pursuant to a decision of the Assembly in respect of grave circumstances, namely: war crimes, genocide and crimes against humanity ...

This meant that when the African Union was launched in 2002 there had already been a conscious shift from the politics of non-intervention to the politics of non-indifference with regard to mass atrocity crimes on the continent. The impact this had on policy-makers and opinion shapers outside of Africa and in building support for R2P is often underestimated.

R2P was an explicit rejection of 'humanitarian intervention'. The doctrine of humanitarian intervention may be summed up as, 'military intervention in a state, without the approval of its authorities, and with the purpose of preventing widespread suffering or death among the inhabitants' (Roberts, 2000). As such it overlooks the broad range of preventive, non-coercive measures that are central to R2P. By contrast, the Responsibility to Protect was predicated upon the notion that sovereignty entails responsibility, building upon the ideas of Francis Deng, previously the UN Secretary-General's Special Advisor on the Prevention of Genocide and now South Sudan's Ambassador to the UN. Although R2P evolved as a preventive doctrine, in the words of one of the ICISS commissioners, Ramesh Thakur, the Responsibility to Protect also rejected both 'unilateral interference and institutionalised indifference' (Thakur, 2011) with regard to any situation that required coercive measures. Rather than compromising sovereignty, R2P seeks to respond to extreme crises in a way that is both legitimate and legal.

Following the UN World Summit the R2P principle was reaffirmed in Security Council Resolution 1674 (2006) and Resolution 1894 (2009). The council also made reference to R2P in Resolution 1706 (2006) on Darfur. On a pragmatic level, R2P played an important role in framing the international community's response, led by now ex-Secretary-General Annan, to the crisis in Kenya in 2007–2008. It directly influenced the robust mandate given to peacekeepers in Ivory Coast in 2011. But the development of R2P has not been without tragic disappointments and setbacks. Although there have been very divisive debates about R2P with regard to Sri Lanka and elsewhere, Libya and Syria have provided R2P with its biggest challenges. These cases are difficult precisely because they raise issues of accountability and coercion to halt mass atrocities – matters the UN Security Council has always struggled to address in a consistent manner.

R2P after Libya and Syria

From the start of Libyan leader Muammar al-Qaddafi's violent crackdown against protesters in February 2011, R2P informed the UN Security Council's response. While R2P had played some role in preventing an escalation of deadly ethnic conflict in Kenya during 2007, it had never been utilised to mobilise the Security Council to take coercive action against a UN member state before. It was for this reason that Resolution 1970 of 26 February was hailed as a groundbreaking diplomatic moment. Similarly, Resolution 1973, which followed on 17 March, was initially seen as a timely and proportional intervention to ensure the protection of civilians at grave risk of mass atrocities. It was seen as a necessary measure of last resort.

Over the course of the following months the debate regarding the meaning of the resolutions and their implementation became increasingly bitter. Some UN member states argued that the Libyan intervention had been hijacked by partisans of 'regime change'. The alternative view was that 'all necessary measures' were being used by the NATO-led alliance to prevent atrocities and protect civilians. Questions of proportionality and motivation began to undermine the unanimity that initially existed.

The fall of Qaddafi's government in August 2011, the challenges of rebuilding Libya from the ruins of civil war, and the destabilising effect of an uncontrolled flow of weapons to neighbouring Mali, mean that Libya continues to provide a focus for debates over R2P. Moreover, the contrast between the Security Council's response in Libya and its inability to take any kind of united action with regard to mass atrocities in nearby Syria, has widened the divide between supporters and critics of the implementation of R2P.

In the final analysis, international military intervention in Libya saved lives. Approximately 1,000 civilians were killed by Libyan government forces while the Security Council authorised a range of non-military measures that sought to persuade the Gaddafi regime to stop perpetrating atrocities. Despite these efforts, Gaddafi openly incited further crimes, threatening to exterminate all 'rats', 'cockroaches' and 'traitors' in Benghazi and elsewhere. The impending assault of Gaddafi's army on Benghazi moved the Security Council to pass Resolution 1973. At the opening session of the 66th UN General Assembly on 22 September 2011, British Prime Minister David Cameron correctly claimed that the resulting action, 'stopped Benghazi from joining Srebrenica and Rwanda in history's painful roll call of massacres the world failed to prevent'. The fact that Resolution 1973 was adopted without a single negative vote on the Security Council reflected that, at the time, even those with serious reservations about a NATO-led operation recognised that the world needed to act.

If for some critics Libya represented a possible case of R2P-overreach, Syria, by contrast, was yet another example of dysfunction and deadlock inside the UN Security Council. Inspired by the Arab spring uprisings, in mid-March 2011 mass protests broke out in Syria. Over the following two years more than 70,000 civilians would be killed as the Syrian state used troops, tanks, artillery, attack helicopters and fighter jets in an attempt to crush popular opposition to its rule. With the Security Council initially distracted by Libya, and with permanent member Russia a long-standing ally, the government of President Bashar al-Assad was able to prevaricate, break numerous promises to reform and avoid UN action. As the popular uprising degenerated into a bitter civil war the Security Council was left immobilised.

There are five factors that explain the different ways in which the Security Council responded to Libya and Syria. First, key actors in the region played a different role in both crises. The Arab League's rapid condemnation of Gaddafi's actions and calls for a no-fly zone in Libya contrasted with its initially cautious response to the situation in Syria. Lebanon, the only Arab League member on the Security Council at the time, pushed the council to take decisive action regarding Libya but initially defended the Syrian government.

Second, whereas a sizable number of key Libyan officials defected from the regime (including the leadership of Libya's Permanent Mission to the UN, who made compelling statements during Security Council discussions), in Syria the regime maintained the formal allegiance of most senior government officials. The Ambassador of Syria to the UN, Bashar Ja'afari, remained an enthusiastic defender of the Assad government's actions.

Third, Libya's status as a pariah state without powerful allies contrasts with Syria, which maintains close relationships with Russia and Iran. Fourth, public statements by Gaddafi that he would 'cleanse' the nation of 'cockroaches' and 'rats' were viewed as incitement to commit crimes against humanity, whereas Assad initially made statements that were viewed as conciliatory despite all evidence to the contrary. Finally, several Security Council members were nervous about the council being drawn into another armed intervention, despite the fact that there was no desire by any state or regional body to directly militarily intervene in Syria. Indeed, arguing that armed intervention would greatly worsen the political and humanitarian crisis in Syria was *de rigueur* for virtually every discussion by diplomats or civil society advocates operating at UN headquarters in New York during 2011 or 2012.

Since March 2011, despite ongoing mass atrocity crimes, Russia and China have vetoed three Security Council resolutions that sought to impose sanctions, an arms embargo and travel bans on the Syrian government. The ostensible justification was that Russia and China were nervous that such UN-authorised measures might eventually lead to Syria becoming 'the next Libya'. Their vetoes were, therefore, also an explicit challenge to the Responsibility to Protect.

The reality is that Russia would have vetoed the Syria resolutions even if the Libyan intervention had never happened and R2P did not exist. During the cold war the Soviet Union was Syria's major military supplier and the government allowed the Kremlin to establish a naval base at Tartus, the Soviets' only military outpost in the Mediterranean and Middle East. Tartus remains a key component of Russia's plan to rebuild a global military presence befitting a recovering superpower. In the bitter recriminations after Libya it was also forgotten, for example, that the first major attempted misuse of R2P was in August 2008 when invoked by Russian Foreign Minister Sergei Lavrov while militarily intervening in South Ossetia. In short, the strategic clash between 'the West' and Russia over Syria has little to do with R2P and much to do with the Kremlin's foreign policy priorities for a resurgent Russia.

Lacking any direct interest in Libya and facing a world outraged by Qaddafi's crimes against his own people, China abstained from the crucial Security Council resolutions that led to the Libyan intervention. Given that China has no direct stake in the Syrian conflict, their decision to cast three veto votes alongside Russia appeared to many UN insiders to have been a strategic decision relating to the balance of power within the Security Council. Despite these actions with regard to Syria, China continued to use other fora to cautiously voice its support for the Responsibility to Protect.

While the failure of the Security Council to respond in a decisive way to the crisis in Syria exposed the council to intense criticism regarding selectivity in application of R2P, the issue of international obligation could not be excluded or ignored. During the debate that preceded the second Syria veto in February 2012, for example, the Guatemalan Foreign Minister insisted that:

Non-intervention in the internal affairs of sovereign States and the respect for their territorial integrity are cardinal principles of our foreign policy. But we also acknowledge the obligation of all States to observe certain norms of conduct in relation to their own populations ... That is why, in an era when the principle of the Responsibility to Protect (R2P) is being questioned, we are not ashamed to affirm that, with some nuances that we have explained in other forums, we support that principle. (Caballeros, 2012)

Russia may have the strategic support of China on the Security Council with regard to Syria, but it is isolated on the broader question of the need for the international community to hold the Syrian government accountable for its 'crimes'. The December 2012 vote in the UN General Assembly saw 135 states support of a resolution condemning mass atrocities committed by Assad's forces, criticising human rights abuses by the armed opposition, and calling upon the Security Council to live up to its responsibilities. Only 12 states voted against the resolution.

Moreover, despite deep cracks within the Security Council over Syria, the council still invoked R2P more often in the year after Libya and the start of Syria crisis than it had done in the five years prior.[2] The reality is that Syria and Libya both moved the emerging norm from moral abstraction to practical debates about implementation. And as Secretary-General Ban Ki-moon argued with regard to R2P at the end of 2011, 'I would far prefer the growing pains of an idea whose time has come to sterile debates about principles that are never put into practice.'

---

[2] In addition to R2P resolutions on Libya (Res. 1970 and Res. 1973), between March 2011 and March 2012 the Security Council invoked R2P in resolutions on Ivory Coast (Res. 1975, 30 March), South Sudan (Res. 1996, 8 July), and Yemen (Res. 2014, 21 October). There were also two follow-up resolutions on Libya (Res. 2016, 27 October; Res. 2040, 12 March). R2P was also invoked in several presidential statements by the Council.

The Preventive Lens: Kenya

In many ways Kenya provides a better lens through which to consider the current state of health of R2P. On 4 March 2013 Kenyans voted in general elections. This was the first national ballot since devastating ethnic violence tore across the country in the aftermath of the December 2007 presidential elections. The 2007–2008 internecine violence, mainly between Kenya's three largest ethnic groups, lasted two months and resulted in the death of 1,133 people. More than 600,000 Kenyans were driven from their homes. It took weeks of mediation by former UN Secretary-General Kofi Annan to find a way out of the crisis and negotiate a power-sharing arrangement. Afterwards, Annan remarked that his role had been guided by the Responsibility to Protect and that intense diplomatic pressure had assisted in pushing the main political players towards a negotiated solution. Extinguishing the flames in Kenya was widely hailed as the first major example of 'R2P in practice'.

In the aftermath of the 2007–2008 conflagration the International Criminal Court indicted four Kenyans for directing the violence. Although one of the accused, Uhuru Kenyatta, was elected President on 4 March 2013, the recent elections passed with relatively few incidents of political or ethnic violence. This was due, in part, to the fact that since 2007 Kenya has enacted significant reforms. Legislation banning incitement and other forms of hate speech, devolution of political authority, a new constitution and ongoing efforts at security sector reform all contributed to a more peaceful election. However, although the country has made undeniable progress, mass unemployment, intractable poverty and endemic corruption continue to fuel the deep distrust many Kenyans still feel towards their government and one another. According to the UN, last year more than 400 Kenyans were killed and 112,000 displaced by deadly localised inter-communal violence.

Nevertheless, the international community's ongoing engagement with the Kenyan government and civil society has been a paragon of engagement under pillars one and two of R2P. The domestic and international response showed that non-coercive tools, such as mediation, can help rebuild fractured societies and avoid further mass atrocities when undertaken with sustained determination. Working in cooperation with local actors, funding ethnic reconciliation efforts and strengthening the rule of law via electoral reform do not make for dramatic photo opportunities, but such work is representative of the broader struggle to prevent mass atrocities in divided societies.

R2P is concerned with the prevention of mass atrocity crimes, not election outcomes. But in Kenya the R2P not only offered an analytical lens to understand the nature of threat facing the country, but also provided a practical tool for mobilising both proximate and long-term preventive action via the UN, the Kenyan government, international partners and civil society. In all likelihood, in the future R2P will be more commonly implemented in 'Kenya-like' pillar one and two situations, than via strategic air strikes and coercive military measures under pillar three.

What Next?

For R2P to continue to develop as an international norm there is a need for its supporters to transform the way the United Nations conducts its business. This should include:

Institutionalising Atrocity Prevention

Since 2010 the governments of Australia, Costa Rica, Denmark and Ghana, in association with the Global Centre for the Responsibility to Protect, have asked that states appoint a senior government official to coordinate national strategies to prevent mass atrocities domestically and regionally. These officials collaborate through an international network to enhance efforts to anticipate and prevent mass atrocity crimes before they occur.

Twenty-eight governments have already appointed Focal Points and almost 40 states attended the second meeting of the R2P Focal

Points network in September 2012.[3] The initiative represents a mix of big and small powers from all regions of world. In early 2012 the Global Centre for the Responsibility to Protect also co-hosted, with the Community of West African States (ECOWAS), a major regional forum on R2P in West Africa. There is real and genuine enthusiasm for the Focal Points idea as a means of building architecture for early warning in a region with an unfortunate history of deadly conflict. A similar European regional meeting, attended by 31 governments, was held in Slovenia during April 2013. Central to the advancement of R2P will be a more developed early warning system via a global network of national R2P Focal Points within governments.

Responsibility Not to Veto

In March 2011 the 'Small 5' (S5) submitted a detailed plan for reform of the United Nations. The S5 – Costa Rica, Jordan, Liechtenstein, Singapore and Switzerland – submitted a draft resolution to the General Assembly with an annex that included 20 recommendations, including suggested reforms to the working methods of the Security Council. The S5's eventual withdrawal of the resolution was due to diplomatic pressure exerted by the powerful five permanent members (or P5) of the Security Council: China, France, Russia, United Kingdom and the United States.

Of particular importance in the S5 proposal was the recommendation that the P5 refrain from using their veto power on the Security Council to block action aimed at preventing or halting mass atrocities. During 2011 and 2012 China and Russia used their veto at the Security Council to block attempts to hold the Syrian government responsible for mass atrocity crimes committed against its own people. The international community's ability to respond to mass

---

[3] The governments that have appointed R2P Focal Points so far are: Argentina, Australia, Austria, Belgium, Bosnia-Herzegovina, Botswana, Bulgaria, Costa Rica, Czech Republic, Denmark, Finland, France, Germany, Ghana, Greece, Guatemala, Hungary, Ireland, Italy, Ivory Coast, the Netherlands, Slovenia, Spain, Sweden, Switzerland, United Kingdom, United States of America and Uruguay.

atrocity crimes should not be contingent upon the partisan interests and political alliances of the permanent members of the council. The Responsibility to Protect means that the P5 have a responsibility not to veto in mass atrocity situations.

Strengthening the International Criminal Court

During 2013 the International Criminal Court (ICC) will conduct important trials that will fundamentally challenge the culture of impunity with regard to mass atrocities in Ivory Coast and Kenya. At a meeting in New York during 2012, ICC Prosecutor Fatou Bensouda stated that, 'the ICC is the legal arm of R2P'. She is correct in the sense that you cannot pursue an end to mass atrocities without supporting the Responsibility to Protect and a more formidable ICC. The Hague is both the departure point and end point for enhanced accountability. Ending impunity for past crimes is one of the most powerful tools for preventing future ones.

While other crucial issues, such as reforming the Security Council or developing prudential criteria for use-of-force mandates, continue to be fiercely debated, the above three issues represent terrain upon which global consensus could be carefully constructed. R2P's champions, including the United Kingdom, should support this agenda.

The UK and R2P

The government of the United Kingdom has a significant stake in R2P's future. During the late 1990s the UK's then Prime Minister, Tony Blair, was a vocal advocate of 'humanitarian intervention', arguing that the international community needed a 'more subtle blend of mutual self-interest and moral purpose in defending the values we cherish' (Blair, 1999). British military forces participated in NATO-led operations aimed at stopping ethnic cleansing in Bosnia in 1995 and in Kosovo in 1999. British military intervention in Sierra Leone in 2000 not only halted atrocities, but also directly contributed to ending the country's decade-long civil war.

With regard to international law, the United Kingdom was one of the first signatories of the Rome Statute of the ICC. The 1998 decision of the British House of Lords to allow the extradition of former Chilean military dictator Augusto Pinochet also represented a significant blow against impunity for former heads of state charged with international crimes. By the turn of the millennium therefore, the United Kingdom government was advocating foreign policy perspectives that sought to integrate 'moral purpose' with global interests, while consolidating its commitment to international legal norms aimed at punishing those deemed responsible for mass atrocities.

With the invasion of Iraq in March 2003 whatever credibility Prime Minister Blair had regarding matters of human rights and civilian protection was irrevocably destroyed. Even prior to Iraq, the doctrine of 'humanitarian intervention' was already under siege. As a military doctrine that underplayed or ignored preventive, mediated and non-violent coercive measures, humanitarian intervention was incapable of appealing to more than a thin layer of western leaders. As former Australian Foreign Minister Gareth Evans, widely credited as the 'inventor' of R2P, later wrote, 'Blair knew how to rally the North, but his doctrine fell on very deaf ears in the South' (Evans, 2008: 34).

Despite the moral impediment of the Iraq war, the UK played a role in facilitating the adoption of the Responsibility to Protect at the 2005 UN World Summit. Since then it has been a steadfast supporter of R2P in both theory and practice. The UK has appointed a senior government official from its conflict prevention team as a designated 'R2P Focal Point', it has attended all of the annual R2P Ministerial Meetings held on the margins of the UN General Assembly each year, and it has been an strong advocate of R2P perspectives inside the Security Council.

While the UK has at times appeared impatient regarding criticisms by Brazil and other countries regarding the way the R2P mandate was implemented in Libya, Prime Minister Cameron has hinted that he would be prepared to take military action to stop mass atrocities without UN Security Council authorisation. For example, when asked about the deteriorating situation in Syria and the deadlock in the Security Council, in March 2012 Cameron responded by saying that:

> I think Kosovo proved that there are occasions when your responsibility to protect … to save lives, to stop slaughter, to act in a way that is both morally right but also in your own national interest – that there are occasions when you can do that without a UN resolution … I've always thought it odd the argument that because there's a Russian veto, suddenly all the other moral arguments are washed away. I don't believe that. (Ferguson, 2012)

Such action, although morally justifiable, would not be consistent with R2P and would definitely damage the development of the norm. By contrast, the UK has invested heavily in conflict prevention in fragile states and has extensive experience working with local partners in ameliorating conflicts that may result in mass atrocity crimes. At the 2012 interactive dialogue on R2P in the UN General Assembly, Ambassador Tatham captured the essence of this approach:

> The United Kingdom believes that the Responsibility to Protect should be a governing principle of all Member States' work across the conflict spectrum, as well as on human rights and development. Building good governance, the rule of law, inclusive and equal societies, and effective judicial and security sectors all contribute to building a preventive environment in which Responsibility to Protect crimes are less likely to take place.

As the UK government considers its future in a truly multi-polar global political environment it should build upon these laudable achievements.

'Faraway Places' and Global Responsibilities

Ideas have a life of their own. In political terms, 'appeasement' will forever be associated with Neville Chamberlain's 1938 gifting of part of Czechoslovakia to Adolf Hitler. Chamberlain's justification was not just that by giving Hitler someone else's country he could hopefully prevent a wider European war, but also that the German–Czechoslovakian conflict was occurring in 'a faraway country between people of whom we know nothing' (Chamberlain, 1938). For Chamberlain, Czechoslovakia and Germany were strange lands that Britishers need not concern themselves about.

Much has changed since then. Despite the deadening influence of the cold war upon the effectiveness of the UN, the new century has seen genuine progress. Although the UN's inability to halt Syria's horror has been a historic tragedy, it is worth noting that no world leader has suggested that this conflict was simply too distant or obscure for us to be concerned. The magnitude of the crime demands our attention. In this context, the 2005 adoption by the UN of the concept of the 'Responsibility to Protect', represented a historic turning point.

We have won the battle of ideas. Within the UN the debate now is about how R2P should be meaningfully implemented in specific cases, not whether an abstract responsibility exists. Moreover, as of 1 January 2013, we currently have the most pro-R2P UN Security Council in its history. Ten out of 15 members, including the UK, are strong advocates of R2P. We also have a UN Secretary-General who recently stated at a Holocaust memorial, that 'the Responsibility to Protect applies everywhere and all the time' (Ban, 2013).

Rwanda and Srebrenica shaped our understanding of mass atrocities during the 1990s and the magnitude of the UN's failure to live up to a core promise to protect all human beings from crimes that offend our common humanity. But our ability to respond adequately to mass atrocities and implement R2P is still fundamentally a question of political will. The Responsibility to Protect is a pledge our governments made to humanity in 2005. It is a promise we need to hold them to.

POWER AND DIPLOMACY IN THE 21ST CENTURY

CHAPTER 14

What is power in the 21st century?

by Lawrence Korb and Max Hoffman

This century has yet to see its Machiavelli; the most sophisticated analysts of power struggle to do more than ask the right questions. Indeed, we are unlikely to see a magisterial definition of or guide to power comparable to Machiavelli's; the complexity of our world and of the sources and forms of power have multiplied. The very effort to define power in today's world is crowded and contested. In that context, this chapter can be seen as a rebellion against the constant demand for a grand system or strategy through which to understand and deal with the changing international order. Many scholars and practitioners of power seem to require a mechanism into which you enter inputs, push the lever, and receive a desired course of action. But the drive for a system that fits all eventualities may be foolish. North Korea, for example, is an anomaly in the history of the nation-state and no exception by which to judge a potential rule. How can we design a system which accurately grapples with North Korea alongside the European Union or sub-Saharan Africa? Such efforts necessarily require us to dull our analytical edge and downplay the specifics of a situation or place in order to reconcile it with a wider theory. While the search itself may be informative, when theories become prescriptive rather than descriptive they become dangerous. Such prescriptions have led to repeated follies over the early years of the new century and, indeed, the past half-century.

How, then, to understand power in the 21st century? We will establish a more complete definition below, but power itself remains what it has always been: control or influence derived from some combination of force, threats, bribery, and attraction. Continuing to describe the continuity of power in this century, the United States remains the only actor capable of projecting power globally or mobilising large-scale international action.

While the definition of power remains relatively static, the sources and limits of power have been rapidly changing, generating a welter of theories and catchphrases. The world has seen a well-documented diffusion of power since the end of the cold war. There are many more 'vetoes' on the international stage and much more resistive capacity worldwide. This is not just a matter of the much ballyhooed shift away from the United States or 'the West' toward Asia or the collection of rising regional powers, but also a diffusion of power from governments to societies and a diverse array of non-state actors.

Other, longer-running changes continue to gradually reshape the context and composition of power. Rising connectivity between people and countries, encompassing the revolution in digital communication and the continuing growth of international trade, has expanded global access to information and established complex networks of interdependence. Increasing prosperity and mobility have greatly expanded the global middle class, creating new political actors and imposing new demands on governments. This prosperity and connectivity has combined with normative changes to restrict the use of force and shift the needle from the 'hard' end of the power spectrum toward the 'soft' end.

So what does this mean for practitioners of power? First, it demands a transnational focus. There is no need to belabour the litany of transnational problems confronting the international community, from climate change to terrorism, global financial regulation to pandemics. Just because this constant refrain has become tired with use does not diminish its importance, and any country or group capable of mobilising action to address these universal problems will find adherents and power. Equally, any nation ignoring these problems to focus on a narrowly self-interested agenda will engender resistance, both internally and internationally.

Second, interactions on the global stage are increasingly shaped by 'intermestic' concerns. The prosperity, connectivity, and normative shifts outlined above mean that international and domestic politics have become more intertwined than ever before. The rise of new political classes and forms of communication mean that it is possible to interact directly with segments of societies, not just governments or elites. This has important consequences for those in power, requiring them to balance international goals with domestic political and economic concerns more than ever before. Equally, concerns surrounding domestic stability can drive international disputes; one only has to examine the political motives behind Japan and China's brinksmanship in the East China Sea.

Third, legitimacy is increasingly critical to the use of power. Establishing legitimacy – either through democratic elections or by conforming to widely acceptable standards of behavior and rule – has always been central to government. But expanding access to information, newly empowered and politically active global middle classes, the diffusion of power from government to society, and the ability of external actors to interact with segments of a nation's society independent of government all combine to elevate the importance of legitimacy in supporting and sustaining power. Legitimacy also interacts with another source of power, efficiency, by which we mean the capacity of government to take quick, effective action. Both legitimacy and efficiency are sources of power, but it is often necessary to sacrifice one to enhance the other. By way of an example (which we will revisit later), the United States is generally willing to sacrifice some efficiency to increase legitimacy and widen support for a given action. China's current system, in contrast, stresses efficiency of action, generally sparing less concern for questions of legitimacy. But the Chinese Communist Party (CCP) has managed to establish a degree of legitimacy *through* efficiency, premising their rule on rapid economic development and nationalism. We will revisit the complexities of this comparison later, but the CCP's choices have important consequences for their use of power, requiring them to devote resources to domestic security which might otherwise be spent projecting power or influence abroad and reducing their transparency, undermining China's attractiveness to outsiders.

One of the major challenges facing leaders today is a widespread deficit – or crisis – of legitimacy, both nationally and internationally. The concept of legitimacy itself seems to be under assault or decaying, even in places holding free and fair elections, like the United States, Japan, or Turkey. The United States' inability to pass a budget is the most important and highest-profile example of this trend, but entrenched and estranged political opposition along with widespread public mistrust of government itself is slowing or paralyzing many governments around the developed world. Meanwhile, deep cynicism surrounding the legitimacy and efficacy of multilateral bodies has hindered progress on transnational issues. This gridlock at the national and multilateral level will become increasingly dangerous as accessing resources – particularly energy and water – becomes harder. Government legitimacy rests on the ability to meet their people's basic demands. Rising standards of living and population growth have increased these demands, making them harder to meet. Continuing economic and population growth, climate change and resource scarcity, and government gridlock will further complicate this endeavor. Perhaps the central challenge for leaders in the years to come will be to meet the demands of the global middle class while keeping disputes over resources out of the 'hard' power domain and within the confines of 'soft' power.

Defining Power

Joseph Nye, perhaps the preeminent scholar of power active today and the man who coined the phrase 'soft power,' defines power simply as 'getting others to do what you want.' Nye outlines three basic forms of power: coercive power (force them to do as you want), transactional power (buy them), and persuasive power (convince them that your interests align). As you might expect, Nye favours a combination of these three forms of power, a carrot and stick approach he now calls 'smart power.' (Nye, 2011) This 'smart power' model was adopted by President Obama and Secretary Clinton in 2009, manifesting itself largely through the withdrawal from Iraq, reorganisation of and increased funding for the State Department and USAID, and a rhetorical shift away from the aggressive unilateral tone of the Bush administration.

Leslie Gelb, the Pulitzer Prize-winning president emeritus of the Council on Foreign Relations, represents a sharper-edged understanding of power. Gelb is skeptical that power has changed much since the end of the cold war and believes it remains: 'getting others to do what they don't want to do.' Gelb does make concessions to the intervening decades, however, agreeing that great power conflicts have become too costly to be considered due to nuclear weapons and deep economic ties. Likewise, he concedes that the weak powers' ability to resist, at least on home turf, has grown significantly. The outright use of force has been further constrained by normative changes, particularly the rise of international institutions and domestic political constraints enhanced by ubiquitous and instantaneous news coverage. The shortcoming of this aspect of his analysis is that it does not fully acknowledge that many of these shifts were already under way even during the cold war.

But Gelb's approach is a useful corrective to those who go too far in extrapolating current trends, ignoring or underplaying the aspects of continuity on the world stage. He points out that the *balance* of power – by which he means hard power – is still important, pointing to the way in which the United States is still used to balance regional powers, for example in Asia against a more assertive China, in Europe against Russian energy politics, or in the Sunni Arab world against Iran's regional influence. This balancing continues, Gelb argues, because power is inherently psychological and based on the threat of force, though the actual use of force is a concession that your power has failed. Therefore, Gelb sees power today as pyramidal and concentrated at the top with the United States, but with many actors possessing the power to resist, making it tough to get things done or address big problems (Gelb, 2009).

Both Nye and Gelb understand that power is grounded in psychological influence, but they reach different conclusions from that core understanding. To Nye, this central psychological aspect means that power can be wielded through persuasion and attraction, though not in all cases. Gelb doubts the prospect of achieving meaningful influence through persuasion or attraction, and believes the psychological underpinnings of power mean it must, at its core, be based upon the credible threat of force. But Gelb's definitions still essentially deal with force or deterrence, reflecting the cold war context with which he's most familiar. His is an enlightened exposition on hard power and its limits, and a useful corrective to those who venture too far in their rush to redefine power, but narrow in its scope.

Moisés Naím of the Carnegie Endowment for International Peace, on the other hand, is less concerned with uncovering the psychology of power and more focused on understanding how it is changing in today's world. To Naím, power is the 'ability to impose and retain control over a country, a marketplace, a constituency, a population of adherents, a network of trade routes.' And he sees trouble on the horizon for those who wish to maintain such control (Naím, 2013). With this as background, we will turn now outline the basics of hard and soft power, identify the balance of power as it stands today, before delving into the changes to the contours of power on which Naím focuses.

Hard Power

Hard power is essentially the use of force or the threat of its use. It is the oldest form of power and is often the first resort when people are asked to define power. Unfortunately, leaders often lose sight of the shortcomings of hard power – and particularly military force. Important changes, to which we will return, have contributed to the decay of hard power, and military force has seen its long-term effectiveness repeatedly questioned over the last half-century, as its impacts have become more destructive.

At the level of hard power, the United States remains the world's only superpower. Even after recent budget cuts, the United States still spends more on defence than the next 14 nations in the world combined, most of whom are allies. The US currently has 3,029 fourth-generation tactical aircraft – three times more than the nearest competitor – and is the only nation fielding a fifth-generation fighter. The US Navy has 57 nuclear-powered attack submarines or cruise missile carrying submarines; China has just 5, and Russia, 25. The US has ten nuclear-powered super-carriers – the most potent tool of hard power projection ever developed – no other country has more than one. And, of course, the United States had 1,722 deployed nuclear warheads as of September 2012 (Korb et al., 2012). The United States is absolutely preponderant in almost every measurable form of military or hard power.

Some prognosticators are already placing China alongside the United States as a military superpower, but this is premature for a number of reasons. First, while China's military budget has been increasing by roughly 10 per cent per year and is the second largest in world, the absolute balance of hard power remains preponderantly in the West; nearly 60 per cent of global military spending came from North America and Western and Central Europe in 2012 (Stockholm International Peace Research Institute, 2013). Second, much of the increase in China's military budget is a result of rising personnel costs – pay raises to keep pace with rapid economic growth and inflation. Third, the weaponry China is developing is overwhelmingly defensive and inappropriate to the projection of power beyond East Asia. And, fourth, part of the increase from the 1990s is a result of Beijing's effort to compensate the military for losses incurred when it was forced to divest itself of commercial holdings and thus may not represent real growth in military spending (Swaine et al., 2013). In sum, China still has a long way to go to match US military power and modernise their military.

But this should not be a cause for triumphalism, for it reflects a deep and costly imbalance in American priorities. While military force remains an important source of hard power, and the United States remains dominant in that space, this scorekeeping is less important than understanding the limits of hard power and the difficulty of maintaining gains secured through force. For one thing, most developed countries now have costly commitments to their own people's well-being that consume resources which might otherwise go to the military. Additionally, it is no longer acceptable simply to destroy an enemy; one must now fill the ensuing vacuum to meet the normative requirements of the international community and prevent transnational problems like terrorism or secure weapons of mass destruction. Equalisers like guerrilla warfare and more prevalent small arms have also leveled the playing field, not just for the US and its allies in Iraq and Afghanistan in the 2000s, but also in Cuba, Vietnam, and Afghanistan during the cold war (Gelb, 2009).

The use of force also carries negative effects internationally and can undermine national reputation and the very legitimacy of interventions. By failing to account for the importance of acquiring international legitimacy in Iraq, the United States made its brand toxic for at least a decade and made it very difficult to get cooperation from foreign governments. After the Iraq invasion the US lost an average of 30 points in attractiveness in polls across the international community (Nye, 2011). Gelb points out that the invasions of Iraq and Afghanistan paradoxically reduced the prospects of using force against other international pariahs like Iran or North Korea; the over-extension of hard power undermines its effectiveness as a deterrent or psychological tool (Gelb, 2009).

Indeed the few successful deployments of force have come when it has been applied in pursuit of narrow strategic goals by a wide, legitimate coalition of nations. The only major examples are the first Gulf War or the interventions in Bosnia and Kosovo, which were fought by broad coalitions under UN or NATO auspices. By marshaling support and resources and not overextending, Presidents H.W. Bush and Clinton orchestrated successful hard power interventions and established moral supremacy as peacemakers and defenders of international norms (Gelb, 2009). But such examples are rare; overall, military power has become progressively less effective over the last quarter century. In 1977 the world had 89 dictators, while today there are only 23; as Naím succinctly states, those who 'rely on coercion face ever-increasing costs simply to maintain market share and patrol their boundaries' (Naím, 2013).

For the UK, therefore, maintaining basic military deterrence and the ability to contribute to international missions in proportion to its size is crucial, but the real value-added comes from shades of soft power we will discuss below. Given this conclusion, one way to enhance British and international security would be to bring the UK under the US nuclear umbrella and devote the resources freed by that move to finance more useful forms of hard and soft power.

Soft Power

Soft power is basically the power to attract others to your cause or persuade them that your interests align. Soft power is difficult to nail down, which has provoked critiques that it cannot force action and is therefore not true power. Gelb, for instance, argues that because ideas and culture are not universal, appeals to such notions are ineffective (Gelb, 2009). But soft power can attract the best people and help bolster economic strength or foster innovation, thereby enhancing total power. Soft powers of persuasion and consultation help provide legitimacy for action, both at home and internationally. President H.W. Bush's diplomatic efforts, a form of soft power, allowed him to execute hard power action effectively when forced to it.

The United States' ability to mobilise sanctions, a form of economic coercion and therefore falling somewhere between hard and soft power, is rooted in legitimacy based on these efforts at persuasion, outreach, and moral example. This carrot and stick approach has also been called 'smart power,' but such distinctions are largely semantic. Another form of this soft power comes through foreign aid, which generates a degree of goodwill while providing leverage, because it can be withdrawn or withheld. More broadly, soft power is a constant source of strength because it attracts investment and people. For much of the international community, the United States is seen as a positive force and therefore enjoys broad support for international action.

Finally, if power is inherently psychological and based in a core understanding of human nature, then narratives matter. Soft power allows nations to craft stories and demonstrate their strength to the world. Joseph Nye submits the 2008 Beijing Olympics as an example of this 'power to attract,' demonstrating efficiency, unity, and legitimacy, thereby broadcasting China's soft power to the world (Nye, 2011). But more lasting instruments of soft power would be well-developed and respected media entities, like the BBC, Agence France-Presse, CNN, or al-Jazeera. The BBC is broadcast in 33 languages worldwide, reaching 300 million households in more than 200 countries and territories (BBC, 2013). Qatar's al-Jazeera networks, meanwhile, now reach 260 million households in 130 countries (ABU, 2013). These networks provide influence to shape understanding and opinion far beyond the UK or Qatar's ability to exert hard power. Overall, the BBC may be a more effective tool of British foreign policy than the Royal Navy or the British Army.

Similarly, the soft power to attract the best people creates lasting nodes of creativity and influence. Great universities like Oxford, Cambridge, Harvard, MIT, or the Sorbonne provide cutting-edge research, tremendous human capital and expertise, powerful narratives, and a positive introduction to foreign attendees. Centres of capital and innovation like Silicon Valley, Wall Street, or London's City likewise exert outsize power on world affairs, granting tremendous power to their host countries. But this is not a zero-sum power game; these centres provide soft power domains for peaceful competition, allowing China to buy up US treasuries or Western pension funds to invest in infrastructure projects in the developing world. Dismissing the importance of persuasion and attraction in creating and maintaining such centres of influence would be foolish.

Where We Stand

Power is diffused in the world today, spread between more countries than it was for most of the last century, and shared more widely outside of governments and militaries. The most hyped international transition is undoubtedly the shift of power toward Asia. The growth of Asia's economic power, and particularly China's rapid ascent, undoubtedly represents a profound shift in international power. The region's military spending has begun to follow suit – in 2012 military expenditures in Asia exceeded those of the European Union for the first time. The five largest arms importers over the last five years were all Asian countries – India, China, Pakistan, South Korea, and Singapore (Stockholm International Peace Research Institute, 2013). As the International Institute for Strategic Studies (IISS) confidently proclaimed in their highly respected annual report of military power, 'the global shift in military power is continuing' (International Institute for Strategic Studies, 2013).

But we should be careful not to lose sight of the present in our rush to predict the future. Most of the projections of future power are based on the simple extrapolation of current trends in gross domestic product growth and expectations that this growth will translate into military power. This approach is not without merit, but it is rooted in a narrow definition of power – economic growth translated directly to military spending – and ignores the many potential pitfalls and internal contradictions facing the rising powers of Asia. Finally, many prophets of Asia's ascent also assume that the rising powers – and China in particular – will seek to project power globally in the same way that the United States and its allies have done for much of the past 70 years; but there is no conclusive evidence that this is true. Indeed, as Gelb points out, China in particular has been very reluctant to assume a global leadership role, and Westerners may be projecting expectations rooted in Europe and America's long history of global action and intervention (Gelb, 2009).

While the question of shifting power from West to East is complex, there is certainly more resistive capacity in the world today than there was at the end of the cold war. Gelb identifies eight regional powers that occupy the second tier of international power (under the United States, at the top of the pyramid). These powers – China, Japan, India, Russia, the United Kingdom, France, Germany, and Brazil – possess sufficient power to stop action which they oppose in international bodies and within their regional domains. These powers can also contribute meaningfully to action in their spheres or internationally, but they cannot project power globally or mobilise significant international action on their own (Gelb, 2009).

Despite acknowledging the new and old (only China, India, and Brazil are fresh players) rank of countries with 'veto' power over international action, Gelb is pushing back against those who would dismiss the United States as a fading power or declare the 'end of history.' The brilliant Zbigniew Brzezinski, President Carter's National Security Advisor, qualifies as a member of this club; he has declared the 21st century a 'post-hegemonic era' where 'no nation has the capacity to impose its will on others in a substantial or permanent way' (Goldstein, 2013). Brzezinski and the other adherents of this post-hegemonic world view rightly identify the 'shift from West to East,' the 'political awakening of populations until recently politically passive or repressed,' political and budgetary dysfunction in the West, widespread adoption of new forms of unconventional warfare, and the adoption of international norms which preclude the outright massacre of people as contributing to the wide dispersal of power (Kakutani, 2012).

Nonetheless, even Brzezinski maintains that the United States remains the one 'indispensable nation,' and argues that the United States should be nudging Russia towards democracy, embracing Turkey, balancing and conciliating China, and leading efforts to address climate change and water scarcity (Kakutani, 2012). Brzezinski's argument is, most of all, a plea for the revitalisation of American power and foreign policy rather than a eulogy. Indeed, despite the declaration of a post-hegemonic world, it would seem more appropriate to say that the United States cannot 'impose its will on others' in a 'substantial' *or* 'permanent' way.

A more important – and potentially dangerous – trend is the diffusion of power *from* governments, rather than between nations. This development encompasses more than political gridlock, though that is both a symptom and contributing cause – in 30 of 34 Organisation for Economic Co-operation and Development (OECD) member states the head of state faces an opposition controlled parliament (*The Economist*, 2013). Rather, it is the established political parties themselves which are under assault in many places. Brian Katulis and Susan Brooks Thistlethwaite of the Center for American Progress argue that the lowering of barriers to entry into politics has led to a new form of 'open source power.' They point to the example of a radical American preacher's ability to spark an international incident, and provoke responses from the Chairman of the Joint Chiefs of Staff and the Secretary of Defense, by announcing his intention to burn the Koran. This upheaval was enabled by the same wide access to digital technology which allowed Bradley Manning and WikiLeaks to release mountains of sensitive US diplomatic data to the world, fundamentally disrupting the only superpower's foreign policy. Katulis and Thistlethwaite also allude to a wider crisis of legitimacy, due in part to widening access to information, noting that 'religious identity is substituting for national identity as the government loses the people's trust' in many fragile states (Katulis and Thistlethwaite, 2010).

This concept of a crisis of legitimacy might reasonably be expanded to encompass the gamut of popular protest movements which have swept the globe. From the Tea Party movement to Occupy Wall Street and the Arab uprisings (and now the liberal protests in Turkey), popular protests have challenged or overthrown democratically elected governments and repressive regimes alike, with many rejecting the basic legitimacy of their elected officials.

Naím attributes these upheavals to three 'revolutions' – the 'more revolution,' the 'mobility revolution,' and the 'mentality revolution' – which have made people more prosperous, mobile, and thus harder to control. He lays out convincing evidence to support his claims. Global economic output is five times the 1950 level and per capita incomes increased 350 per cent over the same period. Since 1981, 660 million Chinese people have emerged from poverty, and the number of Asians living in extreme poverty dropped from 77 per cent in the 1980s to just 14 per cent in 1998. In the last six years alone, the World Bank says 28 formerly low-income countries climbed into the ranks of middle-income nations. This prosperity has been achieved alongside staggering population growth – there are 2 billion more people today than there were in 1950, and by 2050 the world population will have quadrupled from the 1950 baseline. These trends have swollen the ranks of the global middle class – now comprising 84 per cent of the global population – and widened the pool of literate people with the inclination and means to become politically active (Naím, 2013).

Increased mobility has also made it more difficult for governments to control people. Urbanisation has shaped cities where the sheer scale of human activity creates ungoverned or ungovernable spaces – in 2007, for the first time in history, more people live in cities than rural areas. Internationally, the United Nations estimates that there are currently 214 million migrants worldwide, a 37 per cent increase in the last 20 years. This growth and mobility are interconnected, of course, with remittances reaching $449 million in 2010, five times higher than global foreign aid and more than total foreign direct investment to developing countries (Naím 2013).

Naím's persuasive thesis is that greater prosperity, literacy, mobility, and access to information have combined to greatly expand the body of politically active people worldwide and increase their expectations for representation, responsiveness, inclusion, and the efficient provision of basic government services. These expectations essentially amount to simultaneous demands for greater government legitimacy and efficiency – a challenging goal given the overlapping and inverse interaction between the two impulses. Reaching that goal is also complicated by the demographic youth bulge which has reached adulthood in the past five years and – particularly in the Arab world – by water scarcity and volatile food prices. Increasingly, governments have been unable to meet these high demands, resulting in the turmoil and protest which has overturned the established order across the Mediterranean littoral and shaken its foundations elsewhere.

The paradox of this antipodal power and upheaval is that it has left the actual ability to project power internationally more concentrated in the hands of the United States. While America cannot dictate affairs – far from it, as we have seen in Iraq and Afghanistan – it is left as the only country with the ability to galvanise action in the face of so much resistive capacity and so many actors stymied by chaos or internal transformation. This preeminence – though not hegemony – has not been overturned by the shifting of primacy from military force to economic power. The United States is still the largest economy and consumer market, and is the 'closest thing there is to a manager of the global economy.' Even the financial crisis – which began in America – reaffirmed this reality, as the international response was organised by a weak, lame-duck Bush administration, and skittish investors fled to the safety of the American dollar (Gelb, 2009). What is perhaps most striking today is the success the West has had channeling the quest for economic power through peaceful mechanisms, and keeping economic policy separate from power politics and military or strategic aims. This separation – with relatively rare interactions – is a remarkable departure from past precedent, and deserves greater investigation.

So is the present international condition something wholly new or a reversion to norm – more continuity or more change? How has power itself – or its component parts – shifted?

Has Power Changed?

Many of the trends reshaping the use of power today are not entirely new and were visible through the later stages of the cold war and into the 1990s. The elevation of economic over military power was obscured by the superpowers' frozen military confrontation, but the contest was ultimately won because the United States and the West managed to maintain their economic viability while the Soviet political system collapsed as a result of its economic decline. The capacity of minor powers to resist locally is also not a new phenomenon, as America found in Vietnam and the Soviets discovered in Afghanistan, though it has now become a more widely accepted tenet of international relations. Even the adoption of new norms governing the use of force is not a new development but rather the continuation of a long-term trend. But the elevation of transnational problems and of problems within nations rather than between nations is a new and important dynamic.

Power itself remains the ability to get other people to do what you want, but the change in the discourse surrounding the use of force indicates that normative changes – and the new communications which monitor and enforce those norms – mean nations can no longer 'get away with' the naked use of hard power as they once could. The cost of imposing authority on other countries has become prohibitive, requiring the sacrifice of valuable connections (primarily trade) and the violation of widely held standards of acceptable behavior, which undermines legitimacy and therefore power. Maintaining legitimacy and dealing with and providing for newly politicised segments of society has become more important than traditional geostrategic maneuvering. Only by addressing the demands of these new actors can nations maintain basic functionality and influence on the international stage and avoid being forced into turmoil or constant, costly internal repression.

Therefore, the pursuit of power gains, in the traditional sense as Machiavelli or Hans Morgenthau or John Mearsheimer would understand it, is increasingly self-defeating. In 1990, exports and imports comprised 39 per cent of the world economy; by 2010 they totaled 56 per cent. In the first decade of this century alone the value of merchandise traded across borders nearly doubled, from $6.5 trillion to $12.5 trillion. Foreign direct investment made up 6.5 per cent of the world's economy in 1980, but had risen to 30 per cent by 2010, when $4 trillion changed hands across borders *every day* (Naím, 2013). For countries enmeshed in this network there is far more to lose than to gain by attempting to impose their will upon others through hard power. Large-scale military conflict between the major powers has become unthinkable except in the event of madness, mishap, or internal collapse.

In this connected world 'intermestic' relations and the ability to engage with segments of societies, and not just governments, will continue to grow in importance. The new middle classes in countries like China, India, and Brazil represent huge new markets for political discourse and the 'soft power' tools of persuasion Nye advances. The infrastructure for such engagement is in place: in 2010, mobile subscriptions reached 78 people per 100, up from 0.2

per 100 in 1990, and internet users comprised 30 per cent of the world population and 73 per cent of the developed world (Naím, 2013). The US embassy in Beijing's practice of tweeting independent air-quality readings is an example of this form of interaction (US Department of State, 2013). The spread of access to information makes these new global citizens potential targets of interaction, coercion, and persuasion.

This new terrain of competition and persuasion lends greater importance to the central question of legitimacy, a core component of power and authority generally maintained through democratic elections or by conforming to widely acceptable standards of behavior and rule. Legitimacy combines with efficiency – the capacity of a government to take quick, effective action – to constitute a reservoir of power or political capital which can be spent to take action domestically or internationally. Efficiency can enhance or even replace legitimacy, but is becoming increasingly difficult to sustain as the middle class expands, population growth continues, and competition for resources increases.

As outlined above, expectations of government legitimacy and efficiency have changed with the emergence of new middle classes around the world, and failing to meet these requirements can lead to potentially crippling discontent. These shifting obligations are visible in the polling of the World Values Survey, which has found a growing global consensus on the importance of individual rights, equality, and the rejection of authoritarian rule (Naím, 2013). This trend was dramatically demonstrated in the Arab uprisings, where illegitimate governments failed basic efficiency tests and were overthrown by newly empowered political sectors. Where legitimacy was more secure, as in the United States or Turkey, the political systems have been able to weather storms caused by inefficiency or a minority's perception of illegitimacy. Examples include the Tea Party and Occupy Wall Street movements in the United States or the Gezi Park protesters in Turkey.

But the trend is playing out in less spectacular ways elsewhere. China offers a fascinating counterpoint to the Arab world and the West, and casts light on the exact interaction of legitimacy and efficiency. China's recent leadership transition was a carefully orchestrated effort to achieve internal consensus among the CCP – a limited form of legitimacy – to ensure continuity in the eyes of a citizenry who, 'despite living under an authoritarian regime, are finding myriad ways to express their deep frustration with the direction their nation is headed' (Hart, 2012). The CCP has premised their legitimacy upon efficiency – delivering economic growth and lifting millions of Chinese people out of poverty.

But that form of power gets progressively more difficult to maintain. For one thing, it requires a completely unified public façade, but 'negotiations get more contentious with every leadership transition, each [more] removed from the Communist Party strongman eras.' Likewise, the core proposition of efficient government is made more difficult by success; as people rise into the middle class their expectations grow higher. Melanie Hart, a China expert at the Center for American Progress, captures this challenge, writing that:

> the transition from export- and investment-led growth to domestic consumption-led growth … and from lifting tens of millions out of abject poverty to satisfying a more demanding middle class will be even harder for the party to execute. The reason: It will require the kind of deft governing skills that authoritarian regimes are generally not good at using. (Hart, 2012)

This captures the quandary facing China's leadership; by eschewing transparency and the shades of soft power and persuasion necessary to win elections, they limit the legitimacy they can acquire. Lacking legitimacy in the usual sense of the word, the CCP must rely on an efficient mix of hard power – domestic security forces and repression – and bribery – consistent economic growth – to maintain power.

China's choice of power has important international repercussions, requiring them to spend more money on internal security than on defence from other nations. The CCP's lack of transparency also undermines their international power; foreign powers and investors are interested in China's currency reserves and economic opportunities, but few global elites choose to move to China or send their children to be educated there. The Shanghai Cooperation Organisation, China's answer to NATO, has likewise failed to attract other nations to its ranks. China possesses great economic clout and many traditional tools of power, but is reluctant or unable to use them to greatly influence events outside East Asia. China has become a world power, but it is unclear if it can be a world leader. The regime's lack of transparency means many of the new global middle class mistrust the CCP's intentions and doubt their commitment to promoting universal values.

Conclusion

How then will the West respond to this new international terrain? First, we must preserve and expand the normative shifts achieved over the past half-century. Limits on hard power may at times frustrate our ability to achieve narrow strategic goals, but they are crucial to the central challenge of keeping looming resource disputes out of the hard power domain. Moreover, these normative changes – the fact that, broadly speaking, it is no longer acceptable to destroy cities or massacre people, even in a widely accepted 'just cause' – reflect the finest values of the West and the new international community.

Hopefully, reinforcing this normative system will provide more countries with a sense of security and allow for more resources to be devoted to transnational problems, for we face a daunting array of challenges in this field. Adapting to and mitigating climate change should be top of the list, and will require far deeper and more sustained commitment from the international community. Climate change will exacerbate already dire water shortages, increase volatile and rising food prices, disrupt commodity markets, contribute to migratory movements, and strain basic governance with its slow- and sudden-onset impacts. Other tasks include crafting new rules for cyber interaction, shaping more effective financial regulations, combating extremism, and continuing progress on the Millennium Development Goals.

To make progress on these problems, the United States and its allies are still the primary global actor(s). For the UK, international power will increasingly become the ability to foster legitimacy and cooperate with the United States and the international community to solve these transnational problems. With the certainty of offending our British colleagues, we believe the UK is now much like the junior partner in a parliamentary coalition; they are only capable of meaningful action as part of the coalition, and so must pull their share while using their clout to demand moral and legitimate courses of action. But the UK – and other NATO allies – has competitive advantages in many soft power domains, due in part the enduring importance of London and Britain's great universities, and in part to deep historical ties to problematic regions. The United States cannot hope to match the influence of the BBC in Africa, for example, nor can its State Department match the depth and breadth of Britain's connections to India. Britain provides expertise, experience, and long-standing diplomatic and economic ties in areas where others lack influence.

Once more, then, what is power in the 21st century? The power to understand, not just your own situation but the way in which your partners or contestants understand the situation, has become more important than ever. Attempting to precisely calculate power, something which cannot be quantified, demonstrates an interesting phenomenon. You end up changing your inputs until your output reflects some deeply held pre-conception of who is most powerful and who is least powerful. Everyone knows in their heart of hearts that the United States is the most powerful country in the world, with China and Russia still far behind. To be sure, this understanding has roots in quantifiable sources like divisions and airplanes and gross domestic product. But equally sure is the fact that it is heavily influenced by unscientific, psychological, or emotional instinct. And it is that source of power, ephemeral as it is, which is so hard to pin down and understand.

The difficulty inherent in understanding this ephemeral source of power is illustrative. 'Soft power,' or whatever you choose to call it, is fleeting and fragile. Often, as the United States has found, when you reach for the tool of soft power, you find it evaporates in your hand. But the fragility of soft power does not diminish its importance, for it helps shape the perception and context of hard power, particularly the use and the threat of force. We should therefore be exceedingly careful in taking steps which can damage this reservoir of soft power, and instead marshal resources to counter truly important threats to the global order.

In the end, power is intensely contextual, and ascribing a static definition to power is folly – the form of power that matters is the form of power your opponent values, shifting with your gaze. And so the requirement for a grand system of belief is self-defeating and will continue to guide us into costly mistakes, because the world is simply too complex for all-encompassing systems. We should instead rely on soft barriers rather than hard-and-fast rules, and let general goals and principles guide case-by-case cost-benefit analyses.

CHAPTER 15

New challenges for diplomacy in the digital age

by Alec Ross and Ben Scott

Mass protests in 20 countries denounce the United States. Thousands demonstrate at the walls of US embassies across the Middle East – breaching the perimeters. Violent clashes leave dozens of dead and wounded. These were the tragic headlines in September 2012 as a wave of anti-American protest swept Muslim-majority countries. The high drama of diplomatic crisis in Cairo drew out the Egyptian President to calm the conflict between security forces and angry crowds that scaled the walls of the US embassy. More than 200 were reported injured. In neighbouring Libya, an opportunistic terror attack – operating in the thrum of public outrage across the region – stormed the US diplomatic outpost in Benghazi, killing the ambassador and three of his staff. An American school in Tunis was attacked and looted. Tens of thousands marched in Baghdad and Gaza; 100,000 in Islamabad; 125,000 in Karachi.

What triggered this terrible rage and the carnage that followed? It was not a drone strike or a midnight commando raid. It was not an incendiary remark from a White House official or an errant Congressman. It was not an act of any kind by the US government, its military, or its intelligence services. It was a 14-minute YouTube video entitled 'The Innocence of Muslims.' An absurd and grotesque production, it depicted scenes featuring savage acts ostensibly committed by Muslims. It was made with very little money for the express purposes of insulting Islam. It was most likely uploaded in July 2012 by a 55-year-old man with absolutely zero involvement in the US government, zero claim to representing anyone in American politics, and zero credibility as a voice in international affairs. In fact, he was just out of jail on parole after his conviction for financial fraud.

This episode provides an alarming example of how diplomacy and international politics have been disrupted by network technologies and the information revolution. Consider that 72 hours of video are uploaded to YouTube worldwide every minute of every day. Consider that this particular video sat idly on YouTube for two months before its circulation became viral and exposed it to a global audience. Of course, this video was not itself sufficient to cause protests and riots. It was a match that fell into a tinderbox of pent-up frustration and anger. But it is undeniably true that the actions of this unknown bigot in California led directly to the deaths of dozens and the injury of hundreds – not to mention a global diplomatic crisis whose impact will ripple across the Middle East for years.

The point here is simple. In the internet age, anyone with a laptop or a smart-phone has the potential to become a potent actor on the global stage. The disruption of international relations is no longer exclusively the business of nation states, armies, or global economic forces. It can be triggered by individuals and groups of individuals using the power of the internet. Of course there is no such thing as a Twitter or a YouTube revolution. Technology does not cause social and political change by itself. But it enables, catalyzes, and accelerates existing forces of change in ways that were previously impossible. The phenomenon at play in 'The Innocence of Muslims' has parallels in the use of social media to build political movements during the Arab spring. We can also see it when mobile phones become recording devices that bring images of war crimes and atrocities to the world; or critical tools for election monitoring at far-flung polling stations; or information networks for political candidates who reject the mainstream media as the primary means to promote their views.

Our challenge in diplomacy is not to predict the path of these changes. That is all but impossible. Our challenge is to understand the logic of social and political change as it intersects with digital networks. And our job is to modernise a diplomacy that can respond quickly and effectively to this new logic. Diplomats are in the information business. The information business is fundamentally changing. And so diplomats must change with it or risk becoming considerably less relevant.

Part 1: Expanding Access and Agency in a Global Network

The internet is not a new technology – people have been connected since the 1980s and the mass distribution of the web browser in the mid 1990s ensured a rapid global expansion. However, for many of the world's internet users, it remains a relatively new experience. The extension of undersea cables, the modernisation of broadband infrastructure, and the deployment of 3G and 4G mobile networks have converged to create rapid expansions of affordable internet access in many countries just in the last few years. Currently, more than 2 billion people are online. A very substantial number (soon to be a majority) live in developing countries. Of those, a majority are connected through smart-phones. As the number of global internet users doubles in the years ahead, these trends toward Global South and mobile will continue. This means that the kinds of disruptive changes to politics, society and economics that hit the West in the late 1990s are just about to arrive in much of the world. Access to infinite information resources and ubiquitous global communications at low cost is transformative. What remains to be seen is exactly what will be transformed, when, and by whom.

The foundational work for building new kinds of diplomatic practice begins with a serious effort to understand the nature of the relationship between network technologies and social change. At the centre of the transformation is a convergence of information networks – what we have often called the 'triple paradigm shift.' This idea simply describes our current situation in the context of history. In the last three centuries of modern society, three different types of information networks have evolved: (1) economic information systems; (2) mass media; and (3) personal communications. The first of these refers to the way in which buyers and sellers in the marketplace exchange information about prices, purchase orders, inventories, and other matters of commercial trade. This information network has long coincided with the transportation system. Shipping lanes, railroads, highways and then skyways carried not only goods and materials, but also the bill of sale. Today, the internet has become the new and dominant information infrastructure of the global economy. The evolution of networks is easier to see in mass media. Through the 20th century, newspapers gave way to radio, broadcast television, cable/satellite television, and now the internet. And personal communications have moved through the postal system to the telegraph, telephone, and now to the internet. All three paradigms have shifted together in the 21st century to converge on the same information infrastructure. It is governed by every nation state in part but no one as a whole. Interlocking networks are ubiquitous, interdependent, and their functions inseparable. It is no longer possible to talk about governing the mass media system separately from the information networks of the economy and society.

Add to this structural change in the information system a new logic of information production, consumption and distribution. Broadly speaking, we are moving away from a 'hub-and-spoke' model towards a network model. The traditional, 'vertical' institutions of information creation and distribution – mass media companies, brand-name newsrooms, government information offices, and prominent social leaders – have lost a significant measure of control and influence. Citizen reporters, blogosphere echo-chambers, social media chatter, and constant interaction among internet users have created a 'lateral' movement of information that moves peer-to-peer across the network. The power brokers of modern information systems are not in the centre – there is no centre any more – they are in the nodes of the network. On the whole, this process has led to a decentralisation of power in our societies. This does not happen all at once or in the same way everywhere. It is gradual, oscillating, and apolitical. But it is the reason why a delusional ex-convict in southern California can make a YouTube video that causes mass protests around the world. Diplomacy must recognise these new power dynamics and assess how they will impact the business of foreign relations.

The logic of networked information and shifting power dynamics shapes the course of social, political and economic events. Among these, the impacts on the market have been the best documented elsewhere. And although these economic changes are highly relevant to the work of diplomats, we will not dwell on them here. Instead, we will focus our attention on new kinds of policy issues and the changes in diplomatic practices that they portend.

Foreign policy-makers must increasingly focus on three over-lapping fields of policy development – internet freedom, internet governance, and cyber-security. The first is a rights-based agenda that addresses the extension of traditional human rights issues into the digital environment – freedom of expression, freedom of the press, and freedom of association and assembly. Although none of these rights is new to foreign policy, the application of these rights on the internet brings a host of risks and opportunities. For example, when a country chooses to violate the human rights of individuals who voice dissent from a soapbox on the street corner, there is little the international community can do other than condemn the practice and pressure the perpetrating government to reverse course. The results here are often frustratingly meager. When the dissenting voices are online, the situation changes. The offended government may still take steps to arrest the author – assuming they can identify and locate the individual inside their physical borders. And the international community may take the same traditional course of condemnation. However, there are now other alternatives. Led by the US State Department, many governments have begun to support the creation and distribution of technologies designed to support human rights by enabling the circumvention of content censorship and the evasion of surveillance using encryption. In addition, governments may place controls on the export of technologies that enable the kind of surveillance that may restrict human rights. In this context, the right to privacy has become a core part of the digital foreign policy agenda. These practices are now firmly a part of diplomatic practice in some ministries, but we are at the beginning rather than the end of their development.

A second area of policy change consists of a large group of questions under the heading of internet governance. Most specifically, these issues deal with the specific administration of the physical networks that make up the internet, the adoption of global technical standards, and the allocation of domain names and IP (internet protocol) addresses that form the nervous system of the internet. From its inception, these tasks of internet governance have been handled by multi-stakeholder institutions that include government, commercial, and civil society participation. Decisions are usually consensus based, and the organisational principle is mutual cooperation for mutual benefit. As the power of the internet to create economic growth and political disruption grows, the control over these decisions has come into hot dispute. Many governments – led by China, Russia and certain Gulf States – have sought to wrest control away from distributed international organisations and re-centralise it in the hands of governments and intergovernmental organisations. The consequences of this debate could be severe, including the balkanisation of the internet into national and regional networks that operate according to different rules and standards.

Mixed into this power struggle over technical administration are other major policy decisions about the shape and functions of the global internet. These issues include: (1) the deployment of new mobile networks that interconnect technically and physically at the borders; (2) the spread of cross-border social media and with it content and services that are legal in one nation and illegal in others; (3) the growing dominance of so-called 'cloud' services that place data storage and processing in distributed data centres outside the legal jurisdiction of national governments; (4) and, finally, the emergence of 'big data' as the social and economic asset that will drive development in the next generation of services on the network. Policies rooted in social values – privacy, transparency, cultural norms, law enforcement, intellectual property, and taxation – must each be negotiated through international norms of behavior that are consistent or reconcilable with legal norms at home. In short, each nation governs these outcomes for its own people, but depends upon interoperability to take part in the international marketplace of ideas and commerce. This makes for a delicate and difficult balance among conflicting visions for the future of the internet.

A third area of policy focus – with a political profile far larger than the others – is cyber-security. Of course, much of this issue will be settled by defence, military, and intelligence policy making. But there are a variety of problems that are essentially diplomatic. The basic question is simple: what should a nation do to protect itself from cyber-attacks that do not rise to the level of military conflicts but nonetheless result in significant economic loss through espionage and theft of valuable information? Governments have done fairly well working together to address problems they all share – non-state actors (such as transnational criminal organisations) committing cyber-crimes that result in economic loss. Diplomats have helped to negotiate important multilateral cooperation to track criminals who exploit the internet. The much more difficult problem emerges when the origin of the cyber-espionage or cyber-attack is state-sponsored. Of course, governments will not acknowledge responsibility. And precise attribution is notoriously difficult. Consequently, almost all of this behavior occurs with impunity. The costs are mounting. The best response of diplomacy thus far is to conduct painstaking international dialogues to establish norms and confidence-building measures. Results are elusive and tangible changes in behavior seem far in the future. The most sophisticated cyber intrusions continue unabated. The security weaknesses in critical infrastructure networks – both public and privately operated – make this stalemate an alarming situation. Yet there are no clear answers yet devised. If and when there is a serious cyber-incident that results in major loss of life or economic disruption, we may see a far more serious effort to address these problems. But at that point, it is not likely to be a nuanced policy that takes into consideration human rights and the delicate balancing act of internet governance.

For years, these issues have been designated as peripheral to the central matters of foreign policy. But they are not. They are deeply tied to major questions of global geo-politics. For example – view the current situation in Russia through this lens. A meaningful part of the current centralisation of power by Putin and his allies is in response to the protest movements in the last two years that were catalyzed by the internet. The original protests in late 2011 were triggered by allegations of corruption in the Duma elections – much of it documented by mobile phone images and videos of dubious activity at polling stations. Alexei Navalny is among the most prominent opposition leaders to face a show trial – and his power and influence are almost entirely derived from his following as a popular blogger exposing political corruption. The international furore over the jailing of the young women in the punk band 'Pussy Riot' was triggered by the social media accounts of their political protest, arrest, and prosecution. No other incident has focused so much international attention on the Russian government's control over freedom of expression. Meanwhile, the government has put significant resources into its own online communications apparatus. Setting aside investment in and attention to digital surveillance, the online influence of United Russia and other forces aligned with Putin have increased substantially in the last year. In the policy arena, the Russian government has been at the forefront of the effort to challenge the distributed system of internet governance and demand its centralisation. On internet freedom and cyber-security, its cooperation with international organisations might be generously characterised as foot-dragging and double-speak.

But the news about technology policy and foreign affairs is not all bad. For example, during the conflict in Libya, Gaddafi cut off all communications networks bound for the rebel-held territories in the east of the country. In an unprecedented effort that mirrors the logic of a decentralised internet, a variety of different counter-measures were taken. In Benghazi, a group of engineers managed to reconfigure infrastructure to re-start one of the mobile telephone networks for internal calling. A group led by a Libyan ex-pat arranged for support and equipment from Gulf state telecommunications companies to set up a satellite link that gave internet access to the rebel government. Another group succeeded in a technical and diplomatic effort to connect eastern Libya via fiber-optic cables to Egyptian telecommunications lines stretching through the desert. All of this work was driven by the belief of Libyan leaders and the supporters of their political revolution that network communications would be an essential part of their success – not only for government and military communications but also so that the people might tell their stories of conflict, tragedy and triumph to the world. Today, the new Libyan government has put a premium on building a knowledge economy. And some of the leaders of the ad hoc revolutionary technology projects are now in charge of building a network of international partners (government, commercial and civil society) to help expand affordable access to the internet, train a generation of young engineers and entrepreneurs, and foster a vibrant marketplace of ideas online.

In Tunisia, the revolution was famously stoked by a generation of young people connected via Facebook and deeply resentful of the censorship and surveillance practiced by the Ben Ali dictatorship. The meme of '404 error' (the message that appears on screen when a web browser attempts to access a page that has been blocked) became a symbol of the revolution and an organising slogan of the youth movement. In post-revolutionary Tunisia, a remarkable transformation has occurred. The Tunisian internet Agency – once the leading edge of Ben Ali's censorship apparatus – has become a champion for internet freedom and digital economic growth. Tunisia has become a member of the Freedom Online Coalition – a group of 19 countries that have pledged commitments to freedom of expression online and coordinated international advocacy. The censorship equipment that once policed the internet in Tunisia now sits stacked in a dusty corner – a stark reminder to the leadership of an agency with a renewed mission to promote affordable access, open networks, and freedom online.

The risks and opportunities opened at the intersection of technology and foreign policy are numerous and will continue to rise in importance on the ledger of international politics. We are just at the tipping point of the powerful changes driven by 2 billion global internet users. This is just the beginning. To respond effectively, diplomacy will have to adapt quickly and adapt now.

Part 2: Adapting the Institutions of Diplomacy

The US Department of State is known for many things. Nimble, innovative leadership in technology policy and practice had never been among them. When Hillary Clinton became Secretary of State in 2009, she determined to change that. Her objective was not to create a new structure within the department bureaucracy to tackle internet issues. Her objective was to integrate technology policy and practice – a new way of thinking about networks and diplomacy – into every office and embassy in the system. She called this initiative 21st-century Statecraft. It did not seek to invent diplomacy anew, but to build on existing practices of diplomacy and adapt them to harness the power of network technologies to advance the diplomatic and development goals of US foreign policy. Under her leadership, it was remarkably and rapidly successful.

The work that built 21st-century Statecraft stretched across the institution, from the headquarters in Washington to the most far-flung embassy. Its success was based on the ingenuity of hundreds of people enabled by a directive from the top that experimentation in new forms of digital diplomacy would be encouraged. In an environment that encourages innovation, mistakes of commission are better than mistakes of omission. Occasional short term failures are a part of the recipe for longer-term success. We experienced plenty of both. In an ironic twist, it was traditional hierarchical leadership (from Hillary Clinton) that enabled edge-of-network innovation.

Comprehensive Reform

On the surface, 21st-century Statecraft became best known for social media. And indeed, the use of social media as a part of diplomatic communications became widespread under Secretary Clinton, and it has slowly been normalised into the work of many foreign ministries. But the larger story of reform is that the highly visible practices of digital communications are linked to a comprehensive agenda that includes technology policy and programmatic work that leverages information and communications networks. Technology is not important for its own sake. It is important only insofar as it is integrated into the overall strategy for diplomatic engagement.

What do we mean by the strategic integration of new technology into diplomatic practice? Let's unpack the use of social media as a tool of public diplomacy. It is not just about public relations – reaching new audiences with the same message distributed via traditional media. That is the most common understanding and use of social media, but it is not the most important. As a diplomatic tool, social media should be primarily a listening and engagement tool. Diplomats are deployed around the world to better understand what is happening there, describe and analyze what they see and hear, and use those reports to inform better foreign policy decisions. In this context, social media's most valuable features are the insights it yields about political views and social movements among people whose voices are otherwise hard to find. In countries that make broad use of social media, it is no longer necessary to rely merely on our instincts to speculate about the views of particular social groups. They have public voices of their own, media channels for their communities, and active engagement with anyone willing to listen.

If engagement is the true strategic goal of social media as public diplomacy, that necessarily changes the way speakers choose content, tone, frequency, and target audiences. Illustrative and occasionally provocative content matters. Responsiveness matters. Social media is not a glorified press list – it is a community. This thesis informed the State Department's digital strategy. We were surprised at the results. Millions followed US government diplomats on Facebook, Twitter, and other language-specific social media forums. A study by the Brookings Institution projected that the US State Department would reach more than 20 million people per day on Facebook and Twitter alone by the middle of 2013.

But 21st-century Statecraft does not begin and end with good tweets. The way that we *use* the internet – social media and other demonstrations of digital competence – is linked to our policy views *about* the internet and our real-world practices to promote internet access and adoption. Take an issue like internet freedom. It is a moral principle – a value proposition that we seek to promote around the world, largely by trying to persuade other governments and societies to value it in the way that we do. How is that done? In part, it is about practicing what we preach. It is about having policies at home that demonstrate our own commitments to internet freedom. It is about using the internet as a tool of speaking, listening, and convening that embraces and embodies those principles of openness. And it is about using our resources (financial, human, and knowledge) to promote access and adoption of the internet in places where people are disconnected.

Virtually every challenge in the foreign policy work surrounding internet issues requires this multi-layered strategy. It comes with the 'triple paradigm shift' we described earlier. Facebook isn't just a personal communications network. It is a platform for commerce. And it is a new distribution system for mass media outlets. In diplomatic practice, we have to consider it in each of these ways. Returning to the example of Tunisia, this takes on a very practical meaning for diplomats at headquarters or in the embassy responsible for bilateral engagement.

On the surface, we can see that Tunisia is a remarkably heavy social media using country. More than 30 per cent of adults are on Facebook. Any communications plan that doesn't include social media is a failure. Meanwhile, Tunisia is a budding champion for internet freedom – a signature policy issue of a digital human rights agenda that requires partnership, support, and coordination. Linked to these are big opportunities to support the development of a digital economy in Tunisia through cooperation to extend infrastructure, improve network capacity, incubate entrepreneurial businesses and forge partnerships to encourage investment. Add to this work consultations on international policy issues like internet governance, cyber-security, and digital commerce. Development work can also take its cue from Tunisia's technology adoption rates. In the wake of the Tunisian revolution, the State Department partnered with a Tunisian telecommunications provider to offer a free mobile phone application with English-language lessons. It was an experimental project that enjoyed considerable success and popularity.

Human Capital

The pace of change in technology and foreign policy is rapid. The recipes for success today will be outdated within two to three years and require fresh ideas. The natural comfort zone of bureaucratic institutions – to establish a conventional practice and repeat that practice – is ill-suited to this work. Consequently, the most important prescription for ministries that seek to excel in this space is a to focus investments and development on human capital. Bringing diplomatic practice into the 21st century isn't about adding an advisor, an office, or even a bureau. It's about integrating a new way of thinking into the core of what we do – cutting across all elements of diplomacy, policy, and development. To do that, you have to have a great many people who believe it is important, exciting, interesting and worth their time and effort to push through disappointments and growing pains to find successful practices. To that end, foreign ministries must:

- create space for non-traditional thinking;
- change practices in leadership, management;
- retool the workforce through extensive training and non-hierarchical advancement;
- lean toward transparency rather than secrecy in diplomatic reporting;
- focus on recruitment, examination and hiring processes to find new kinds of talent;
- cycle experts and specialists at middle/senior levels into the workforce on a biannual basis;
- promote and support a culture of new diplomatic practice.

To be successful in continuous innovation in diplomacy, we must internalise a new model of what it means to be a diplomat. That is not to say that conventional diplomatic engagement and state-to-state consultations have been turned upside down. They have not.

It means simply that these practices must adapt to a new logic of information systems. This logic is what informs political decisions in governments, guides public opinion, and shapes new social and political movements. The sources of information production have decentralised. Distribution is now networked peer-to-peer in addition to hub-and-spoke. And consumption patterns are accelerated, diversified, and intensified. All of these trends change the methods of belief formation, social cohesion, and personal decision-making. Our diplomatic practices and self-identification must adjust to this new reality.

It is an exciting if daunting opportunity, but it is hard to pretend that foreign ministries are not due for a change. Our model of diplomacy is premised on a 19th-century idea of information scarcity – that we carried forward into the 20th century. The idea is that we have diplomats posted around the world who are there to help our citizens in those countries, but also to collect and process information about what is happening in those parts of the world to help inform foreign policy making back home in the capital. The scarce resource that we invested time to gather and nurture was valuable information and insightful analysis – largely distilled from political elites and what exposure we could get to the general public.

In the 21st century, that information is no longer particularly scarce. The internet makes it possible for anyone anywhere to read, hear, and watch the primary information sources in virtually every country in the world – and, what's more, social media allows that same global audience to hear from thousands of new voices that are closer to the communities that they represent. We have an information abundance problem; not an information scarcity problem.

What is most interesting in retrospect about the WikiLeaks cables now is not how many contained incendiary secrets or embarrassing disclosures. It is the high per centage that did not, but rather exposed the State Department officials who wrote them as very intelligent, competent observers of their environment. We need to begin asking ourselves about the return on investment of all of this information processing and look at other ways we might allocate our resources – financial and human.

Such a review is likely to find that we can begin to back off of the information gathering and distilling business. Much of what is gathered, summarised and distributed is not read – and even more of it is already available somewhere on the internet. A part of our long-term digital strategy should be to focus on the value that can be added exclusively by public engagement via a highly talented diplomatic corps. This means more time spent outside the embassy. More time spent talking and less writing. To the extent that we are relying on local observers to make meaning and insight out of local media sources – we should focus on combinatorial analysis that integrates a conventional media, new media, and interpersonal interaction. For forward-leaning leaders in diplomacy, none of these recommendations will be newsworthy. They are evident and driving change already. But until this analysis becomes conventional wisdom, we are unlikely to see the kind of systemic change that will optimise results in a 21st-century Statecraft.

Conclusion: Adaptability – Key to Success

The measure of our success will not be predicting the future, it will lie in our versatility, open-mindedness, and willingness to experiment and innovate. Our mission should be first to increase the speed of our adaptation to change. Second, we should focus on reducing the practices of our institutions that resist experimentation, punish innovation, and enforce old models and standards. These simple strategies will look different for different institutions at different times and places – but the motivations will be the same. This is a process that we should expect to take a generation. And while that may give comfort to those who favour slow change – the advantages to be gained from successful digital practice (and the disadvantages that will burden those that do not have these skills) will be considerable. We will mark a major step forward when the idea of 21st-century Statecraft is an anachronism that describes what contemporaries view as the perfectly normal business of diplomacy.

CHAPTER 16

Insider and outsider: The UK's enduring capacity for influence

by Robin Niblett

Previous chapters in this book have focused upon the international context for British foreign policy. The authors have addressed the global changes and challenges that will affect the UK, from nuclear proliferation to climate change; the status of the United States, which remains the UK's principal ally on the world stage; the rise of new powers; and the health of those international institutions within which the UK concentrates its diplomatic effort. This chapter assesses the UK's capacity to exert international influence within a changing international context. It explores the resources available to the UK, relative to others, and the political and popular support upon which its leaders seek to take action. The chapter also considers the UK's current role within international institutions. If there is one distinguishing feature of the 21st century it appears to be the inability of countries to address international challenges on their own or to exert genuine international leadership. It is important, therefore, to consider the effectiveness of the international institutions through which the UK conducts its diplomacy and seeks to leverage its power. Are these institutions in the ascendance or in decline? Is the UK's position within them becoming stronger or weaker?

In this chapter, I argue that Britain has the potential to retain its capacity for international influence, even though it faces a number of near-term challenges. In order to live up to its potential, Britain's leaders must concentrate on two factors. The first is to ensure that the UK sets its economy on a path to sustainable and productive growth. Without a strong economic base, Britain's many attributes for international influence will begin to erode. Second, the UK will need to leverage its national and diplomatic strengths more proactively and challenge the status quo more frequently if it is to be influential in promoting its values and interests. Britain's position within those key institutions and relationships that helped promote its interests over the past 60 or so years is now more precarious. It risks being less influential in the UN Security Council in a world of rising powers; less relevant to the United States as US leaders focus more on Asia; less significant in a leaderless G20 world than one led by the G8; and a more detached member of the European Union. It will need to adapt, therefore, to being more of a 'fringe insider' at the multilateral level. Diplomatic excellence will be measured increasingly by the UK's ability to set specific policy agendas in a globally competitive international environment and less by its capacity to serve as a highly regarded mediator between sometimes divergent Western views.

A Changing and Challenging Context

As the title of this book indicates, British diplomacy is seeking to adapt to a rapidly changing world. A number of studies have outlined the key features of this emerging context.[1] Among the most prominent trends are a global economic re-balancing from West to East and North to South and a longer-term shift in global political power in the same direction. At the same time, the power of the state is

---

[1] US National Intelligence Council (NIC), *Global Trends 2030: Alternative Worlds* (Washington, DC: NIC, 2012), http://www.dni.gov/files/documents/ GlobalTrends_2030.pdf; European Union Institute for Security Studies (EUISS), *Citizens in an Interconnected and Polycentric World* (Paris: EUISS, 2012) ; and Robin Niblett, *Playing to its Strengths: Rethinking the UK's Role in a Changing World* (London: Chatham House, 2010).

being challenged by unpredictable forces of individual 'empowerment', involving ever-more influential non-state actors and a mass
middle class connected through information networks. This 'polycentric world' poses particular challenges to the UK, both to its
future prosperity and to the influence it can project internationally.
The UK has enjoyed a privileged position in a Western-led world
order that may soon be eclipsed.

A country's power and influence in international affairs reflect
a combination of factors. The first are national and build upon its
material and human capabilities, along with the ability to apply political will-power towards international objectives. By this measure, the
UK is in relative decline, and has been so for the last few decades.
Following the global financial crisis of 2008, its economic position
has subsided further relative to that of most of the rest of the world.[2]
In the first quarter of 2013, the UK's GDP was estimated to be
3.9 per cent below its 2008 pre-crisis peak.[3] The global financial
crisis has exerted severe pressure on an economy that was especially
dependent on credit to drive growth through the first half of the
2000s and on tax revenue from the financial sector in order to pay
rising bills for public services. Nor can the UK rely any longer on
windfall profits from the domestic oil and gas sector which will form
a declining proportion of government revenues and national wealth
in the coming decades. The impact of the eurozone crisis on the
rest of the EU has also highlighted the UK's under-achievement in
penetrating emerging economies with manufactured exports. The
UK's share of global GDP declined from 3.2 per cent in 2008 to

---

[2] See, for example, the UK's ranking in terms of household disposable income
per head. According to the OECD, the UK ranked twelfth in the world, falling
down a list of other advanced economies including the United States, Australia,
Canada and a number of Britain's European counterparts. Claire Jones,
'Britons slip down world ready-cash table', *Financial Times*, 14 May 2013,
http://www.ft.com/cms/s/0/02703f38-bcac-11e2-b344-00144feab7de.
html#axzz2XtaMGnIq.
[3] Office of National Statistics, *Quarterly National Accounts, Q1 2013*, Statistical
Bulletin, 27 June 2013 (London: ONS, 2013), http://www.ons.gov.uk/ons/
dcp171778_314093.pdf, p. 2.

a projected 2.7 per cent in 2013.[4] In addition, the UK's share of world exports fell from 6 per cent in 1980 to 2 per cent in 2011.[5] As a result, the coalition government is focused on re-balancing the economy towards the world's growth markets.

Like its counterparts in all other European states, the government is also in the midst of reforming its welfare system and reducing the cost of welfare payments as a share of overall government spending. The ever-expanding costs of the state-funded benefits system, pensions and health care in particular, have become unsustainable for many EU members at a time when they are under pressure to concentrate more of their resources on retaining their competitive position internationally.

As in the rest of the EU, making such fundamental changes to Britain's political economy is exceptionally difficult. It also poses challenges for the UK's international role. Like other European states, the UK has decided to cut back on defence expenditure and military procurement as part of the overall effort to reduce the size of government spending. Cuts to the Ministry of Defence's resource budget will lead to further reductions of £249 million in 2013/14 and £247 million in 2014/15.[6] This decline in UK defence spending coincides with rising investments in military capabilities by a number of significant countries, including China, Russia, India, Turkey and Saudi Arabia. The difference with the majority of

---

[4] Measured by purchasing power parity; International Monetary Fund, 'United Kingdom: gross domestic product based on PPP share of world total', *World Economic Outlook Database*, April 2013, http://www.imf.org/external/pubs/ft/weo/2013/01/weodata/weorept.aspx?sy=2008&ey=2013&scsm=1&ssd=1&sort=country&ds=.&br=1&pr1.x=45&pr1.y=12&c=112&s=PPPSH&grp=0&a=#notes.

[5] In addition, 'while the UK was the 5th largest exporter in cash terms between 1980 and 2000, in 2011 it was ranked 12th'. See Grahame Allen, 'UK trade statistics', House of Commons, 8 October 2012, http://www.parliament.uk/briefing-papers/SN06211.

[6] These figures exclude capital spending. See Malcolm Chalmers, *The Squeeze Continues: UK Defence Spending and the 2013 Budget*, RUSI Analysis, 25 March 2013, http://www.rusi.org/analysis/commentary/ref:C51506B24A254C/#.UdL16TvCbTp.

its EU partners is that persistent and severe cuts in UK defence spending undermine the UK's still special relationship with the US in defence matters, where the capacity to deploy and fight alongside US forces gives the UK a more credible and valued voice (among many US voices, admittedly) in the process of US decision-making. UK defence cuts could also undermine the credibility and legitimacy of the UK's position as one of the five permanent members of the UN Security Council.

British public opinion is also playing an ambivalent role in the debate over the international issues that government should prioritise in the future. The Chatham House-YouGov surveys of general public and opinion-former views on the UK's international priorities reveal some important contradictions. In the 2012 survey, the general public ranked international terrorism as the greatest threat to the British way of life, whereas opinion-formers regarded the failure of the international financial system as the leading concern. More generally, the general public selected hard security issues such as terrorism and the proliferation of weapons of mass destruction more often than opinion-formers, who expressed greater concern with threats related to economics, resources and energy.[7]

The UK faces two additional challenges in terms of domestic political support for international diplomatic engagement. First, like other European states, the country's leading political parties, Conservative and Labour, have seen an erosion of their membership base in the past decade[8]. Britain may be entering a period of protracted coalition government that will inevitably affect the country's flexibility of action on the international stage, as can be seen by the recent decision to give Members of Parliament the vote on whether or not to arm the Syrian opposition. Strong executive leadership on international

---

[7] See Jonathan Knight, Robin Niblett and Thomas Raines, *Hard Choices Ahead: The Chatham House–YouGov Survey 2012* (London: Chatham House, 2012), p. 6.
[8] According to *The Economist*, 'In 1951 the Tories and Labour together won 98 per cent of the vote. In 2010 they won 65 per cent and neither could win a majority in Parliament'. See 'The little party behind the throne', 29 June 2013, http://www.economist.com/news/britain/21580139-liberal-democrats-can-expect-be-smaller-more-powerful-little-party-behind.

affairs, as epitomised by the governments of Margaret Thatcher and Tony Blair, may be in temporary or structural retreat. The axioms of the UK's post-war foreign policy – in particular, the pro-Atlanticism of the Conservative Party and New Labour – can no longer be taken for granted. And the persistent Euro-scepticism of the activist base of the Conservative Party and many of its MPs, alongside the emergence of the UK Independence Party as a serious force in national politics, further constrain the government's room for political manoeuvre in international affairs.

Even as domestic politics may weaken the political base for an activist British foreign policy, the main institutional avenues for British influence are also in retreat. The US decision to re-balance the focus of its foreign policy to the Asia-Pacific region reduces the pivotal role that the UK played for the past 50 years within the Atlantic alliance, when the Euro-Atlantic area was at the centre of American foreign policy. NATO has become more of an insurance policy for its members than an alliance of like-minded states capable of acting proactively on the world stage.[9]

Within the EU, most member states remain focused on their internal recovery from the financial crisis and on overcoming the structural weaknesses that this crisis revealed in the construction of the single currency. Hopes that the EU might serve as a vehicle for its members to play a more influential role across a range of international dossiers, from climate change negotiations to assisting in the political and economic transitions in the Arab world, have been undercut by the EU's loss of credibility during this period and persistent weaknesses in the structures of EU foreign policy.

At the same time, the euro crisis has stoked fears that deepening political integration within the eurozone will be to the UK's disadvantage, especially in terms of the Single Market. And it has emboldened British critics of the EU who would prefer the country

---

[9] For further discussion, see Robin Niblett, *The UK's Relationship with NATO: Strategic Challenges to the Alliance*, Evidence to the National Security Strategy Committee's Third Review, House of Commons, May 2013, http://www. chathamhouse.org/sites/default/files/public/Research/Europe/0513pmnt_ niblett.pdf.

to leave altogether. Prime Minister David Cameron's decision to promise a referendum on the UK's EU membership in the next Parliament, should the Conservative Party win the 2015 general election, is designed in part to assuage his party's political base and their allies among the Conservative backbenches. The decision also aims to provide leverage to the UK to negotiate sufficient EU reforms to protect the interests of countries outside the single currency as integration deepens within the eurozone. But this is a high-risk strategy: it remains to be seen whether the government can use the fear of a British exit as a means to focus other EU governments on a largely UK-instigated and -driven reform agenda, or whether negotiating 'while keeping a hand on the door handle',[10] as EU President Herman Van Rompuy put it, will reduce the UK's leverage across a range of EU policy areas.

Under any circumstances, the UK's ambivalence about its future inside the EU has encouraged US leaders to deepen other bilateral relationships in Europe, focusing on Germany in particular. For leaders of the world's (re-)emerging powers, such as China and India, the UK was already one among a number of important European counterparts, rather than a *primus inter pares*. Britain's status as a potential EU 'outsider' may encourage them to try to isolate the UK, believing that the other EU members may now be less willing to show solidarity with the UK at moments of diplomatic tension. This calculation appears to have contributed to the Chinese decision to put the UK into diplomatic 'purdah' for a whole year after David Cameron and Nick Clegg met with the Dalai Lama in the summer of 2012.

Finally, while the UK was able to host a successful G8 Presidency in 2012–13, this grouping is now more of a Western caucus within the larger, more globally representative G20 than a gathering of the world's most influential nations. At the same time, alternative institutional avenues for international and regional influence have gained strength in the past 10 years. This includes regional group-

---

[10] Herman Van Rompuy, 'Britain in Europe: channelling change together', speech at the Policy Network Annual Conference, London, 28 February 2013, http://www.consilium.europa.eu/uedocs/cms_data/docs/pressdata/en/ec/135747.pdf.

ings such as the African Union, MERCOSUL and ASEAN, and more expansive groupings including the Shanghai Cooperation Organisation (SCO) and the BRICS summit gatherings. While the capacity for these groups to lead change internationally or project influence regionally remains limited at this stage in their evolution, they have created a far more competitive space within which the UK and other established powers must project their voice and interests.

A Continuing Capacity for Influence

So, is the UK's international influence in irreversible decline? It is important to balance the risks to the UK arising from the changing international context with an assessment of the country's remaining capabilities – in other words, its capacity for influence. Change is relative and, when considered in these terms, the UK retains considerable potential for international influence early in the 21st century, despite the challenges described above.

The list of UK strengths relative to other countries in the world is well known within policy circles.[11] Britain still ranks among the world's leading mid-sized countries from a combined demographic and economic perspective. Retaining this status will be an essential platform for broader UK influence in the future. According to the UN, the UK's population will reach at least 73 million in 2050, which may make it the most populous country in the EU, overtaking Germany at some point in the 2040s.[12] This means that the UK remains a relatively young country by European standards, with a potential competitive edge if British governments can set the right policy mix to unlock its demographic potential.

The UK could benefit from a better balanced economy than in the past. The manufacturing sector has the potential to stage a competitive

---

[11] For a summary, see Robin Niblett, *Playing to its Strengths*.

[12] See United Nations Department of Economic and Social Affairs, *World Population Prospects: The 2012 Revision* (New York: UN, 2012), http://esa.un.org/unpd/wpp/index.htm.

revival, as UK companies respond to the combination of low interest rates, new R&D incentives and lower rates of corporate tax and seek new opportunities to meet the growing demand for advanced manufacturing products in emerging markets. In addition, the service sector, the UK's main area of relative economic competitiveness, is well-positioned to take advantage of growing demand from the emerging economies in the world's South and East. The UK is second only to the US in the export of services, and leads the world on a per capita basis.[13] UK-based financial, legal and accounting services are not only major contributors to UK prosperity; they also place UK firms at the heart of global corporate deal-making and negotiation, connecting companies and governments and helping define the norms and rules under which international commerce is undertaken.

The UK services sector possesses a number of other structural advantages. English is the world's *de facto* international language, a status which has entrenched the country's competitive strengths in the financial, legal and accounting sectors, while continuing to benefit the education and communications sectors. Added to the unique benefit of the country's time zone between Asia and the Americas, the strength of the UK services sector has helped make London one of the world's first global capitals and one of the most competitive centres of economic activity in the world.

At the same time, the UK remains one of the most open economies in the world and one of the most successful in attracting foreign direct investment (FDI). According to the UN Conference on Trade and Development (UNCTAD), the UK ranks fifth in the world in terms of FDI; and investment into the UK rose 22 per cent in 2012.[14] Britain has allowed foreign firms to buy up much

---

[13] See World Trade Organisation, 'Trade growth to slow in 2012 after strong deceleration in 2011', 12 April 2012, http://www.wto.org/english/news_e/pres12_e/pr658_e.htm.

[14] This is in contrast to Germany (an 85 per cent drop) and Europe as a whole (a 42 per cent drop). Figures from UNCTAD, see Katie Allen, 'Foreign investment in UK rises despite slump across rest of Europe', *The Guardian*, 26 June 2013, http://www.guardian.co.uk/world/2013/jun/26/foreign-investment-uk-rises-europe.

of its manufacturing sector and is now vying for foreign invest-ment into its under-funded physical infrastructure. As a result, the country serves as one of the preferred destinations for major multi-national companies to carry out their globally integrated business operations.

The UK has the potential, therefore, to carry out the internal re-balancing of its economy which all of the major UK parties support. There are numerous obstacles to success, of course, ranging from the growing cost of servicing its post-financial crisis debt to declining standards in primary and secondary education relative to other countries; an ageing transportation and energy infrastructure; and difficulties in enabling small and medium-sized companies to gain access to the sort of 'patient capital' necessary for sustainable growth. Nevertheless, given its relative economic under-performance in recent years, the UK has the potential to grow its way out of its current economic stagnation. And its prospects do not suffer from the risks facing the many emerging economies which need to break through their middle-income ceil-ings at some point in the next five years. Recent developments in China, Russia, Brazil and Turkey have exposed how the rising powers face their own structural challenges of demography, rising social expectations, weak political legitimacy, resource insecurity, growing pollution, and endemic corruption.[15]

If the UK can re-set itself on a path of sustainable economic growth, this will provide an essential platform for it to maintain or increase its capacity for international influence.[16] First, economic

---

[15] For further analysis of these developments, see Ruchir Sharma, 'Broken BRICS: why the Rest Stopped Rising', *Foreign Affairs*, Vol. 91,, No. 6, November/December 2012, pp. 2–7; and Gideon Rachman, 'The Brics have taken an unhappy turn', *Financial Times*, 8 October 2012, http://www.ft.com/cms/s/0/af6e8b08-1136-11e2-8d5f-00144feabdc0.html#axzz2FIwvVnUD.

[16] The same argument has been made by Richard Haass, President of the Council on Foreign Relations, among others, in terms of restoring the 'economic founda-tions' of American power and foreign policy See Richard N. Haass, *Foreign Policy Begins at Home: The Case for Putting America's House in Order* (New York: Basic Books, 2013).

strength will bring material benefits. UK military spending could increase again, offering the government greater options to contribute to the international peace and stability that also serves the country's political and economic interests. These options would include increasing military and police training missions in key countries, while contributing to the maintenance of international stability through increased patrolling of sea lanes and support of missions for post-conflict reconstruction, peace-keeping or disaster relief. Second, the government could increase its still modest investment in its diplomatic capabilities. Expanding the UK's diplomatic missions in priority countries has been a valuable step, with 50 new posts created in Beijing and 30 in New Delhi. By 2015, 11 new British embassies will open, with 300 more staff in emerging economies, including in South Korea, Malaysia, Nigeria, Angola, Argentina, Peru, Pakistan, Vietnam, and the Philippines.[17] In addition, making greater use of local staff has helped offset the costs of the added investment. But the UK's diplomatic capabilities remain under-funded, from compensation levels to technology infrastructure to overall staff numbers. Third, the UK could meet and maintain its goal of spending 0.7 per cent of GNI on development assistance while increasing the national administrative capacity to manage this increased flow of funds, and ensure that the support is put to good use.

Each of these steps would enhance the UK's soft power; in other words, its power of attraction to others. Training missions, port visits, diplomatic presence, and disaster relief can all be offered without demanding specific returns from the recipients of these British investments. The results can be powerful, in terms of deepening personal ties between Britain and those countries that benefit from

---

[17] See William Hague, 'Our diplomatic network is the essential infrastructure of Britain's influence in the world', speech at the British Academy, 17 October 2012, https://www.gov.uk/government/speeches/foreign-secretary-speech-on-diplomatic-tradecraft; and William Hague, 'For the first time in decades our diplomatic reach will be extended not reduced', speech to the House of Commons, 11 May 2011, https://www.gov.uk/government/news/foreign-secretary-for-the-first-time-in-decades-our-diplomatic-reach-will-be-extended-not-reduced.

these initiatives and by creating the networks through which the UK can later engage in dialogue, press its case or make its own appeals for support. For example, the UK's response to the Great Eastern Earthquake and ensuing nuclear disaster in Japan in March 2011 has reinforced the bilateral relationship in ways that will carry multiple benefits for both sides. Strengthening the British economy can also enhance Britain's soft power in other ways, not least by making it a more attractive destination for foreign investment, underpinning its commercial diplomacy and its voice within EU-led trade negotiations, and giving it added weight in discussions in the G20 and other fora on the reform of international financial regulations and institutions. In other words, economic success will increase the UK's power of attraction to others: increasing the degree to which other states seek out the UK's support, associate themselves with its initiatives, and look to follow its example.

Leveraging institutions

While it is possible to paint a relatively rosy picture of future UK influence on the world stage, it is important to remember that the UK will generally need to act in partnership with others in order to bring about outcomes that match its values and interests. The disadvantage of collective action, with its tendency towards lowest common denominator outcomes, is well known. The UN Security Council, for example, stands out as an organisation that more often than not constrains (as it was designed to do) the capacity for forceful action on the world stage rather than enabling it. However, collective action offers the only pathway to respond to the challenges to peace and security in a world of ever-deepening interdependence. The world's major powers, including China and the US, are learning the same painful lesson as the UK and its European counterparts have learned that transnational threats, such as from climate change and international financial instability, cannot be resolved successfully through sovereign actions alone. And the growing pressures on emerging powers from their expanding middle classes, with rising expectations and real-time, unfiltered access to information, will demand their engagement alongside fully developed countries in trying to find common solutions to the challenges of economic growth, environmental sustainability and security.

The question then, is what can Britain offer in a world of deepening interdependence, when it is just one among a growing number of influential players? A key advantage for Britain is that it remains one of the most networked countries in the world, with an important institutional position in the EU, G20, G8, NATO, UN Security Council, IMF/World Bank and the Commonwealth. The UK has traditionally played the role of insider within these institutions, most of which, bar the EU, it was involved in helping to establish. And within them, one of the main roles of UK diplomats has been to serve as diplomatic mediators, trying to bridge differences, for example, between the US and Europe over the decision to go to war with Iraq in 2003.

Now, the UK may need to adapt its approach to its engagement in these institutions. It needs to play to a different set of national strengths in this changing world. Britain may be less powerful in material terms than was the case 30 years ago, but it can still be confident in its position as a dynamic mid-sized economic, diplomatic and military power. In fact, rather than being a weakness, the apparent decline in its position relative to the US and to rising powers such as China and India could be a source of strength, if used intelligently, as mid-sized and smaller states seek to resist the dominance of those larger powers that see themselves as the poles in a new multi-polar world order. Here, the current and future British governments may do well to play up the UK's emerging position as 'fringe insider' within the world's key institutions.

For example, the UK should remain within the EU, embrace the benefits that membership of a rules-based, supra-national single market of some 500 million people confers upon Britain, and accept that, as a non-euro member, it will be on its institutional periphery. Accepting this duality, the UK could turn its self-exclusion from the eurozone into a strength in terms of its influence over the EU's external policies, playing the role of instigator of more coordinated

EU efforts to tackle shared international challenges. If (and only if) the UK government can navigate its way through its EU referendum maze, then its position as a strong European economy with global ties on the institutional and physical periphery of the EU could enable it to serve as one of the most powerful voices within the EU for deepening the EU's international engagement. This could involve driving the EU's current and future trade liberalisation agreements, such as the Transatlantic Trade and Investment Partnership or the EU–Japan Economic Partnership Agreement, or arguing the case for more forceful EU involvement in managing the security risks of its neighbourhood, as it is doing currently alongside France over the crisis in Syria.

In terms of NATO, the UK should use its position as America's closest European security ally (for which it is sometimes viewed with suspicion by European partners) to drive a strategic reassessment of transatlantic burden-sharing at a time when America is turning away from Europe. As mentioned above, NATO risks becoming little more than an insurance policy, under which the United States remains Europe's security guarantor of last resort, but the two sides of the Atlantic gradually lose the capacity to support each other in confronting pressing international security challenges. To avoid such an outcome, the UK should propose how it and its European NATO partners might support the US in regions beyond the Euro-Atlantic area, such as the Gulf and other vital shipping nodes, in ways that play to European capabilities and political sensitivities.

In the case of the Commonwealth, the UK should actively promote rule of law reform as a central tenet for economic development. In the case of the G8, the UK could commit to raising the voice of this Western caucus inside the broader and still quite unfocused G20. It could build on a successful G8 Presidency in 2012–13, for example, in order to promote within the broader G20 the practical value of increased standards of transparency in governance and taxation.

The British government should not forget that its capacity to project international influence goes beyond these state-centric institutions and dimensions. The BBC's reputation for objective analysis has made it one of the most trusted broadcasters in the world. Retaining that role is not only a valuable international public service, it also helps promote the sort of transparency that empowers populations at the expense of entrenched and inefficient authority. The British Council promotes the study of English and an under-standing of British culture across the world, in ways which not only strengthen the role of English as an international language, but also as a tool for cross-cultural research, inquiry and negotiation. British policy institutes offer international analysis and neutral forums for debating policy while drawing on the insights of extensive local dias-poras, especially from the Middle East and sub-Saharan Africa. British universities attract students from across the world and deliver world-class research, and in so doing help build personal networks that can reinforce bilateral relationships. And British-based environmental, humanitarian and human rights NGOs are fearless in challenging illiberal and autocratic regimes that can often block change. A more proactive UK approach to agenda-setting at the international level needs to play to these strengths.

Conclusion

In the last five years, the UK has under-performed economically, which has undercut its international standing and, to a certain degree, its capacity for international influence, both in its hard and soft power. In addition, Britain will experience a degree of relative decline compared to the US and major rising economic powers in the future. However, given its underlying economic strengths, demo-graphic resilience, unique political-economic attributes, including the advantages of language and time zone, and its recent under-per-formance, it is possible that the country may be heading into a period of relatively better economic health.

Despite its recent poor economic performance, the UK has still remained one of the world's most active and influential countries in recent years, especially in terms of leading international debates, such as over the significance of climate change in the past and over approaches to promoting sustainable development, better governance and global health today. 'Punching above its weight' may prove harder to sustain in the future, however, given the rise of other state and non-state actors and the relative decline in influence of international institutions in which the UK has been a lead member.

While rebuilding its economic strength will be a *sine qua non* for future British international influence, this influence will also depend upon how the country's leaders leverage the UK's position within key international institutions in what is now a highly interdependent world. Networks and coalitions will be essential to success. The UK can survive and even prosper alone. But, if it detaches itself completely from its closest and deepest institutional network, the EU, it will likely become a consumer of global public goods, standards and norms, rather than a shaper of its international environment.

CONCLUSION

by Douglas Alexander and Ian Kearns

If you ask a group of the world's leading thinkers on international affairs to contribute to a book of this nature you shouldn't be surprised if they confront you with penetrating insights and a challenging response. In that regard if in no other, we hope readers will agree this volume does not disappoint. Each contributor has not only reviewed current circumstances and challenges but has also tabled policy relevant ideas, for which we are grateful.

In this final chapter, we do not attempt a full synthesis of what has gone before. We have too little space and the terrain covered is too wide to make such a synthesis possible. Nor do we think it is strictly necessary. Our contention is that behind the long list of issues covered, from the rise of China to the Arab revolt and from climate change, humanitarian intervention, and the plight of the bottom billion to the challenge of terrorism, a number of wider themes and ideas are evident and recurrent throughout the book.

These themes and ideas reflect the scale and pace of change that marks the international environment and that will present very different challenges in the middle of this decade than were evident in the middle of the last.

This year, of course, marks the tenth anniversary of the US-led invasion of Iraq, an event that continues to cast a long shadow over British foreign policy. Indeed the consequences of Iraq already seem deeper and broader than those of the Suez crisis in 1956. Important though the lessons of the past are to learn, they should not blind us to the even bigger challenge of a future widely seen as an 'Asian

Century'. Undeniably the events of September 11, and responses to it shaped the last decade. Yet there is little doubt that the global financial crisis of 2007/8, and the shifts of wealth and power it accelerated, will impact on international affairs for far longer than simply a decade.

After what President Obama recently described as a 'decade of war', British foreign policy in the years ahead must reject two fallacies: the hubris that the UK can 'reorder the world' on one hand, and a retreat into simply strategic shrinkage and mercantilism on the other.

That is why it is so pressing to find an alternative approach that avoids this false choice between either hubris or simply a 'smaller UK' outlook. We need to uphold the idea that we can still help shape the world through our alliances and benefit from a more ambitious approach. The starting point must be an analysis of what has changed in the world in recent years, and what the foundations might be for a different British policy that seeks to work with others to shape a world more conducive to our interests and values. We identify these trends in the coming paragraphs before trying to draw insights for specific areas of policy.

The first trend, which shapes everything we are living through, is the diffusion of power – both from the West to the Rest (as the chapters by Mark Leonard and Xenia Dormandy illustrate) and from the nation state to an array of non-governmental organisations, ranging from Oxfam to al-Qaida.

The second trend, as captured in the chapter by Larry Korb and Max Hoffman, is that power is also changing in character. Military capabilities and combat readiness are still important as a last resort but they tell us little about outcomes in the worlds of finance or climate change for example, nor do they tell us much about the ability of non-state actors like al-Qaida to have a major impact on world affairs.

A third trend evident in the contributions to the book relates to the inadequacy of traditional notions of sovereignty in current circumstances. Few could dispute that across the fields of economics, the environment, public health and security issues, our destinies today are not only linked but to a large extent are shared with those living beyond our borders. Governments must therefore look to each other for help in managing problems and seizing opportunities.

Alec Ross and Ben Scott's chapter on digital diplomacy brings home another lesson, namely that in the international politics of tomorrow, traditional diplomatic assumptions about scarcity of information and the influencing of events primarily through private channels of communication with other governments will become increasingly anachronistic. Our diplomacy will have to master the world of decentralised, peer-to-peer information flows.

The Foundations of Tomorrow's Foreign Policy

These four trends require a response involving not only specific policy initiatives but also a wider shift in thinking. If power is increasingly slipping beyond state level to an ungoverned and unregulated global space then a central challenge for all governments is how to regain control of the events that affect your citizens. The most powerful route is extended multilateral cooperation. Bilateral diplomacy can play a useful role on specific topics but it is not sufficient to deal with challenges that are global or regional in nature and the current British government has placed too much expectation upon it. Nor can the multilateral cooperation of tomorrow be the preserve only of a Western club. Institutions grounded in or traditionally dominated by the West, such as NATO, the European Union (EU), the International Monetary Fund (IMF) and the World Bank, while all still vital, are no longer enough on their own.

In the future, we will need to work with old and existing partners but also with new ones in an 'extended' form of multilateralism. In Asia today, in part driven by China's rise, we are seeing the emergence of new potential players, new partnerships and new formats of cooperation. More broadly we will not have the luxury of working only with those who share our values. This does not mean we should abandon those values or ignore violations of them, but it does mean we should seek pragmatic solutions to some of the world's most pressing problems by working with all those relevant to the solution.

Second, as Larry Korb and Max Hoffman reminded us, we will need to place an enhanced emphasis on legitimacy. In a world of diffuse power, where even the most powerful actors can't coerce or buy their way to all the cooperation they need, then cooperation is going to have to come partly through persuasion. This means embracing the view that our foreign policy must focus on citizens, corporations and NGOs as well as the governments of other states through traditional and social media.

If coercion is likely to be less effective in tomorrow's conditions than it has been in the past, then another challenge is how best to tilt the balance from hard power to the available alternatives. American analysts have talked of the idea of aggregating 'hard power' (coercion and bribery) and 'soft power' (attraction and example) instruments into smart power. Behind the jargon this means learning to combine military, political, diplomatic, economic and cultural instruments together to better effect and it means breaking down the barriers and stove-pipes inside Whitehall.

However, any state's potential to influence the environment internationally is heavily impacted by the wealth, vitality and resources it has domestically. As Richard Haas's recent book has it: *Foreign Policy Begins at Home*. Robin Niblett's chapter pointed out that our country remains the seventh largest economy in the world. We are an open, trading country and our capital city is one of the world's pre-eminent financial centres. English remains the primary language of international business, diplomacy and elite education. We are also a top-table member of not just the EU, but also of NATO, the G8, the G20, the Commonwealth, and the United Nations Security Council. These are overlapping and interdependent spheres of influence, not mutually exclusive power bases that we have to choose between and together they give the UK both the opportunity and the responsibility to exercise some international leadership.

But we also face some significant challenges. When the next government takes office in 2015 the reality facing it will include difficult fiscal circumstances and budgets for defence and diplomacy that may either be close to stagnant or in real terms decline. The wider challenge of how to sustain fiscal credibility while stimulating renewed economic growth will also still be with us. So too will the wider question of how we should prepare our businesses and our people with the education and skills they will need to compete in what has been described as an 'Asian' Century. Many of our closest allies will be in a similar or worse position. Addressing this context so that we are able to play a full and active international role will be vital.

However, we should not underestimate the influence that can come from leading by domestic example. International agreements require domestic implementation and the strength of our commitment to multilateralism abroad and the strength of our governance at home can most effectively be demonstrated by our willingness to exercise sovereignty responsibly. Depending on the issue, this might mean ensuring the transparency, monitoring, and effective regulation of legal and financial markets and institutions to make sure they aren't hide-outs for corruption or sources of financial contagion. In the age of climate change, nuclear threats and terrorism it might mean taking other actions to tackle carbon emissions, to secure vulnerable nuclear materials and to ensure that our territory is not being used as a jumping off point for terrorist groups or criminal gangs. The more a state can demonstrate a commitment to this kind of behaviour at home, the more likely it is to be seen as a credible, effective international partner.

Implications for Policy

If these four foundations – extended multilateralism, legitimacy, smart power and domestic strength – are each central to tomorrow's foreign policy for the UK, we turn next to their application in practice. They are not mutually exclusive ideas, and cannot each simply be applied to isolated and discrete areas of policy while having no meaning in relation to others. They must be applied in combination, and can inform a wide range of foreign policy approaches.

We start below with three sets of regional challenges, in Asia, in our own Euro-Atlantic neighbourhood and in the Middle East, in which the notion of extended multilateralism is clearly evident. We turn next to three areas where reinforced legitimacy and smart power are central, namely human rights, the UK's approach to the use of force and armed conflict, and action to help the world's poorest. We then go on to a consideration of the implications of the four foundations for policy toward two major global challenges, namely nuclear weapons and climate change, and to an examination of what the ideas mean for reform of the UN. And we conclude the section by returning to the idea of domestic strength and the notion that successful foreign policy begins at home.

An Asian Step-change

When a Labour government was elected in 1997, its biggest foreign policy challenge was ending the UK's isolation in Europe after the 'Beef Wars' and self-marginalisation of the previous government. The new government announced a 'European Step-change' designed to mobilise the whole of government behind a policy of making the UK as influential in the European Union as France and Germany. It required policy innovation by many government departments – economic, justice, migration, foreign policy – under the leadership of the prime minister. One of the key elements was a campaign to ensure that every British minister met their counterparts in all EU member states, and to launch bilateral initiatives to kick-start European action on a series of topics from European competitiveness to European defence.

Today, as economic wealth and political power shifts from West to East, the UK is lagging behind many European partners in its quest to gain from Asian growth markets and to build political relationships with rising powers. This is particularly true of China – which is already an important fact in almost every major domestic and foreign policy challenge in the UK but which has not been at the heart of a concerted political strategy by the government. It is also in Asia that each of the four foundations of tomorrow's foreign policy come into sharpest focus. So far, in spite of their economic wealth, Asian powers have not played a role in the solution of global problems that is commensurate with their growing economic power, and only a limited number of countries in Asia seem to support multilateralism as a core value. Asian countries such as China and India are unwilling to accept the legitimacy of the West to set a geo-political agenda and are challenging it increasingly in different institutions. Asian countries have also been the most forthright in using economic means to achieve political ends – putting pressures on the openness of the global economy. And, as a vital growth engine of the global economy, Asian countries hold the key to the UK's economic revival.

In order to face up to this challenge, the British government needs to re-orientate its strategic focus to meet the challenges and opportunities of Asian revival. Too much of the current government's shift to Asia has been narrowly focused in the commercial realm, but the evidence suggests that even if the UK's prime interest were mercantile, it would be more likely to benefit from economic openings if its growth strategy were anchored in a broader political approach led from the highest levels of the government. And, as a country that still has some ambitions to help shape the world, the UK should begin to address Asian countries as real partners on a range of issues – from the future of the Middle East and Africa to technology and climate change.

For that reason, the government should set up an 'Asian Stepchange' taskforce, supported by the Foreign and Commonwealth Office (FCO), to flesh out the strategic goals for government departments in the most economically dynamic and geo-politically perilous region of the world.

This could include a foreign and security policy strategy with elements on the key global issues as well as Asian security. An important part of this approach should be an attempt to mobilise all parts of the Foreign Office as well as the Ministry of Defence and the Department for International Development (DfID) to draw on their distinctive abilities to build relationships with Asian countries. Of course this approach would involve both a dialogue with China and also one with China's democratic neighbours on how to cope with China's rise. But it should include other areas as well – for example, on the future of the Middle East, where the US is seeking less engagement and where China and other Asian countries are now the biggest consumers of Middle Eastern energy. It could include discussions on crisis management, peacekeeping and the legitimacy of armed conflict (including the challenges posed by drone warfare).The foreign and security policy could try to build wider support for the EU's multilateral trading push – building on the EU's FTA (free trade agreement) with Korea by signing new deals with India and Japan.

This should go hand in hand with a domestic policy push across government to focus our education, infrastructure, inward investment policies and our export promotion policies to allow the UK to benefit from Asian growth. A key element should be a focus on rejuvenating the big cities – not just London, but cities like Manchester, Glasgow and Birmingham – and linking them into opportunities in China and other Asian giants.

The British approach to Asia needs to be aligned with our traditional foreign policy relationships – with Europe and the United States. Ideally, the 'Asian Step-change' would be developed within a wider European context to maximise European power – ideally in partnership with Berlin and Paris – as our interests with these two countries in relation to Asia are virtually identical and our weight will be considerably enhanced. One symbolic way of doing this could be for a joint visit by British, French and German foreign ministers to Beijing, Delhi and Tokyo. It will also be important to deepen and re-orient the transatlantic relationship at a time when both Americans and Europeans are focused on Asia. There needs to be a growth of contact and discussion across the Atlantic on Asian issues and a recognition that both sides will have to defend their distinctive interests. In this context, the best scope for cooperation will be by strengthening the domestic foundations for the West through the Transatlantic Trade and Investment Partnership (TTIP).

Foreign Policy in the Euro-Atlantic Area

Europe today is under stress. But if we allow the strains to turn into open division, the UK will see its own power diffused and its prosperity diminished. To avoid this we must address weaknesses within Europe even while being sensitive to the challenges of a world of rising powers outside Europe.

We should pursue ambitious reforms, not seek exit from the EU. Our membership of the EU gives us access to, and influence in, the biggest global trading bloc and real opportunities to secure new markets across the world for our products. The pooled resources of members help make us safer and more secure – whether through tackling climate change, cross-border crime and terror, or through targeted use of EU sanctions on Iran. And the EU is not just an instrument for amplifying our power but also for promoting our values of securing peace and security and defending democracy and human rights.

That said, significant challenges now face its legitimacy in the UK. These must be addressed. First, the UK needs to advance, with others in Europe, a reform agenda to promote economic growth across the EU. This means not just restraint but also reform of the EU budget. The budget should focus on those items where spending at the EU level can save money at the national level, through economies of scale or by avoiding duplication, and resources should be shifted from the Common Agricultural Policy (CAP) and put into areas of more productive economic development. Despite past reforms, the CAP remains an obstacle to international trade liberalisation and introduces distortions so there is not a level playing field.

Second, the UK needs to set out a credible agenda for institutional reform in Europe. National parliaments should have more say over the making of new EU legislation if that legislation is to be seen as legitimate. The costs of the European Parliament should be brought down and the workings of the Commission made more effective.

We must be much clearer about the final destination of the European project. The future of the European Union is not, and must not be defined as, uniform progress towards a common federal government or the merging of national identities into a United States of Europe. Instead we must pursue a vision of Europe that is flexible and capable of accommodating varying levels of integration among member states. And as the countries in the eurozone take additional steps to manage the single currency, the UK needs to be at the table negotiating institutional safeguards with regard to the single market and the balance of interests between those inside and outside of the

Euro. If we do not so this, it risks further undermining the UK's membership in the eyes of the public.

By addressing these requirements for enhanced legitimacy and effectiveness within the EU, the institution will be better placed to play the external role that is required of it. It will stand a better chance of strategically engaging with rising powers like China and India on a range of pressing issues like trade, climate change and security. And it will be better placed to use access to its own markets to promote important opening of trade.

Wider Europe

Europe does not, of course, stop at the borders of the EU and neither should our efforts to extend multilateral cooperation within Europe. There have recently been some worrying developments in Russian politics, including the intimidation of journalists and the designation of many civil society organisations as foreign agents. Where we disagree with decisions taken by the Russian government, we should say so. But, as the chapter in this volume by Bob Legvold makes clear, we cannot allow these disagreements to become the totality of the relationship with Russia. Russia is a permanent member of the UN Security Council, a partner in P5 (Permanent Five) efforts to address nuclear challenges and the third largest emitter of greenhouse gases in the world. It is an important supplier of energy to many of our key European trading partners, a diplomatic player in the Middle East and a key actor in Euro-Atlantic security affairs. To pursue our core economic, diplomatic, security, and environmental interests, we have to find effective ways of working with Russia.

As Zbigniew Brzezinski argued in his book, *Strategic Vision*, cooperative European goals need to be set within the framework of a longer-term vision (Brzezinski, 2012). One practical starting point for pursuing this longer-term vision could be to take up some of the proposals in *Building Mutual Security in the Euro-Atlantic Region*, the report recently published by Sam Nunn, Igor Ivanov, Wolfgang Ischinger and Des Browne (Nunn et al., 2013). This report suggests a framework for dialogue on political–military relations among all parties in the region, covering nuclear weapons, conventional forces and new challenges related to cyber-security and the possible militarisation of space.

NATO and Transatlantic Relations

Pursuing this dialogue and the goal of greater European cooperation with our neighbours to the east, including with Russia, can be complementary and in no way undermining of our continued partnership with the United States.

That partnership itself needs to be deepened through a Trans-Atlantic Trade and Investment Partnership (TTIP). If a TTIP has not been concluded when the next government comes to office in 2015, it should be concluded as a matter of urgency. Our partnership with the US also rests upon our membership of NATO, the bedrock of our security. As Kori Schake pointed out in her upbeat assessment of its continuing relevance in this volume, claims of a crisis in the alliance have been around for decades. That said, with the United States now accounting for around 75 per cent of all NATO defence expenditure and UK and European defence budgets being cut, an incoming government in 2015 is going to be met with an argument over burden-sharing within the alliance. The European members of NATO must address this. The UK must lead an effort to encourage other Europeans to do more together to make their defence expenditure go further. This is in the interests of Europe and of the US, and it has been put off for too long.

The Middle East

On Europe's southern border too there is a strong case for extended multilateralism. As Shashank Joshi's chapter made clear, we are witnessing change on a truly historic scale in the Middle East. The initial optimism of the Arab spring has been tempered by the horror in Syria, and deep concern that the century-long ordering of nation states in the region is now threatened by a deepening and dangerous sectarian divide between Sunnis and Shia.

In Egypt, turmoil followed the first elections, with President Morsi being ousted by the military after one year in power. If the lesson drawn from these actions by the Muslim Brotherhood is that they will forever be frozen out of democratic politics then the consequences both for Egypt and the broader region will be dangerous. If we are to help these societies to secure a better future, the EU must continue to provide economic assistance and must also take more radical measures to open up European markets to the region. This would benefit European consumers, cement new friendships and help ensure that the political optimism that does exist in the region isn't met with economic disappointment in the medium term.

We must continue the dialogue with Russia on how to address the challenges facing the Middle East. The disagreements with Moscow over Syria have been profound but on other issues, such as Iran's nuclear programme, we have been able to find diplomatic formulas that enable us to work together. We must understand and appreciate Turkey's emergence as a major player across the region and, where we have common cause, work diplomatically together to help stabilise the situation, and promote peace and economic development. We must work to strengthen and build more formal links with multilateral institutions existing in the region too, such as the Arab League and the Gulf Cooperation Council.

The BBC's editorial independence and objectivity helps explain why BBC Arabic online audiences grew 300 per cent during the protests against the Mubarak regime in Egypt, and BBC Persian television has been subject to increasing and aggressive jamming from within Iran. The World Service Trust has also worked with Tunisian TV to help it adapt to being a public service broadcaster rather than a mouth-piece for a discredited and authoritarian regime. It is therefore important that the value of smart power, in the form of public diplomacy, be recognised for the contribution it can make to the region even amidst all the present difficulties.

Protecting Human Rights

The strength of our commitment to universal human rights is a key factor in how the rest of the world judges the UK's place on the world stage. The UK was one of the first signatories to the Universal Declaration on Human Rights and now – even at a time when the ascendance of democracy and human rights is being questioned –

the British government must not only uphold those rights, but be a vocal advocate for all other states in the international system doing the same. This applies as much to our partners or allies in other important economic and security endeavours as it does to states with which we have fewer and less important ties.

Our wider commitment to human rights must extend beyond general support to a clear and unambiguous position with regard to torture, which is not only illegal, but abhorrent. Its use under any circumstances cannot be sanctioned. Where there is evidence that unacceptable practices have occurred, be it in countries that are adversarial to the United Kingdom or even among its allies, those practices must be condemned.

In the 21st century communications environment our commitment to human rights and the credibility of our public diplomacy are linked and both require us to show our support for freedom of expression on the internet. Today, freedom of speech means freedom to blog, to tweet and to discuss ideas with people all across the world. We must give vocal support to those whose rights are being threatened or removed and support the creation and distribution of technologies that help circumvent illegitimate censorship. This means looking afresh at export control regimes with regard to technologies that may be used for these ends and for the abuse of basic human rights. And it means supporting the multilateral institutions, that include governments and commercial and civil society organisations in the administration of the physical infrastructure of the internet.

Today, the internet operates in the way it does because multiple stakeholders have been able to work together to agree global technical standards and a process for allocating domain names and IP (internet provider) addresses. Some governments, including those of China, Russia and some Gulf States, are seeking to re-centralise control of this process in government hands. If such states succeed, the result could not only be loss of individual freedoms but, as Alec Ross and Ben Scott pointed out, the effective Balkanisation of the internet into separate networks that operate by different rules and standards.

Our Approach to Armed Conflict

The gravest decision a government can take is to use military force and put their troops and civilians in harm's way. When circumstances do arise in which the use of force by members of the international community has to be contemplated, the case for taking such action will face intense public scrutiny.

We should welcome this. A decade on, Iraq still holds difficult lessons for any incoming government in the UK. We must recognise that, especially in the post-Iraq era, whether for reasons of self-defence, compelling humanitarian emergency, or following authorisation by the UN Security Council, legal and public clarity around the rationale for any action is vital.

Debates about the use of force must also address the crucial role of the perceived legitimacy of any action taken in determining its eventual success. The aftermath of the invasion of Iraq demonstrated the difficulties of both effective post-war planning and prolonged occupation of another state, even for a country of the military and financial capability of the United States. But it also showed that effective intervention relies on having coordinated and achievable goals backed up with the appropriate levels of knowledge, resources and operational capabilities – and that securing this requires international legitimacy – all of which the Coalition Provisional Authority crucially lacked.

But while the experience of Iraq should inform our foreign policy, it shouldn't paralyse it. Neither neo-conservatism nor neo-isolationism is the right way forward. The recent British military effort aimed at helping to protect the people of Benghazi in 2011 demonstrated a different approach is possible. Libya showed that the choice is not always between doing nothing, or using force on the scale of Iraq, which saw 46,000 UK troops deployed on the eve of the 2003 invasion.

So where the criteria for the legitimate use of force in conflict environments are met, the notion of 'smart power' becomes directly relevant. This sort of approach suggests that force needs to be targeted at a specific threat rather than be open ended. Moreover, the military instrument should not necessarily be used first and should not be used in isolation from many other instruments of policy.

The international community can do more to prevent conflict in the first place. This is often about dealing with governance and development challenges as well as helping local authorities to exercise their sovereignty responsibly. No amount of international support for an intervention in a country will be enough if the authorities locally are perceived as illegitimate and/or wholly ineffective. Mali's government, for example, didn't just lack security at the time of the French intervention in early 2013. It lacked legitimacy after a military coup. Poverty and lawlessness blighted the lives of the population there. Smart power suggests that the development effort must always therefore match the security response. But even when conflict prevention fails, the policy choice, is not always between doing nothing and intervening with British and other Western nations' combat forces. A smart response exhibits restraint in the use of our own military and helps others to help themselves.

This may require the ongoing provision of financing, training and intelligence support to local and regional forces that are deploying to a conflict zone. The time is fast approaching when this assistance should be offered on more than an ad hoc basis. Both Kori Schake and Paul Collier, in their respective chapters in this volume, were right to point out the need for the African Union (AU) to become a more effective, better organised collective security organisation capable of dealing with this challenge in Africa. The incoming government in 2015 should see part of its historic mission as support to African countries who want to work to develop regional bodies and organisations, like the AU and ECOWAS (Economic Community of West African States), and should encourage the US and other NATO allies to do the same.

A 'smart power' approach to conflict also means that, in a world where power is dispersed, in which the range of the challenges is great and the instruments to address them fall under no single jurisdiction, one of the most important things the UK government can do is to learn to do things with others (Ashdown, 2011). Our military is adept at doing this through formal alliances like NATO and through experience at working in less formal coalitions in different conflict environments over many years.

Helping the World's Poorest

Our conflict policy connects directly with our wider effort to help the world's poorest. Here the agenda is changing, with 75 per cent of the world's poorest now living in middle-income countries and aid more concentrated in fragile states, but huge opportunities remain for engagement in other ways, including through both the private sector and NGOs. So here again notions such as legitimacy, smart power and multilateralism apply.

As Paul Collier has reminded us both in this volume and elsewhere, an effective response to this challenge requires pooling a range of policy instruments and working multilaterally with partners to increase our overall effect (Collier, 2008). It also means setting an example by taking necessary steps at home.

The UK's commitment to providing 0.7 per cent of GNI in aid to developing countries is an important component of a progressive international strategy. It is also vital that the UK continues to work for transparent accounting in how aid money is used in recipient countries.

Helping the poorest countries to help themselves is also a key component of any effective international development strategy. It is currently estimated that developing countries are losing more in revenue than they receive in aid, so it is vital that we do more to help these countries strengthen their tax base.

The facilitating processes for this outflow of tax revenue involve shell companies registered in places like London. So the government that comes to power in 2015 should build on progress made on this issue at the G8 meeting in Northern Ireland in June 2013, and take steps to pursue multilateral agreement on better information sharing between tax authorities and efforts to tackle tax havens. A form of country-by-country reporting, agreed internationally, would mean large multinational companies would have to publish the key information on their profits and taxes in each of the countries in which they operate, making it easier to assess the amount of tax they pay. This could prove a vital boost for developing countries and help increase their tax revenues and in turn, reduce their reliance on aid.

Helping African countries deal with the transfer pricing challenge specifically, by encouraging wider implementation of the OECD guidelines will also be key, as well as helping them improve tax collection capabilities more broadly through potentially using aid to help strengthen developing country tax authorities on the ground.

More needs to be done globally to help some of the poorest countries in the world to get a fairer price for their commodities. At the moment governments in some of the poorest countries suffer severe asymmetries of information about resource deposits compared to the companies vying for the rights to extract those resources. The result is often sales of resources at greatly under-valued prices. To tackle this, the UK should maintain its support for efforts to publish contract information and encourage other countries to immediately adopt and implement the Extractive Industries Transparency Initiative, as well as advance transparency initiatives to include other sectors. We should also consider how current efforts to gather and publish geologically relevant survey data could help level the playing field and help developing country governments to negotiate more effectively for their citizens.

Dealing with Existential Threats

Nuclear Weapons

Graham Allison's chapter argues that the nuclear challenges presented by Iran and North Korea are emblematic of a nuclear order that is in trouble. Although the number of nuclear weapons in the world has gone down since the end of the cold war, they now exist in more countries and in more unstable regions than ever before. There is the ongoing risk of antagonism between nuclear-armed states like India and Pakistan, significant new proliferation risks across the Middle East and East Asia, and the threat of nuclear terrorism. And while deterrence may have worked during the cold war stand-off between the United States and the Soviet Union, many credible voices are now warning that in the new nuclear age of more nuclear-armed states, deterrence is going to become increasingly complex and difficult to manage (Shultz et al., 2007).

Addressing these dangers requires action in three areas. First, we need progress on multilateral nuclear disarmament. This needs to be stimulated by a further bilateral arrangement between the United States and Russia, who between them possess 95 per cent of all the nuclear weapons, but thereafter the nuclear reductions talks must be broadened out. At a minimum, this means extending the current dialogue among the P5 nuclear weapon states recognised by the Non-Proliferation Treaty (the UK, US, France, China and Russia) to cover a serious multilateral disarmament dialogue.

To provide wider support for such disarmament efforts the UK should also push for progress on other multilateral instruments. Both the United States and China must be encouraged and pressed to ratify and help bring into force the Comprehensive Test Ban Treaty (CTBT) and the UK should pursue the goal of a Fissile Material Cut-Off Treaty (FMCT) which would effectively ban future production of material that is essential in the production of nuclear weapons.

Second, we need to shore up the Non-Proliferation Treaty (NPT) – the one key multilateral instrument that has done most to deliver nuclear security. Demonstrating progress on disarmament is important to this goal, since disarmament by the nuclear-haves is a key feature of the grand bargain with the nuclear have-nots that the NPT represents. All states, including Iran, must comply with their NPT obligations to allow full inspections of their nuclear activities and we must commit to the long haul of diplomacy required to create a WMD Free Zone in the Middle East.

Third, in a world that must confront the threat of nuclear terrorism, we need a more effective way of managing the security of nuclear weapons and weapon-related materials. Currently, while each nuclear-armed state is responsible for its own security arrangements, there are no international mechanisms through which states can demonstrate to each other that they are exercising their sovereignty responsibly in this area (NTI, 2012). The UK should therefore support the development of workable international assurance mechanisms on nuclear security to enhance the confidence and security of all. It should also encourage those states that wish to exercise their sovereignty responsibly in this area but may not have sufficient money or technical expertise and capacity to do so.

Climate Change

We must continue to pursue a global multilateral deal to cut carbon emissions and head off some of the worst possible consequences of climate change. As Jeff Mazo's chapter pointed out, with 0.7°C of warming already having occurred, and a further 0.6°C bound to occur from emissions already in the atmosphere, it may be too late to avoid exceeding global warming of 2°C since pre-industrial times, a level that is widely accepted as dangerous. The projected consequences of sea-level rise, droughts, floods, water scarcity and large-scale population displacement are well known. Warming to even higher levels is possible and, without action, is certain.

The UK must therefore continue to play a lead role, including via the European Union, in multilateral efforts to ensure an effective and enforceable agreement to cut global carbon emissions is in effect by 2020. The UK should also ensure that the security implications of climate change remain on the agenda of the UN Security Council. Yet we must also be willing to form new alliances. There are already professional international networks and cross-country alliances and the UK should consider what further role it can play to develop new alliances and new instruments to achieve progress.

Nonetheless for many of the poorest countries climate change is no longer a future threat but is already a contemporary crisis. So any development assistance must continue to be targeted and effectively focused on the related challenges of poverty reduction.

Reforming the UN

Lastly, in this brief review of international issues seen in the context of the foundations of tomorrow's foreign policy for the UK, we turn to reform of the United Nations, the body that, like no other, has the potential to speak on behalf of the whole international community.

As a founder member of the UN and as host to its very first meeting in January 1946, the UK cannot shirk its responsibilities towards reforming the UN. First and foremost is an open recognition by the UK that a structure that was fit for purpose 70 years ago no longer commands unquestioned credibility. In that regard the UK should be forthcoming in its commitment to reform of the Security Council and, especially, the role and number of Permanent Members. One starting point for discussion could be Kofi Annan's proposals of 2005, which envisaged either an addition of six Permanent Members or the creation of a new category of non-Permanent Members that would occupy their seats for four years, renewable once, and not the customary two years as now. The year 2015 marks the seventieth anniversary of the founding of the UN here in the UK. The UK could that year initiate work to develop a consensus on Security Council reform. Of course the veto would be a key issue. Trying to build a consensus on limiting the use of the veto and, ideally, confining its use to vital national security issues would not be easy but as enlargement of the Security Council is addressed this issue must be too.

Second, the P5, and the Security Council generally, have allowed peacekeeping missions to be led by countries which sometimes have weak armies or are deficient in key capabilities such as helicopters, engineering units or military hospitals. Inevitably this has impacted on their performance. Countries such as the UK, with effective militaries, should therefore look afresh at what role they could contribute to UN peacekeeping. It could also offer, with others, to boost military planning within the Department of Peacekeeping Operations (DPKO) by seconding UK military officers or offering training to officers from developing countries to enhance their professional capabilities.

Third, we have assessed the growing impact of climate change and other environmental threats and challenges earlier in this volume. The UN Environment Programme (UNEP) based in Nairobi is currently ill-equipped to deal with this challenge and remains underfunded. The UK should therefore consider working to build a consensus around its replacement with a new and more powerful United Nations Environment Organization (UNEO), with its own secretariat and based in New York or Geneva.

Finally, we have noted the growing role of regional organisations alongside member states in addressing global issues. One way by which these partnerships could be both better recognised and reflected in the international system would be for the UN to convene annually a Congress of Regional Organizations to include the OAS (Organization of American States), the EU, AU, Arab League, SAARC (South Asian Association for Regional Cooperation) and ASEAN (Association of Southeast Asian Nations) to meet at Secretary-General level in New York simultaneously with the UN General Assembly.

Foreign Policy Begins at Home

A key challenge for UK foreign policy is to keep pace with the present pace of change. The government coming to power in 2015 should conduct a Strategic Diplomacy Review. This should assess diplomatic priorities and the relative distribution of expenditure in relation to those priorities, including an assessment of expenditure on conflict prevention as compared to the costs of conflict and post-conflict reconstruction, and an assessment of expenditure on multilateral activities as compared to bilateral activities and the costs of the embassy network. The review would also allow a diplomatic service skills assessment to be undertaken.

More widely however, if as a nation we are to help influence tomorrow effectively, we must acknowledge our overall position internationally, especially in relation to other countries experiencing record levels of economic and demographic growth and we must focus clearly on the issue of our domestic strength. Rebuilding our economic strength, as Robin Niblett notes, will be a *sine qua non* for future British international influence.

Rebuilding that strength is going to require the development of an effective strategy for sustainable and productive growth in the post-crash world. Without a strong economic foundation, the United Kingdom's capacity to influence foreign affairs will erode. That strategy will involve renewed investments in infrastructure and a sharper focus on steps to promote growth and jobs. It is going to require looking afresh at our education and skills policies to ensure we are preparing our own citizens and students with the cultural, linguistic and other skills they will need to be successful in the global markets opening up. And it is going to require a fresh look at energy strategy, to ensure a balanced approach whereby diversity of supply means that we are a little less reliant on unstable and expensive energy imports, and therefore less vulnerable to instability in regions rich in energy.

Done well, renewal at home will not only improve the lives of our citizens but will also provide the resources we need to engage successfully in the world for the long term. Indeed if we can re-create an economic and social model that others want to emulate, it will strengthen our soft power abroad.

If the UK approaches the challenge of the future by acknowledging the ways in which foreign and domestic policy can support each other in this way, then there is no reason why the country cannot continue to be effective and influential on the international stage for many years come.

Conclusion

We have tried in this chapter to reflect on the depth of the analysis and expertise on show throughout the rest of the book. We have drawn on that expertise and analysis to call for an approach to British foreign policy that is multilateral in character, innovative in the use of the power the UK still has, and respectful of international law. We have called for an approach that is simultaneously Asia-conscious and pro-European, and simultaneously focused on a mutually beneficial partnership with the United States while still being concerned with matters across wider Europe. And we have called for an approach that is responsible as it exercises sovereignty and is informed by the challenges and opportunities presented by new technology.

Inevitably, not all contributors or readers will agree with some of the judgments we have made. Some will complain that multi-lateralism is fine in principle, for example, but often unworkable in practice. Others will argue that we don't always get to choose which armed conflicts we are involved in, or when. Still others may complain that it is fine to set out assumptions about the future direction of foreign policy, so long as one remains aware that those assumptions are unlikely to survive first contact with reality.

We are aware of these arguments and have rejected them. One can believe it is worth setting out the underlying trends and founda-tions that can and should inform our foreign policy without falling into the trap of naivety. Certainly a radically changed global contract means now, more than ever, that all states are buffeted by events and none can fully command the external environment. The choice on offer is whether to be buffeted within the framework of a strategic vision or whether to be buffeted without.

Similarly, one can either encounter the difficulties of multilat-eral cooperation and work to improve it anyway, or concede that the world will have no effective multilateral governance. There is no easier third way. And one can retain hard power capabilities and a realistic acknowledgement that they will sometimes have to be used while still believing in a smart power approach.

We believe the concepts set out in this chapter, combine a strong sense of idealism with a determined sense of practicability. Making progress certainly requires a realistic understanding of power and its location but our approach needs also to be rooted in our values. That is the progressive approach, and it should be applied to foreign policy every bit as much as it must be applied to policy at home.

REFERENCES

Introduction

Cukier, Kenneth and Viktor Mayer-Schoenberger (2013) 'The Rise of Big Data', *Foreign Affairs*, May/June.

Foreign Policy/Fund for Peace (2013) *Failed States Index 2013*, http://ffp. statesindex.org/rankings-2013-sortable

Institute for Public Policy Research (2008) *Shared Destinies: The Interim Report of the IPPR Commission on National Security in the 21st Century.* London: IPPR/

Leonard, Mark and Kundnani, Hans (2013) 'Think Again: European Decline', *Foreign Policy*, May/June, pp. 46–50.

Rose, Chris (2009) 'Nicholas Stern: Climate and Economic Crises Can Be Tackled Jointly', *Words To Remember*, Wind Direction, March 2009 [accessed 12 July 2013] Available at:

http://www.ewea.org/fileadmin/ewea_documents/documents/ publications/WD/2009_february/Words_to_remember_Nicholas_ Stern__February_March_.pdf

Schmidt, Eric and Cohen, Jared (2013) *The New Digital Age: Reshaping the Future of People, Nations and Business.* New York: Knopf.

UN (2012) *World Population Prospects: The 2012 Revision.* Population Division of the Department of Economic and Social Affairs of the United Nations Secretariat. Available at: http://esa.un.org/unpd/wpp/index.htm

Zakaria, Fareed (2012) 'An Age of Progress', text of a Harvard Commencement Address, 24 May. Available at: http://news.harvard. edu/gazette/story/2012/05/text-of-fareed-zakarias-commencement-address/

Chapter 4

BBC News (2013) 'UK Risks 'Turning Inwards' over EU Referendum – US Official', http://www.bbc.co.uk/news/uk-politics-20961651, accessed 9 January 2013.

Bureau of Labor Statistics (2013)'Bureau of Labor Statistics Data', http:// data.bls.gov/timeseries/LNS14000000 , accessed 24 May 2013.

Carroll, R. et al. (2008) 'Who Is More Liberal, Obama or Clinton?', Vote View, 18 April 2008.

Congressional Research Service (2005) 'European Union's Arms Embargo on China: Implications and Options for US Policy', 15 April.

Deininger, K. and Squire, L. (1996) 'A New Data Set Measuring Income Inequality', *World Bank Economic Review* 10(3): 565–91.

EUISS (EU Institute for Security Studies) (2012) *Global Trends 2030 – Citizens in an Interconnected and Polycentric World*, edited by A. de Vasconcelos. Paris: EUISS.

Hormats, Robert D. (2013) 'Keynote Address', speech to Pacific Energy Summit, Vancouver, British Columbia, Canada, 3 April.

IMF (International Monetary Fund) (2012) 'World Economic Outlook Database, October 2012', http://www.imf.org/external/pubs/ft/weo/2012/02/weodata/index.aspx.

Lowrey, Annie, (2012) 'Income Inequality May Take Toll on Growth', *The New York Times*, 16 October.

Mather, Mark (2012) 'Income Inequality Rises Across the United States – Population Reference Bureau', Population Reference Bureau, http://www.prb.org/Articles/2012/us-income-inequality.aspx?p=1, accessed September 2012.

NIC (National Intelligence Council) (2012) *Global Trends 2030: Alternative Worlds*, Washington, DC, NIC.

Obama, B. (2009) 'US President Barack Obama Inaugural Address', speech to the people of the United States, Washington, DC, 20 January.

Obama, B. (2011) 'US President Barack Obama speech to the UK Parliament', London, 25 May.

Office of the Clerk (2009) 'Final Vote Results for Roll Call 46', http://clerk.house.gov/evs/2009/roll046.xml, accessed 28 January 2009.

Panetta, Leon (2011) 'Remarks by Secretary Panetta at Carnegie Europe (NATO)', Brussels, Belgium, 5 October.

Perlo-Freeman S., Sköns, E., Solmirano, C. and Wilandh, H. (2012) 'Trends in World Military Expenditure, 2012', Sipri Fact Sheet, SIPRI.

Pew Global Attitudes Project (2009) 'Confidence in Obama Lifts US Image Around the World', http://www.pewglobal.org/2009/07/23/confidence-in-obama-lifts-us-image-around-the-world, accessed 23 July 2009.

Pew Global Attitudes Project (2012) 'Global Opinion of Obama Slips, International Policies Faulted', http://www.pewglobal.org/2012/06/13/global-opinion-of-obama-slips-international-policies-faulted, accessed 13 June 2012.

Pew Research Global Attitudes Project (2012) 'World's Leading Economic Power: Percent Responding China', http://www.pewglobal.org/database/

?indicator=17&survey=14&response=China&mode=chart, accessed 5 April 2013.

Pew Research Center (2012) 'Nones on the Rise: One-in-Five Adults Have No Religious Affiliation', Washington, DC: Pew Research Center.

Pew Social and Demographic Trends (2012) 'The Lost Decade of the Middle Class', http://www.pewsocialtrends.org/2012/08/22/the-lost-decade-of-the-middle-class/, accessed 22 August 2012.

Roggio, Bill and Mayer, Alexander (2013) 'Charting the Data for US Airstrikes in Pakistan, 2004–2013', *The Long War Journal*, http://www.longwarjournal.org/pakistan-strikes.php, accessed 17 April 2013.

Slaughter, Anne-Marie, (2009) 'America's Edge', *Foreign Affairs*, 1 January.

The Economist (2011) 'Economics Focus: How to Get a Date', http://www.economist.com/node/21542155, 31 December.

The White House (2010) 'National Security Strategy', The White House, Washington, DC, May.

World Bank (2013) 'GDP Growth (Annual %) Data Table', http://data.worldbank.org/indicator/NY.GDP.MKTP.KD.ZG, accessed 5 April 2013.

Chapter 5

Allen, Grahame (2012) 'UK–Russia trade statistics', House of Commons Library, 22 October.

Aron, Leon (2013) 'Structure and context in US–Russian relations at the outset of Barack Obama's second term', *Outlook*, American Enterprise Institute, winter.

Browne, Des, Ischinger, Wolfgang, Ivanov, Igor and Nunn, Sam (2013) *Building Mutual Security in the Euro-Atlantic Region*. Washington, DC: Nuclear Threat Initiative.

Cameron, David (2011) Speech to Moscow State University, Moscow, 12 September, in *New Statesman*, http://www.newstatesman.com/2011/09/russia-britain-stability-work-3

de Nevers, Renée (2002) 'Is Russia really an ally?', *PONARS Policy Memo 295*, October.

de Quincey, Paul (2013) 'How 2014 became the UK/Russia Year of Culture', British Council, *Voices*, http://blog.britishcouncil.org/2013/03/13/uk-russia-year-of-culture/, 13 March.

Dvorkin, Vladimir (2013) 'The prospects for cooperation between US/NATO and Russia on BMD', in Alexei Arbatov and Vladimir Dvorkin, *Missile Defense: Confrontation and Cooperation*. Washington, DC: Carnegie Endowment for International Peace: pp. 215–24.

EASI Working Group on Energy (2012) *Energy as a Building Block in Creating a Euro-Atlantic Security Community*, http://carnegieendowment.org/2012/02/03/energy-as-building-block-in-creating-euro-atlantic-security-community/9cvy, 3 February.

EASI Working Group on Missile Defense (2012) *Missile Defense: Toward a New Paradigm*, http://carnegieendowment.org/2012/02/03/missile-defense-toward-new-paradigm/9cvz, 3 February.

Feneko, Alexei (2010) 'Slozhnoe nasledstvo (Complicated legacy)', *Nezavisimaya gazeta*, 15 October: 7

Golovanova, Olga (2013) 'U nas est neskolko kliuchevykh razlichii (We have a number of key differences)', *Kommersant Daily*, 13 March: 8.

Graham, Thomas and Trenin, Dmitry (2012) 'Why the reset should be reset', *The New York Times*, 12 December.

Grove, Thomas (2012) 'Russia's Putin says West on the decline', *Reuters*, http://www.reuters.com/article/2012/07/09/us-russia-putin-west-idUSBRE86818020120709, 9 July.

Harding, Luke (2013) 'Moscow warns UK against arming Syrian opposition', *Guardian International*, 14 March: 25.

Ignatius, David (2013) 'Wooing Russia and its influence', *Washington Post*, 21 February.

ITAR/TASS (2013) 'Shell becomes Gazprom's partner on Russia's Arctic shelf', *Russian Press Review*, http://www.itar-tass.com/en/c142/700694.html, 9 April.

Kendall, Bridget (2009) '"Respectful disagreement' in Moscow', BBC News, http://news.bbc.co.uk/2/hi/uk_news/8339292.stm, 3 November.

Lieven, Anatol (2005) 'The Essential Vladimir Putin', *Foreign Policy*, 146: 72–3.

Lucas, Edward (2008) *The New cold war: The Future of Russia and the West*. London: Palgrave/Macmillan.

Pushkov, Alexei (2013) 'Senior Russian MP concerned about new European values', Interfax, http://russialist.org/senior-russian-mp-concerned-about-new-european-values, 18 April.

Ralph, Jason and Clark, David (2013) 'FPC conversation piece: Labour's next foreign policy. A response', The Foreign Policy Centre, February.

Select Committee on Energy and Climate Change (2011) 'UK energy supply: security or independence?', *Energy and Climate Change – Eighth Report*, www.parliament.uk, 10 October 2012.

Shestakov, Evgeny (2013) 'Opyat dvoika (Again a deuce)', *Rossiiskaya gazeta*, 14 March: 8

Shevtsova, Lilia and Wood, Andrew (2011) *Change or Decay? Russia's*

Dilemma and the West's Response. Washington, DC: Carnegie Endowment for International Peace.

Sweeney, Kate (2012) 'Lord Green urges companies to explore Russia', *Business Weekly*, http://www.businessweekly.co.uk/export-to/europe/14902-lord-green-urges-companies-to-explore-russia, 12 December.

The White House, Office of the Press Secretary (1992) 'A Charter for American–Russian Partnership and Friendship', http://www.fas.org/spp/starwars/offdocs/b920617k.htm 16 June 1992.

Trenin, Dmitry (2012) 'Koncts prezhnikh otnoshenii Evrocouz-Rossiya (The end of the former EU–Russia relationship)', inoСМИ.Ru, http://www.inosmi.ru/russia/20121227/203876010.html, 27 December.

Chapter 6

Ajrash, Kadhim, and Razzouk, Nayla (2013) 'Iraq Revises Its Oil Reserves to 150 Billion Barrels', *Bloomberg*. http://www.bloomberg.com/news/2013-04-10/iraq-revises-its-oil-reserves-to-150-billion-barrels.html.

Arnold, Tom (2013) 'Gulf States Counting Even More on Oil Price', *The National*, 6 January. http://www.thenational.ae/thenational conversation/industry-insights/energy/gulf-states-counting-even-more-on-oil-price.

Axworthy, Michael (2008) *Iran: Empire of the Mind: A History from Zoroaster to the Present Day*, Penguin.

Baldor, Lolita C. (2013) 'US to Cut Carrier Fleet in Persian Gulf to 1', Associated Press. 6 February http://bigstory.ap.org/article/panetta-defense-budget-cuts-will-damage-economy.

Barnes-Dacey, Julien (2013) 'Lebanon: Locked into Escalation?', European Council on Foreign Relations, 26 March. http://ecfr.eu/content/entry/commentary_lebanon_locked_into_escalation_125.

Blitz, James (2013) 'David Cameron's Twin-track Policy Pits Human Rights Against Trade', *Financial Times*, 1 May. http://www.ft.com/cms/s/0/c87551b4-b27f-11e2-a388-00144feabdc0.html#axzz2ScyVygyU.

Brown, Nathan J. (2013) 'Islam and Politics in the New Egypt', The Carnegie Papers, Washington D.C.: Carnegie Endowment for International Peace.

Brownlee, Jason (2012) *Democracy Prevention: The Politics of the U.S.-Egyptian Alliance*, Cambridge University Press.

Byman, Daniel, and Sachs. Natan (2013) 'Israel's Three Gambles', *Foreign Policy*, 7 May. http://www.foreignpolicy.com/articles/2013/05/06/israel_three_gambles_syria.

Chivers, C. J., and Schmitt, Eric (2013) 'Arms Airlift to Syrian Rebels Expands, With C.I.A. Aid', *New York Times*, 24 March. http://www.

nytimes.com/2013/03/25/world/middleeast/arms-airlift-to-syrian-rebels-expands-with-cia-aid.html.

Chulov, Martin, and Black, Ian (2013) 'Syria: Jordan to Spearhead Saudi Arabian Arms Drive', *Guardian*, 14 April. http://www.guardian.co.uk/world/2013/apr/14/syria-jordan-spearhead-saudi-arms-drive.

Davidson, Christopher (2013) *After the Sheikhs: The Coming Collapse of the Gulf Monarchies*, Oxford University Press.

Dodge, Toby (2013) *Iraq: From War to a New Authoritarianism*, Adelphi Series, Routledge.

Dueck, Colin (2013) 'Obama's Strategic Denial', *The National Interest*, 7 May. http://nationalinterest.org/commentary/obamas-strategic-denial-8275.

Gause, F. Gregory (1994) *Oil Monarchies: Domestic and Security Challenges in the Arab Gulf States*, Council on Foreign Relations.

Gavlak, Dale (2013) 'Syrian Women Giving Birth in Exile of Refugee Camp', Associated Press, 7 May. http://bigstory.ap.org/article/syrian-women-giving-birth-exile-refugee-camp.

Gordon, Joy (2010) 'Lessons We Should Have Learned from the Iraqi Sanctions', *Foreign Policy*. http://mideast.foreignpolicy.com/posts/2010/07/08/lessons_we_should_have_learned_from_the_iraqi_sanctions.

Halliday, Fred (2005) *The Middle East in International Relations: Power, Politics and Ideology*, Cambridge University Press.

Harling, Peter, and Birke, Sarah (2013) 'The Syrian Heartbreak', Middle East Research and Information Project (MERIP). http://www.merip.org/mero/mero041613.

Healy, Jack (2012) 'Saudi Arabia Names Ambassador to Iraq', *New York Times*, 21 February. http://www.nytimes.com/2012/02/22/world/middleeast/saudi-arabia-names-ambassador-to-iraq.html.

Hollis, Rosemary (2010) *Britain and the Middle East in the 9/11 Era*, John Wiley & Sons.

International Crisis Group (2012), 'Israel and Hamas: Fire and Ceasefire in a New Middle East', Middle East Report 133.

Jilani, Hamza (2013) 'Focus on 'Asianisation' in GCC at QU Seminar', *Gulf-Times*, 2 May. http://www.gulf-times.com/qatar/178/details/351286/focus-on-%E2%80%98asianisation%E2%80%99-in-gcc-at-qu-seminar.

Johnsen, Gregory (2013) 'Yemen Has One More Year to Save Itself from Collapse', *The National*, 13 February. http://www.thenational.ae/thenationalconversation/comment/yemen-has-one-more-year-to-save-itself-from-collapse.

Johnstone, Sarah, and Mazo, Jeffrey (2011) 'Global Warming and the Arab Spring', *Survival* 53 (2): 11–17. doi:10.1080/00396338.2011.571006.

Joshi, Shashank (2012) *The Permanent Crisis: Iran's Nuclear Trajectory*, Whitehall Paper, Royal United Services Institute 79, London: Routledge.

Joshi, Shashank, and Chalmers, Hugh (2013) 'Iran: Red Lines and Grey Areas', briefing paper, London: Royal United Services Institute. http://www.rusi.org/downloads/assets/Iran_Red_Lines.pdf.

Joshi, Shashank, and Stein, Aaron (2013) 'The Turkey-Israel Rapprochement', *Foreign Policy*, 3 April. http://mideast.foreignpolicy.com/posts/2013/04/03/the_turkey_israel_rapprochement.

Kahl, Colin H., and Lynch, Marc (2013) 'US Strategy after the Arab Uprisings: Toward Progressive Engagement', *Washington Quarterly* 13 (2): 39–60.

Kamrava, Mehran (2012) 'The Arab Spring and the Saudi-Led Counterrevolution', *Orbis* 56 (1): 96–104. doi:10.1016/j.orbis.2011.10.011.

Kerr, Malcolm H. (1971) *The Arab cold war: Gamal 'Abd al-Nasir and His Rivals, 1958-1970*, 3rd ed., Oxford University Press.

Kinninmont, Jane, Sirri, Omar, and Stansfield, Gareth (2013) 'Iraq's Foreign Policy, Ten Years On', in *Iraq Ten Years On*, edited by Claire Spencer, Jane Kinninmont and Omar Sirri, 37–40, London: Chatham House.

Lynch, Marc (2011) 'The What Cooperation Council?' *Foreign Policy*. http://lynch.foreignpolicy.com/posts/2011/05/11/the_what_cooperation_council.

Lynch, Marc (2013) 'The Middle East's Kings of Cowardice', *Foreign Policy*, 18 April. http://www.foreignpolicy.com/articles/2013/04/18/middle_east_kings_of_cowardice.

Miller, Aaron David (2013) 'Tribes With Flags' *Foreign Policy*, 27 February. http://www.foreignpolicy.com/articles/2013/02/27/tribes_with_flags_arab_spring_states.

Mills, Robin (2011) 'Asia and Gulf States Need to Deepen Energy Relationship', *The National*, 18 October. http://www.thenational.ae/thenationalconversation/industry-insights/energy/asia-and-gulf-states-need-to-deepen-energy-relationship.

Mousavian, Seyed Hossein (2012) *The Iranian Nuclear Crisis*, Washington D.C.: Carnegie Endowment for International Peace.

Nasr, Vali (2007) *The Shia Revival: How Conflicts Within Islam Will Shape the Future*, W. W. Norton & Company.

O'Bagy, Elizabeth (2012) 'Jihad in Syria', Middle East Security Report 6, Washington D.C.: The Institute for the Study of War (ISW). http://understandingwar.org/sites/default/files/Jihad-In-Syria-17SEPT.pdf.

Pantucci, Raffaello (2013) 'The al-Nusra Front 'Merger': Underscoring the Growing Regionalisation of Al-Qa'ida', *Royal United Services*

Institute, 15 April. http://www.rusi.org/go.php?structureID=
commentary&ref=C516C202F5D8B5#.UYpxhCsjqXQ.

Pew Research Center (2013) 'Widespread Middle East Fears That Syrian
Violence Will Spread', *Pew Research Global Attitudes Project*, 1 May.
http://www.pewglobal.org/2013/05/01/widespread-middle-east-
fears-that-syrian-violence-will-spread/.

Prothero, Mitch (2012) 'Syria's War Comes to Beirut', *Foreign Policy*, 21 May.
http://www.foreignpolicy.com/articles/2012/05/21/syria_s_war_
comes_to_beirut?

Roberts, David (2012) 'Examining Qatari-Saudi Relations', *The Gulf
Blog*. http://thegulfblog.com/2012/02/28/examining-qatari-saudi-
relations/.

Ryan, Curtis R. (2013) 'Jordan's Unfinished Journey: Parliamentary
Elections and the State of Reform', policy brief, Washington D.C.: Project
on Middle East Democracy (POMED).

Sanger, David E. (2012) 'Jihadists Receiving Most Arms Sent to
Syrian Rebels', *New York Times*, 14 October. http://www.nytimes.
com/2012/10/15/world/middleeast/jihadists-receiving-most-arms-
sent-to-syrian-rebels.html.

Shanker, Thom, Schmitt, Eric, and Sanger, David E. (2012) 'US Adds
Forces in Persian Gulf, a Signal to Iran', *New York Times*, 3 July. http://
www.nytimes.com/2012/07/03/world/middleeast/us-adds-forces-in-
persian-gulf-a-signal-to-iran.html.

Springborg, Robert (2013) 'Sisi's Islamist Agenda for Egypt: The General's
Radical Political Vision', *Foreign Affairs*, 28 July.
www.foreignaffairs.com/articles/139605/robert-springborg/sisis-islamist-
agenda-for-egypt?page=show

Stansfield, Gareth, and Kelly, Saul (2013) 'A Return to East of Suez?
UK Military Deployment to the Gulf', London: Royal United Services
Institute. http://www.rusi.org/downloads/assets/East_of_Suez_
Return_042013.pdf.

Strauss, Delphine, and Gardner, David (2010) 'Turkey: The Sentinel Swivels',
Financial Times, 20 July. http://www.ft.com/cms/s/0/50cdc5ea-942a-
11df-a3fe-00144feab49a.html#axzz1tpwMJ5Gu.

'The Arab Opinion Project' (2012) Doha, Qatar: The Arab Center
for Research and Policy Studies. http://english.dohainstitute.org/
Home/Details?entityID=5ea4b31b-155d-4a9f-8f4d-a5b428135cd5&
resourceId=5083cf8e-38f8-4e4a-8bc5-fc91660608b0#1.

Ulrichsen, Kristian Coates (2011) *Insecure Gulf: the End of Certainty and
the Transition to the Post-oil Era*, New York: Columbia University Press.

Wehrey, Frederic M. Green, Jerrold D.; Nichiporuk, Brian; Nader, Alireza;

Hansell, Lydia; Nafisi, Rasool; and Bohandy, S.R. (2009) 'The Rise of the Pasdaran: Assessing the Domestic Roles of Iran's Islamic Revolutionary Guards Corps', product page, Santa Monica, CA: RAND Corporation. http://www.rand.org/pubs/monographs/MG821.html.

Worth, Robert F. and C. J. Chivers (2013), 'Seized Arms Off Yemen Raise Alarm Over Iran', *New York Times*, 2 March. http://www.nytimes.com/2013/03/03/world/middleeast/seized-arms-off-yemen-raise-alarm-over-iran.html.

Worth, Robert F. Mazzetti, Mark, and Shane, Scott (2013) 'With Brennan Pick, a Light on Drone Strikes' Hazards', *New York Times*, 5 February. http://www.nytimes.com/2013/02/06/world/middleeast/with-brennan-pick-a-light-on-drone-strikes-hazards.html.

Yom, Sean, and Gause, Gregory (2012) 'Resilient Royals: How Arab Monarchies Hang On', *Journal of Democracy* 23 (4): 74–88.

Zelin, Aaron Y. (2013) 'European Foreign Fighters in Syria', *The International Centre for the Study of Radicalisation*, 2 April. http://icsr.info/2013/04/icsr-insight-european-foreign-fighters-in-syria-2/.

Chapter 8

Eide, E. B. (2012) 'The Future of European Defense and Transatlantic Solidarity,' Center for Strategic and International Studies, 12 January, http://csis.org/event/honorable-espen-barth-eide-minister-defense-norway (accessed July 2013).

NATO (2010) 'Active Engagement, Modern Defense: Strategic Concept for Defense and Security of the Members of the North Atlantic Treaty Association,' http://www.nato.int/cps/en/natolive/official_texts_68580.htm (accessed July 2013).

NATO Parliamentary Assembly (2013) 'The Growing Strategic Relevance of Asia: Implications for NATO,' May.

Rasmussen, A. F. (2012a) Secretary General's Annual Report 2012, NATO.

Rasmussen, A. F. (2012b) 'NATO 2020: Shared Leadership for a Shared Future,' NATO, 23 March.

Roughead, G. and Schake, K. (2013) 'National Defense in a Time of Change,' Hamilton Project, February.

Stuster, J. D. (2013) 'The Obama Administration Just Can't Seem to Pivot to Asia,' *Foreign Policy*, 7 June.

Sloan, S. (2008) 'How and Why Did NATO Survive the Bush Doctrine?' NATO Defense College.

Wall Street Journal (2011) Transcript of Defense Secretary Gates' Speech on NATO's Future, 10 June.

Chapter 9

Annan, K. (2012) *Interventions: A Life in War and Peace*. London: Allen Lane.

Der Spiegel (2012) 'Norway Takes Aim at G-20: One of the Greatest Setbacks Since World War II', 22 June.

Weiss, T. G. and Kalbacher, D. Z. (2013) 'The United Nations', in Paul D. Williams (ed.) *Security Studies*. London: Routledge.

Chapter 10

Allison, G. (2004) *Nuclear Terrorism*. New York: Owl Books.

Allison, G. (2012a) 'Slinking toward the bomb,' *Scientific American*, 306(6).

Allison, G. (2012b) 'Living in the era of megaterror,' *International Herald Tribune*, 8 September.

Allison, G. (2013) 'North Korea's lesson: nukes for sale,' *New York Times* website, 12 February. http://www.nytimes.com/2013/02/12/opinion/north-koreas-lesson-nukes-for-sale.html.

Bracken, P. (2012) *The Second Nuclear Age: Strategy, Danger, and the New Power Politics*. New York: Times Books.

Broad, W. Sanger, D. and Bonner, R. (2004) 'A tale of nuclear proliferation: how Pakistani built his network,' *New York Times*, 12 February.

Cameron, D. (2013) 'We need a nuclear deterrent more than ever,' *Daily Telegraph*, 3 April. http://www.telegraph.co.uk/news/politics/david-cameron/9969596/David-Cameron-We-need-a-nuclear-deterrent-more-than-ever.html.

Choe, S. and Sanger, D. (2013) 'Pyongyang, bluster, fakery and real risks,' *New York Times*, 30 March.

CNN (2004) 'Transcript of Rice's 9/11 commission statement,' 19 May. http://edition.cnn.com/2004/ALLPOLITICS/04/08/rice.transcript/.

Dalton, T. and Yoon, H. J. (2013) 'Reading into South Korea's nuclear debate,' Pacific Forum CSIS, Center for Strategic and International Studies website, 18 March. http://csis.org/publication/pacnet-20-reading-south-koreas-nuclear-debate.

Erdbrink, T. (2012) 'Nonaligned nations back Iran on nuclear power, but not on Syria,' *New York Times*, 1 September.

Foradori, P. and Malin, M. (2012) 'A WMD-free zone in the Middle East,' Belfer Center for Science and International Affairs, Harvard Kennedy School, December. http://belfercenter.ksg.harvard.edu/files/WMDFZ_PDF.pdf.

Foster, J. (1973) 'Nuclear weapons,' *Encyclopedia Americana*, 20: 520–22

Gates, R. (2010) 'Remarks by Secretary Gates at the Shangri-La Dialogue,' International Institute of Strategic Studies, Singapore, 4 June. http://

www.defense.gov/transcripts/transcript.aspx?transcriptid=4634.

Graham, B. and Talent, J. (chairs) (2008) *World at Risk*, Commission on the Prevention of Weapons of Mass Destruction Proliferation and Terrorism. New York: Vintage Books.

Hague, W. (2009) 'The future of British foreign policy with a Conservative government,' speech at International Institute of Strategic Studies, London, 21 July. http://www.iiss.org/recent-key-addresses/william-hague-address-jul-09/.

Hague, W. (2010) Testimony before the House of Commons, London, 26 May. http://www.publications.parliament.uk/pa/cm201011/cmhansrd/cm100526/debtext/100526-0005.htm.

Hope, C. (2012) 'David Cameron: Iran could 'trigger nuclear arms race',' *Daily Telegraph*, 5 November. http://www.telegraph.co.uk/news/uknews/defence/9655968/David-Cameron-Iran-could-trigger-nuclear-arms-race.html.

Hymans, J. (2011) 'Veto players, nuclear energy, and nonproliferation,' *International Security*, 36(2).

IAEA (International Atomic Energy Agency) (2013a) 'Power reactor information system,' IAEA website, last updated 6 June 2013. http://www.iaea.org/PRIS/home.aspx.

IAEA (International Atomic Energy Agency) (2013b) 'Implementation of the NPT safeguards agreement and relevant provisions of Security Council resolutions in the Islamic Republic of Iran,' IAEA board report, 21 February. http://www.iaea.org/Publications/Documents/Board/2013/gov2013-6.pdf.

International Panel on Fissile Materials (2009) 'Global fissile material report 2009,' October. http://fissilematerials.org/library/gfmr09.pdf.

International Panel on Fissile Materials (2010) 'Global fissile material report 2010,' December. http://fissilematerials.org/library/gfmr10.pdf.

International Panel on Fissile Materials (2013) 'Fissile material stocks,' International Panel on Fissile Materials website, last updated January 2013. http://fissilematerials.org/.

Kissinger, H. (2006) in Graham Allison et al., *Nuclear Proliferation: Risk and Responsibility*. Washington, DC: Trilateral Commission.

Korea News Service (2013) 'DPRK has no idea of negotiating with US unless it rolls back its hostile policy towards it,' 16 March. http://www.kcna.co.jp/item/2013/201303/news16/20130316-25ee.html.

Martinez, L. and Ferran, L. (2013) 'US Gen: an Iranian nuke would spark arms race,' ABC News website, 5 March. http://abcnews.go.com/Blotter/us-gen-james-mattis-iranian-nuke-spark-arms/story?id=18659131#.UWhqRaKR-ct.

Miller, S. (2003) 'Is the NPT system slowly dying? Seven challenges to the regime,' paper prepared for the Athens Conference on Nuclear Proliferation, May. http://belfercenter.hks.harvard.edu/files/miller_athens.pdf.

Miller S (2012) 'Nuclear collisions: discord, reform, and the nuclear nonproliferation regime,' American Academy of Arts & Sciences. http://www.amacad.org/pdfs/nonproliferation.pdf.

Mowatt-Larssen, R. (2010) 'Al-Qaida weapons of mass destruction threat: hype or reality?' Belfer Center for Science and International Affairs, Harvard Kennedy School, January. http://belfercenter.ksg.harvard.edu/files/al-Qaida-wmd-threat.pdf.

Narang, V. (2010) 'Posturing for peace?' International Security, 34(3).

Norris, R. and Kristensen, H. (2006) 'Global nuclear stockpiles, 1945–2006,' Bulletin of Atomic Scientists, July/August, 62: 64–66.

Norris, R. and Kristensen, H. (2011) 'British nuclear forces, 2011,' Bulletin of Atomic Scientists, September/October, 67: 89–97.

Norris, R. and Kristensen, H. (2013a) 'Russian nuclear forces, 2013,' Bulletin of Atomic Scientists, May/June, 69: 71–81.

Norris, R. and Kristensen, H. (2013b) 'US nuclear forces, 2013,' Bulletin of Atomic Scientists, March/April, 69: 77–86.

Nuclear Threat Initiative (2013) 'Global nuclear security gains: NTI Nuclear Materials Security Index, one-year progress report,' 30 January. http://www.nti.org/analysis/articles/global-nuclear-security-gains-nti-nuclear-materials-security-index-one-year-progress-report/.

Nunn, S. (2005) 'The day after an attack, what would we wish we had done? Why aren't we doing it now?,' testimony before the 9/11 Public Discourse Project, 27 June. http://www.nti.org/analysis/testimonies/day-after-attack-what-would-we-wish-we-had-done-why-arent-we-doing-it-now/.

Obama, B. (2009a) 'Remarks by President Obama in Prague as delivered,' 5 April. http://www.whitehouse.gov/the_press_office/Remarks-By-President-Barack-Obama-In-Prague-As-Delivered.

Obama, B. (2009b) 'Remarks by the President at the United Nations Security Council Summit on Nuclear Non-Proliferation and Nuclear Disarmament,' UN Security Council, New York, 24 September. http://www.whitehouse.gov/the_press_office/Remarks-By-The-President-At-the-UN-Security-Council-Summit-On-Nuclear-Non-Proliferation-And-Nuclear-Disarmament.

Office of the Secretary of Defense (2013) 'Military and security developments involving the Democratic People's Republic of Korea,' annual report to Congress, 15 February. http://info.publicintelligence.net/DoD-DPRK-2012.pdf.

Présidence de la République (2013) 'Défense et sécurité nationale,' white paper, 29 April. http://www.gouvernement.fr/sites/default/files/fichiers_joints/livre-blanc-sur-la-defense-et-la-securite-nationale_2013.pdf.

Reuters (2011) 'Saudi Prince Turki urges nuclear option after Iran,' Reuters News website, 6 December. http://www.reuters.com/article/2011/12/06/nuclear-saudi-idAFL5E7N62G920111206.

Risen, J. (2012) 'Seeking nuclear insight in fog of the Ayatollah's utterances,' *New York Times*, 14 April.

Royal Society (2007) 'Strategy options for the UK's separated plutonium,' policy document 24/07, September. http://royalsociety.org/uploadedFiles/Royal_Society_Content/policy/publications/2007/8018.pdf.

Rumsfeld, D. (2002) 'DoD news briefing – Secretary Rumsfeld and Gen. Myers,' news transcript, U.S. Department of Defense, 12 February. http://www.defense.gov/transcripts/transcript.aspx?transcriptid=2636.

Sanger, D. (2013) 'In US, South Korean makes case for nuclear arms,' *New York Times* website, 9 April. http://www.nytimes.com/2013/04/10/world/asia/in-us-south-korean-makes-case-for-nuclear-arms.html.

Schlesinger, A. (2002) *A Thousand Days: John F. Kennedy in the White House*, 2nd edn. New York: First Mariner Books.

Shanker, T., Sanger, D., and Schmitt, E. (2013) 'Pentagon finds nuclear strides by North Korea,' *New York Times*, 12 April.

Shultz, G., Perry, W., Kissinger, H., and Nunn, S. (2007) 'A world free of nuclear weapons,' *Wall Street Journal*, 4 January.

Shultz, G., Perry, W., Kissinger, H. and Nunn, S. (2008) 'Toward a nuclear-free world,' *Wall Street Journal*, 15 January.

UK Foreign and Commonwealth Office (2012) 'National counter proliferation strategy 2012–2015,' policy paper, 23 March. https://www.gov.uk/government/uploads/system/uploads/attachment_data/file/36194/counter-proliferation-strat.pdf.

UN Office for Disarmament Affairs (2013) 'Treaty on the non-proliferation of nuclear weapons,' last updated 2013. http://www.un.org/disarmament/WMD/Nuclear/NPTtext.shtml.

US Department of Defense (2010) 'Nuclear posture review report,' April. http://www.defense.gov/npr/docs/2010%20nuclear%20posture%20review%20report.pdf.

Von Hippel, F. and Takubo, M. (2012) 'Japan's nuclear mistake,' *New York Times*, 29 November.

Chapter 11

Al-Arabiya (2011) 'Two dead and 400 injured in Algeria riots: minister', *Al-Arabiya* website, 8 January.

ACD (Armed Conflict Database) (no date) 'Sudan (Darfur): historical background'. Http://acd.iiss.org, accessed 31 May 2013.

Balmaseda, M. A,, Trenberth, K. E, and Källén E (2013) 'Distinctive climate signals in reanalysis of global ocean heat content', *Geophysical Research Letters*, online version of record, DOI: 10.1002/grl.50382.

Ban Ki-moon (2007) 'A climate culprit in Darfur', *Washington Post*, 16 June.

Brooks, N. (2006) 'Climate change, drought and pastoralism in the Sahel', discussion note for the World Initiative on Sustainable Pastoralism. http://community.eldis.org/.5994ce60/WISP_climate_change_en.doc

Burke, M. B., Miguel, E., Satyanath, S., Dykema, J. A. and Lobell, D. B. (2009) 'Warming increases the risk of civil war in Africa', *Proceedings of the National Academy of Sciences*, 106(49): 20670–20674.

Cabinet Office (2010) *Securing Britain in an Age of Uncertainty: The Strategic Defence and Security Review*, CM7948. London.

CNA Corporation (2006) *National Security and the Threat of Climate Change*. Alexandria, VA.

Coumou, D. and Rahmstorf, S. (2012) 'A decade of weather extremes', *Nature Climate Change*, 2(7): 491–496.

CEU (Council of the European Union) (2008) *Climate Change and International Security*. Report from the Commission and the Secretary-General/High Representative to the European Council, 7249/08. Brussels.

Curtis, M., Kersley, R. and Rana, M. (2011) *Emerging Consumer Survey 2011*. Zurich: Credit Suisse Research Institute.

Femia, F. and Werrell, C. (2013) 'Climate change before and after the Arab Awakening: the cases of Syria and Libya', in Werrell C and Femia F (eds) *The Arab Spring and Climate Change*. Washington, DC: Center for American Progress.

Global Humanitarian Forum (2009) *Climate Change: The Anatomy of a Silent Crisis*. Geneva.

Good, P., Gosling, S. N., Bernie, D., Caesar, J., Warren, R., Arnell, N. W. and Lowe, J. A. (2010) *An Updated Review of Developments in Climate Science Research since the IPCC Fourth Assessment Report*. Report submitted to the Committee on Climate Change. Exeter: AVOID programme. http://downloads.theccc.org.uk.s3.amazonaws.com/4th%20 Budget/fourthbudget_supporting_research_reviewofclimatescience_ developements_since_IPPC_AR4.pdf.

Gore, A. (2006) *An Inconvenient Truth: The Planetary Emergency of Global Warming and What We Can Do about It*. Emmaus, PA: Rodale.

Hawkins, E. and Sutton, R. (2009) 'The potential to narrow uncertainty in regional climate predictions', *Bulletin of the American Meteorological Society*, 90(8): 1095–1107.

HLP (High-Level Panel of Eminent Persons on the Post-2015 Development Agenda) (2013) *A New Global Partnership: Eradicate Poverty and Transform Economies through Sustainable Development.* Report to the Secretary-General. New York: United Nations.

Holland, A. and Vagg, X. (2013) 'A clear and present danger: the Security Council and Climate Change', American Security Project Flashpoint blog, 1 April.

Hsiang, S. M., Meng, K. C. and Cane, M. A. (2011) 'Civil conflicts are associated with climate change', *Nature*, 476(7361): 438–440.

IPPC (Intergovernmental Panel on Climate Change) (2001) *Climate Change 2001: Impacts, Adaptation and Vulnerability.* Cambridge: Cambridge University Press.

IPPC (Intergovernmental Panel on Climate Change) (2007a) *Climate Change 2007: Impacts, Adaptation and Vulnerability.* Cambridge: Cambridge University Press.

IPPC (Intergovernmental Panel on Climate Change) (2007b) *Climate Change 2007: The Physical Science Basis.* Cambridge: Cambridge University Press.

IISS (International Institute for Strategic Studies) (2011a) 'Climate change and human security', in *Strategic Survey 2011: The Annual Review of World Affairs.* Abingdon: Routledge.

IISS (International Institute for Strategic Studies) (2011b) 'Global agriculture and food security', in *Strategic Survey 2011: The Annual Review of World Affairs.* Abingdon: Routledge.

Jayaram, D. (2013) 'Six reasons why the UN Security Council should not discuss climate change', e-International Relations blog, 26 April.

Johnstone, S. and Mazo, J. (2011) 'Global warming and the Arab Spring', *Survival*, 53(2): 11–17.

Johnstone, S. and Mazo, J. (2013) 'Global warming and the Arab Spring', in Werrell C and Femia F (eds) *The Arab Spring and Climate Change*, Washington, DC: Center for American Progress.

Kevane, M. and Gray, L. (2008) 'Darfur: rainfall and conflict', *Environmental Research Letters*, 3. http://papers.ssrn.com/sol3/papers.cfm?abstract_id=1147303.

Lowrey, A. (2011) 'Protesting on an empty stomach', *Slate* website, 31 January.

Mazo, J. (2010) *Climate Conflict: How Global Warming Threatens Security and What to Do about It.* Abingdon: Routledge for the International Institute for Strategic Studies.

Mazo, J. (2011) 'Climate change and energy security as military issues', in Dane F (ed.) *Security and Responsibility in a Multipolar World*, Rio de Janeiro: Konrad Adenauer Stiftung.

Mohamed, Y. A. (2006) 'Land tenure, land use and conflicts in Darfur', in *Environmental Degradation as a Cause of Conflict in Darfur, Conference Proceedings, Khartoum, December 2004*. Addis Ababa: University for Peace Africa Programme.

NOAA (National Oceanic and Atmospheric Administration) (2013) 'Carbon dioxide at NOAA's Mauna Loa Observatory reaches new milestone: tops 400 ppm', press release, 10 May.

O'Fahey, R. S. (2006) 'Conflict in Darfur: historical and contemporary perspectives', in *Environmental Degradation as a Cause of Conflict in Darfur, Conference Proceedings, Khartoum, December 2004*. Addis Ababa: University for Peace Africa Programme.

Oreskes, N. (2007) 'The scientific consensus on climate change: how do we know we're not wrong?', in DiMento, J. F. C. and Doughman, P. M. (eds) *Climate Change: What It Means for Us, Our Children, and Our Grandchildren*. Cambridge, MA: MIT Press.

Otto, A., Otto, F. E. L., Boucher, B., Church, J., Hegerl, G., Forster, P. M. et al. (2013) 'Energy budget constraints on climate response', *Nature Geoscience*, 6(6): 415–416.

Prunier, G. (2005) *Darfur: The Ambiguous Genocide*. London: Hurst.

Rahmstorf, S. and Coumou, D. (2011) 'Increase of extreme events in a warming world', *Proceedings of the National Academy of Sciences*, 108(44): 17905–17909.

Reynolds, P. (2007) 'Security Council takes on global warming', BBC News website, 18 April.

Scheffran, J., Brzoska, M., Kominek, J., Link, P. M. and Schilling, J. (2012) 'Disentangling the climate–conflict nexus: empirical and theoretical assessment of vulnerabilities and pathways', *Review of European Studies*, 4(5), doi;10.5539/res.v4n5p1.

Schubert, R., Schellnhuber, H. J., Buchmann, N., Epiney, A., Greisshammer, R., Kulessa, M. E. et al. (2008) *World in Transition: Climate Change as a Security Risk*. London: Earthscan for the German Advisory Council on Global Change.

Smith, J. B., Schenider, S. H., Oppenheimer, M., Yohe, G. W., Hare, W., Mastrandrea, M. D. et al. (2009) 'Assessing dangerous climate change through an update of the Intergovernmental Panel on Climate Change (IPCC) 'reasons for concern'', *Proceedings of the National Academy of Sciences*, 109(11): 4133–4137.

Sternberg, T. (2013) 'Chinese drought, wheat, and the Egyptian uprising: how a local hazard became globalized', in Werrell, C. and Femia, F. (eds) *The Arab Spring and Climate Change*. Washington, DC: Center for American Progress.

Tertrais, .B (2011) 'The climate wars myth', *Washington Quarterly*, 34(3): 17–29.

UNDP (United Nations Development Programme) (2007) *Fighting Climate Change: Human Solidarity in a Divided World*. Human Development Report 2007/2008. New York.

UNEP (United Nations Environment Programme) (2007) *Sudan: Post-conflict Environment Assessment*. Nairobi.

UNEP (United Nations Environment Programme) (2012) *The Emissions Gap Report 2012*. Nairobi.

UNFCCC (United Nations Framework Convention on Climate Change) (1992). Text of the Convention. UN document FCCC/INFORMAL/84.

UNFCCC (United Nations Framework Convention on Climate Change) (2009) Copenhagen Accord. UN document FCCC/CP/2009/L.7.

UNFCCC (United Nations Framework Convention on Climate Change) (2011) Establishment of an Ad Hoc Working Group on the Durban Platform for Enhanced Action. UN document FCCC/CP/2011/L.10 .

USAID (United States Agency for International Development) (2010) *Sudan – Complex Emergency*. Situation report no 4.

USDoD (United States Department of Defense) (2010) *Quadrennial Defense Review Report*. Washington, DC.

Webersik, C. (2008) 'Sudan climate change and security factsheet', UN University Institute of Advanced Studies fact sheet 2008/2.

Werz, M. and Hoffman, M. (2013) 'Climate change, migration and conflict', in Werrell, C. and Femia, F. (eds) *The Arab Spring and Climate Change*. Washington, DC: Center for American Progress.

WHO (World Health Organization) (2008) *Global Burden of Disease: 2004 Update*. Geneva.

Zhang, D. D., Lee, H. F., Wang, C., Li, B., Pei, Q., Zhang, J. et al. (2011) 'The causality analysis of climate change and large-scale human crisis', *Proceedings of the National Academy of Sciences*, 108(42): 17296–17301.

Zoellick RB (2008) 'Fragile states: securing development', *Survival*, 50(6): 67–84.

Chapter 12

Africa Progress Panel (2013) *Equity in Extractives: Stewarding Africa's Natural Resources for All*. Geneva.

Collier, Paul (2007) *The Bottom Billion*. Oxford: Oxford University Press.

Collier, Paul (2009) *Wars, Guns and Votes: Democracy in Dangerous Places*. London: Random House.

Collier, Paul (2010) *The Plundered Planet*. London: Oxford University Press and Penguin.

Collier, Paul and Tony Venables (2011) *Plundered Nations*. Basingstoke: Palgrave Macmillan.

Collier, Paul (2013) *Aid as a Catalyst for Pioneer Investment*. WIDER Working Paper 2013/004. Helsinki: WIDER.

Myrdal, Gunnar (1966) *Asian Drama*. Harmondsworth: Penguin.

Chapter 13

Annan, K. (2000) *We the Peoples: The Role of the United Nations in the 21st Century*. Millennium Report. New York: United Nations.

Ban, K. (2011) United Nations Secretary-General Ban Ki-moon's remarks, as prepared for delivery, at a breakfast round table with Foreign Ministers, on 'The Responsibility to Protect: Responding to Imminent Threats of Mass Atrocities', New York, 23 September.

Ban, K. (2013) United Nations Secretary-General Ban Ki-moon's remarks at the Park East Synagogue commemoration in memory of the victims of the Holocaust, New York, 12 January.

Blair, T. (1999) 'Doctrine of the International Community', Speech delivered at the Chicago Economic Club, 22 April.

Caballeros, H. (2012) Statement by H.E. Harold Caballeros, Minister of Foreign Affairs of Guatemala to United Nations Security Council Debate on the Situation in the Middle East, New York, 31 January.

Chamberlain, N. (1938) Chamberlain's radio broadcast following his meetings with Hitler at Berchtesgaden and at Godesberg concerning the crisis over Czechoslovakia, available at http://www.st-andrews.ac.uk/~pv/munich/czdoc09.html.

Evans, G. (2008) *The Responsibility to Protect: Ending Mass Atrocity Crimes Once and For All*. Washington, DC: Brookings Institution Press.

Ferguson, N. (2012) 'The British Prime Minister is Coming to America', *Newsweek*, 12 March.

Human Security Research Group (2012) *Human Security Report 2012: Sexual Violence, Education and War: Beyond the Mainstream Narrative*. Vancouver: Human Security Press.

Power, S. (2007) *A Problem from Hell: America and the Age of Genocide*. New York: Harper Perennial.

Roberts, A. (2000) 'Humanitarian Issues and Agencies as Triggers for International Military Action', *International Review of the Red Cross*, 82 (839): 673–698.

Tatham, M. (2012) 'The UK is Fully Committed to Implementing the Responsibility to Protect', Statement by Ambassador Michael Tatham at UN General Assembly Interactive Dialogue on the 'Report of the Secretary-General on the Responsibility to Protect: Timely and Decisive Response', New York, 5 September.

Thakur, R. (2011) 'Has R2P Worked in Libya?', *Canberra Times*, 19 September.

Chapter 14

ABU (Asia-Pacific Broadcasting Union (2013) 'Al-Jazeera expands global reach with Orange TV'. http://www.abu.org.my/Latest_News-@-Al_Jazeera_expands_global_reach_with_Orange_TV.aspx.

BBC (2013) 'Around the World'. http://www.bbc.co.uk/aboutthebbc/insidethebbc/whatwedo/aroundtheworld/#section-2.

Kakutani, M. (2012) 'Surveying a global power shift', *The New York Times*, 29 January.

The Economist (2013) 'It ain't what it used to be', 28 March.

Gelb, L. (2009) *Power Rules: How Common Sense Can Rescue American Foreign Policy*. New York: HarperCollins.

Goldstein, G. (2013) "The End of Power from Boardrooms to Battlefields to Churches to States, Why Being in Charge Isn't What It Used to Be' by Moises Naím', *Washington Post*, 8 March.

Hart, M. (2012) 'China's real leadership question', Center for American Progress, 16 August.

International Institute for Strategic Studies (IISS) (2013) *The Military Balance 2013*. London: IISS.

Katulis, B. and Thistlethwaite, S. B. (2010) 'Power shift', Center for American Progress, 16 December.

Korb, L., Rothman, A. and Hoffman, M. (2012) '$100 billion in politically feasible defense cuts for a budget deal', Center for American Progress, 6 December.

Naím, M. (2013) *The End of Power: From Boardrooms to Battlefields and Churches to States, Why Being In Charge Isn't What It Used to Be*. New York: Basic Books.

Naím, M. (2013) 'The End of Power', *Reason* 14 April.

Nye, J. (2011) *The Future of Power*. New York: Perseus Books Group

Perlo-Freeman, S., Sköns, E., Solmirano, C., and Wilandh, H. (2013) *Trends in World Military Expenditure, 2012*. Stockholm International Peace Research Institute (SIPRI).

Swaine, M., Mochizuki, M., Brown, M., Giarra, P., Paal, D., Odell, R. E. et al. (2013) *China's Military and the U.S.–Japan Alliance in 2030: A Strategic Net Assessment*. Carnegie Endowment for International Peace.

United States Department of State (2013) 'Beijing air quality current reading'. http://beijing.usembassy-china.org.cn/aqirecent3.html.

United States Department of Defense (2013) *Military and Security Developments Involving the People's Republic of China 2013*.

Chapter 17

Ashdown, Paddy (2011) 'The global power shift', TED Talk, available at: http://www.ted.com/talks/paddy_ashdown_the_global_power_shift.html

Brzezinski, Zbigniew (2012) *Strategic Vision: America and the Crisis of Global Power*, Basic Books, New York.

Byrne, L. (2013) *Turning to Face the East: How Britain Can Prosper in the Asian Century*. London: Guardian Books.

Collier, Paul (2008) *The Bottom Billion*. Oxford: Oxford University Press.

Haas, Richard N. (2013) *Foreign Policy Begins at Home*. New York: Basic Books.

Nuclear Threat Initiative (NTI) (2012) *Nuclear Materials Security Index*. Washington, DC: NTI.

Nunn, Sam, Igor Ivanov, Des Browne and Wolfgang Ischinger (2013) *Building Mutual Security in the Euro-Atlantic Region*. London: NTI, ELN, RIAC & MSC.

Nye, Joseph (2011) *The Future of Power*. New York: Public Affairs.

Shultz, G. P, William J. Perry, Henry A. Kissinger and Sam Nunn (2007) A World Free of Nuclear Weapons. *Wall Street Journal*, 4 January.

A NOTE ON THE CONTRIBUTORS

Simon Adams
Dr Simon Adams is Executive Director of the Global Centre for the Responsibility to Protect. Dr Adams has previously worked with NGOs, governments and community organisations in South Africa, East Timor, Northern Ireland, Rwanda, Mozambique, Zimbabwe and elsewhere. He is the author of four books and numerous academic articles with a focus on international conflict.

Douglas Alexander MP
Douglas Alexander is Shadow Foreign Secretary and Member of Parliament for Paisley and Renfrewshire South. Between May 2001 and May 2010 he served in a wide range of ministerial positions including Secretary of State for International Development, Minister of State for Trade, Investment and Foreign Affairs, and Minister of State for Europe. Between June 2007 and May 2010 he was the UK's governor to the World Bank. During 2012–13 he was a Fisher Family Fellow at the Belfer Centre for the Future of Diplomacy at Harvard's John F. Kennedy School of Government.

Graham Allison
Graham Allison is Director of the Belfer Center for Science and International Affairs and Douglas Dillon Professor of Government at Harvard's John F. Kennedy School of Government. He served as Special Advisor to the Secretary of Defense under President Reagan and as Assistant Secretary of Defense for policy and plans under President Clinton.

Michael Clarke
Professor Michael Clarke is the Director General of the Royal United Services Institute (RUSI). Until July 2007 he was Deputy

Vice-Principal and Director of Research Development at King's College London, where he is now also visiting Professor of Defence Studies. He was the founding director of the International Policy Institute at King's College London from 2001 to 2005 and head of the School of Social Science and Public Policy at KCL in 2004–05.

Paul Collier
Paul Collier is the Director of the Centre for the Study of African Economies, and Professor of Economics and Public Policy at the Blavatnik School of Government, Oxford. A Professorial Fellow of St Antony's College, he is currently Advisor to the Strategy and Policy Department of the IMF, and advised on the development agenda for the 2013 G8.

Xenia Dormandy
Xenia Dormandy is a Senior Fellow at Chatham House in charge of the programme on America's Changing Role in the World. A former executive director of the PeaceNexus Foundation, a peace-building foundation in Switzerland, Xenia served as director for South Asia on the US National Security Council in 2004–2005.

Rolf Ekéus
Ambassador Rolf Ekéus is Chairman emeritus of the board of the Stockholm International Peace Research Institute. He served as Executive Chairman of the UN Special Commission on Iraq from 1991 to 1997 and was Swedish ambassador to the United States from 1997 to 2000.

Charles Grant
Charles Grant helped to found the Centre for European Reform in 1996 and became its first Director in 1998. Previously Brussels editor at the *Economist*, he has also been Director of the British Council.

Max Hoffman
Max Hoffman is a Research Assistant on the National Security and International Policy team at CAP.

Shashank Joshi

Shashank Joshi is a Research Fellow at the Royal United Services Institute (RUSI) and a PHD candidate in the Department of Government at Harvard University. He specialises in the international security in South Asia and the Middle East.

Ian Kearns

Ian Kearns is Director of the European Leadership Network (ELN), a new London-based think-tank focusing on security in the Euro-Atlantic neighbourhood, with a special emphasis on nuclear and arms control issues. He is a former advisor to the UK parliament on national security strategy and former Deputy Director of the Institute for Public Policy Research, the UK's leading progressive think-tank.

Lawrence J. Korb

Lawrence J. Korb is a Senior Fellow at the Centre for American Progress (CAP). He is also a senior advisor to the Centre for Defense Information and an adjunct professor at Georgetown University. Dr Korb served as Assistant Secretary of Defense (manpower, reserve affairs, installations, and logistics) from 1981 through 1985.

Robert Legvold

Professor Robert Legvold is Marshall D. Shulman Professor emeritus in the Department of Political Science at Columbia and a former Director of the "Euro-Atlantic Security Initiative" sponsored by the Carnegie Endowment for International Peace.

Mark Leonard

Mark Leonard is Co-Founder and Director of the European Council on Foreign Relations. He writes a fortnightly column on European and Global issues for Reuters.com. Mark has spent time as a visiting fellow at the Geman Marshall Fund of the United Staes in Washington and the Chinese Academy of Social Sciences in Beijing. He is author of the best-selling book *What Does China Think?* (2008) translated into 15 languages and *Why Europe Will Run the 21st Century* which was translated into 19 languages.

Jeffrey Mazo

Dr Jeffrey Mazo is Consulting Senior Fellow for Environmental Security and Science Policy and Consulting Editor at Survival International Institute for Strategic Studies.

Robin Niblett

Dr Robin Niblett became the Director of Chatham House (the Royal Institute of International Affairs) in January 2007. Before joining Chatham House, from 2001 to 2006, Dr Niblett was the Executive Vice President and Chief Operating Officer of the Center for Strategic & International Studies (CSIS).

Alec Ross

Alec Ross served as Senior Advisor for innovation in the office of US Secretary of State Hillary Clinton. Prior to his service at the State Department, Alec worked on the Obama-Biden Presidential Transition Team and served as Convener for Obama for America's Technology, Media and Telecommunications Policy Committee.

Kori Schake

Kori Schake is a Research Fellow at the Hoover Institution and an Associate Professor of international security studies at the United States Military Academy. She served as the Deputy Director for policy planning in the US State Department from 2007 to 2008.

Ben Scott

Dr Ben Scott is a Program Director at the Stiftung Neue Verantwortung in Berlin and Senior Advisor to the Open Technology Institute at the New America Foundation in Washington DC. Previously, he was policy advisor for Innovation at the US Department of State, where he worked at the intersection of technology and foreign policy.

Michael C. Williams

Lord Michael Williams of Baglan is Distinguished Visiting Fellow and acting head of the Asia Programme at Chatham House. He is former UN Under Secretary for the Middle East and a former special advisor to the UK Foreign Secretary.

ACKNOWLEDGEMENTS

This book reflects the support, advice and contribution of many people who have assisted the editors in their efforts to bring it to publication. We would like to thank in particular Mark Leonard, Robin Niblett and Michael Williams who, as well as contributing chapters, provided insightful observations and wise counsel on the broader themes developed in the book. We would also like to offer a special thanks to the team at IPPR and to Nick Pearce in particular, who has been integral to bringing this book to publication. We would also like to thank our colleagues at the European Leadership Network (ELN) and at the Labour Party, including Michelle Napchan, David Chaplin and Andrew Mackenzie, for their input, advice and support. Finally, we would like to acknowledge the forbearance of our respective families during our work on this book. We hope in time, our children will judge it worthy of their dad's periodic absences.

INDEX